More Unequal

12/08

More Unequal
Aspects of Class in the United States

Edited by
Michael D. Yates

Monthly Review Press
New York

Copyright © 2007 Michael D. Yates

Library of Congress Cataloging-in-Publication Data

More unequal: aspects of class in the United States
        edited By Michael D. Yates.

p. cm.
ISBN 978-1-58367-159-7—ISBN 978-1-58367-160-3.
Social classes—United States. 2. Equality—United States.
3. United States—Social conditions—21st century.
I. Yates, Michael, 1946-HN90.S6M67
2007305.50973'09045—dc22
                        2007017333
design by Terry J. Allen

Monthly Review Press
146 West 29th St. #6W
New York, NY 10001

10 9 8 7 6 5 4 3 2 1

Contents

Acknowledgments

A book such as this is by definition a cooperative effort. This effort began with the preparation of the July/August 2006 issue of *Monthly Review*, titled "Aspects of Class in the U.S." The editorial committee put this issue together, so I want to first acknowledge its members (besides myself): John Bellamy Foster, John Mage, John Simon, Brett Clark, Claude Misukiewicz, Victor Wallis, and Yoshie Furuhashi. Second, I want to thank the contributors, who not only wrote the fine articles in this collection, but also were gracious and accommodating when it came to the editing of their works. Third, thanks go to Brett Clark of Monthly Review Press, who bore the brunt of the sometimes onerous task of getting everything ready for publication. And finally, I want to thank our mentor, the late Harry Magdoff, who died before the summer issue was published but whose spirit is well represented by it and by this book.

Introduction

Michael D. Yates

The glaring increase in economic inequality evident in the United States over the past thirty years has finally made it into the pages of the major media. In the past three years, the *Los Angeles Times*, the *Wall Street Journal*, and the *New York Times* have each published a series of articles on the subject of class. The growing economic divide has also caught the attention of a few prominent economists, like Joseph Stiglitz and Paul Krugman. Even Treasury secretary Henry Paulson has admitted that inequality is on the rise.

The articles in the newspapers are interesting and informative, demonstrating that equality of opportunity, the shibboleth so beloved by our politicians, pundits, and educators, has lost a lot of its power. There is a chasm between the rich and poor, in terms of everything from access to schooling and health care to whom we marry. However, all of the mainstream writing on class focuses on various characteristics of individuals. People are in a class because of their income or their level of schooling. Social class, in other words, is determined by income and education, and society is broken down into rich, poor, and those in the middle. In the examination of the data, writers note that racial minorities are more likely to be poor than whites, that the middle-income group is shrinking, that the gap between rich and poor is growing, that upward mobility (from poorer to richer) is less than it used to be, that in our mass consumption society it is more difficult to discern who is in what class, that inheritance is less important than it used to be, that schooling is more important than ever in determining income and class mobility, and so forth.

Not much is said about what has been driving the increase in inequality. What is said is either wrong (for example, the argument that the growing income divide is the result of computer-generated technological change which has increased the need for skilled and highly educated workers) or superficial (for example, the argument that the policies of the Republican Party have been responsible for much of the growth in inequality). What is never said, because it cannot be said, is that inequality is a normal feature of capitalist economies, and growing inequality is a natural consequence of capitalism when there is a quiescent working class, as is the case in the United States and much of the world.

The evidence for the propositions, that capitalist economies are profoundly unequal and are more unequal the less collectively powerful workers are, is overwhelming. The productive wealth—what we call the means of production—of every capitalist economy is owned by a tiny minority of individuals. And this is true no matter what party is in power or what country we are examining. Material life is always better, on average, in those capitalist economies with well-organized workers. It is no accident that throughout Europe, and especially in the Scandinavian nations, working people enjoy guaranteed vacations and holidays, subsidized or free health care, greater access to higher education, and prohibitions against arbitrary dismissal. Unions are strong there (though in many places increasingly less so). In the United States, however, where unions are rare, workers have none of these things. Since the mid-1970s, the owners of the means of production have waged unrelenting warfare against workers and their unions, and the results are everywhere apparent—workingmen and women have become more and more subservient to the vagaries and cruelties of the marketplace. If you get sick, too bad. If your plant closes, fend for yourself. If you get old, keep working.

To say that there are classes in capitalism and that these are fundamentally connected to the nature of this mode of production—that they in fact define the system—is just a starting point. Marx argued that embedded in capital—whether in its money or physical form—is an antagonistic relationship between workers and their employers. The essence of this relationship is the exploitation of the workers, the extraction of a surplus by the employers from their labor, necessary to fuel the accumulation of capital in a milieu of intense competition. Unlike other modes of production such as slavery or feudalism, this exploitation is hidden by the market; it takes place behind the workers' backs, so to speak. They sell their ability to work in the impersonal market, and it appears that the market dictates their pay. And assuming no overt dishonesty, it appears they get paid for each hour they work. But once they sell their labor power to the employer, it belongs to the boss just as surely as does the machinery. Inside the workplace the freedom of the market disappears, and the workers are driven, as relentlessly as possible, to produce an output far in excess of what they might choose to make if they controlled the production process. This creates an ultimately unresolvable tension between workers and employers, and this tension accounts for much of the historical trajectory of each capitalist economy.

Marx's analysis of capitalism is fruitful, opening many fields of inquiry. If the exploitation of wage labor is central to capitalism's operation, then it follows that the ability to maintain and, when possible, deepen this exploitation will also be central. Employers will be bound to control their workers' labor as much as possible, to prevent them from being able to interfere with their own exploitation. The centralization of workers into factories and the use of the detailed division of labor, mechanization, and lean production can all be seen primarily as control mechanisms aimed at maintaining the surplus. That they serve to alienate workers and at the same time create a reserve army of labor only adds to the power of capital and makes it still harder for workers to intervene on their own behalf. Employers will be bound as well to do whatever they can to prevent workers from organizing collectively, since this is the one thing that can throw a monkey wrench into the drive to accumulate capital. If they can divide workers on any basis, they will—by skill, race, gender, religion, or employment. They will also organize themselves politically, using their superior monetary resources and their near-monopoly of society's productive forces, to pressure the state to control labor, by force if necessary. They will wage ceaseless propaganda in favor of capitalism and against the system's enemies.

Perhaps the most enlightening part of Marx's theory of capitalism, though also the part most difficult for most people to embrace, is that if capitalism requires exploitation and all that goes with it, then exploitation cannot be eliminated within its confines. Reforms of various sorts are possible, even reforms that last a long time, but the liberation of human beings—their ability to control their own destinies, to develop their full human capacities, to live in relative harmony with one another and with the world around them—cannot be achieved in capitalism. Poverty and misery, grotesque inequality, alienation, the pillage of the environment—all will and must continue so long as we have capitalism. It's that simple.

But if seeing capitalism through the lens of class and class struggle offers profound insights, it also generates many complicating questions. Some of these are examined by the authors of the essays in this book. Can the categories of capital and labor be given empirical reality? Who exactly are the workers? Who are the capitalists? Are there other classes? Who constitutes the ruling class? Capital rules in the logic of the system, but who rules in the concrete world? And how do they rule? What connections are there among class, race, and gender? Are race and gender separate categories that require their own special analysis or can they never be examined isolated from class? How can the rest of society, the cultural dimension, be related to the class structure? Does class determine things like a nation's system of schooling? What about the media? Art and literature? The questions asked by scientists?

All of these questions are germane to what I think is the most important question: How do workers become class conscious? It would be reasonable to think that in the advanced capitalist countries the contradictions implicit in the system would begin to show themselves, and as they wreaked havoc on workers, the workers would begin to understand what was happening to them and act accordingly. Ironically, though labor forces in the rich capitalist nations have done many things to advance their life circumstances, they have not very often radically challenged the system itself. Instead, the most radical upheavals have taken place in poor countries: Russia, China, Vietnam, Cuba, Korea, and a few others. Today revolutionary movements are few in number (Nepal, Colombia, and Venezuela come to mind), and capital is on the offensive and labor in retreat throughout the rich capitalist world.

Many reasons have been put forward for the lack of class consciousness in the United States and its brethren capitalist nations, everything from business control of the media to the bureaucratization of the labor unions. For me two things stand out, which I have described as follows:

> Two important problems confront the unity of the world's workers. First, capitalism has always developed in the context of a nation, with an active and complicit state. Second, capitalism has, from its beginning, developed unevenly in different parts of the world. The original capitalist nations of Europe and, later, those special cases of the United States and Japan subjugated the rest of the world through their military and economic might, creating an imperialist system of rich and poor capitalist nations. These twin developments, nationalism and imperialism, have erected substantial barriers against the unity of the workers of the world.

In this brief introduction, I don't have space to fully develop this idea, but an example might suffice to give readers an idea of what I meant. Consider the U.S. invasion of Iraq. How did working people and their unions respond in the United States? Most workers succumbed immediately to the government and media propaganda frenzy. Most of organized labor, which represents a small fraction of U.S. workers, opposed the war, but the opposition, with some exceptions (such as the group USLAW—U.S. Labor Against War), was tepid and nothing was said about

U.S. imperialism or the imperatives of the capitalist system. Labor's leaders generally understood that the war in Iraq is connected to oil, but there is little evidence that this goes beyond populist arguments critical of big oil and government connivance with the oil companies. Rank-and-file workers, especially those outside the unions, typically supported the war. Much of labor's antagonism to the war ended once U.S. troops actually invaded Iraq. It reappeared as more U.S. soldiers died and as the insanity of the Bush administration became inescapably apparent. However, we seldom hear horror expressed at the Iraqis slaughtered or hear of support for Iraqi workers and the Iraqi labor movement, both of which have been in the crosshairs of the occupiers and their Iraqi allies. It is easy to imagine that should the United States wage war against another country, such as Iran, and especially if this were done under the auspices of a Democratic president, the U.S. labor movement would offer little resistance.

We see in the consciousness of the working class of the United States the impact of scores of years of nationalism within the world's biggest and most aggressive imperialist power. The same impact occurs in all the rich capitalist nations though probably to a lesser degree in most of them. Ignorance, hatred, and feelings of superiority toward the "Other" are so ingrained in U.S. workers, especially the white majority (people of color are "Others," too), that it is very difficult for them to see their own employers, and the government that allies with these employers, as their class enemies. In such circumstances systematic class-conscious thinking and acting become nearly impossible. And turning these arguments around, it is not so hard to understand why class consciousness has been most developed among workers and peasants in the poor capitalist countries.

Some of the essays in this book offer suggestions as to how we might break out of this consciousness impasse. Lots more work needs to be done. But until we figure it out and act upon our knowledge, the class divide will continue to grow and the conditions of the working masses will continue to worsen. We have our work cut out for us.

1

Aspects of Class in the United States:
A Prologue

John Bellamy Foster

If class war is continual in capitalist society, there is no doubt that in recent decades in the United States it has taken a much more virulent form. In a speech delivered at New York University in 2004, Bill Moyers pointed out:

> Class war was declared a generation ago in a powerful paperback polemic by William Simon, who was soon to be Secretary of the Treasury. He called on the financial and business class, in effect, to take back the power and privileges they had lost in the Depression and the New Deal. They got the message, and soon they began a stealthy class war against the rest of the society and the principles of our democracy. They set out to trash the social contract, to cut their workforces and wages, to scour the globe in search of cheap labor, and to shred the social safety net that was supposed to protect people from hardships beyond their control. *Business Week* put it bluntly at the time [in its October 12, 1974 issue]: "Some people will obviously have to do with less . . . . It will be a bitter pill for many Americans to swallow the idea of doing with less so that big business can have more."[1]

The effects of this relentless offensive by the vested interests against the rest of the society are increasingly evident. In 2005, the *New York Times* and the *Wall Street Journal* each published a series of articles focusing on class in the United States. This rare open acknowledgment of the importance of class by the elite media can be attributed in part to rapid increases in income and wealth inequality in U.S. society over the last couple of decades—coupled with the dramatic effects of the Bush tax cuts that have primarily benefited the wealthy. But it also grew out of a host of new statistical studies that have demonstrated that intergenerational class mobility in the United States is far below what was previously supposed, and that the United States is a more class-bound society than its major Western European counterparts, with the exception of Britain. In the words of the *Wall Street Journal* (May 13, 2005):

> Although Americans still think of their land as a place of exceptional opportunity—in contrast to class-bound Europe—the evidence suggests otherwise. And scholars have, over the past decade, come to see America as a less mobile society than they once believed. As recently as the later 1980s, economists argued that not much advantage passed from parent to child, perhaps as little as 20 percent. By that measure, a rich man's grandchild would have barely any edge over a poor man's grandchild . . . . But over the last 10 years, better data and more number-crunching have led economists and sociologists to a new consensus: The escalators of mobility move much more slowly. A substantial body of research finds that at least 45 percent of parents' advantage in income is passed along to their children, and perhaps as much as 60 percent. With the higher estimate, it's not only how much money your parents have that matters— even your great-great grandfather's wealth might give you a noticeable edge today.

As Paul Sweezy once observed, "Self-reproduction is an *essential* characteristic of a class as distinct from a mere stratum."[2] What is clear from recent data is that the upper classes in the United States are extremely effective in reproducing themselves—to a degree that invites no obvious historical comparison in modern capitalist history. According to the *New York Times* (November 14, 2002), "Bhashkar Mazumber of the Federal Reserve Bank of Chicago . . . found that around 65 percent of the earnings advantage of fathers was transmitted to sons." Tom Hertz, an economist at American University, states that "while few would deny that it is *possible* to start poor and end rich, the evidence suggests that this feat is more difficult to accomplish in the United States than in other high-income nations."[3]

The fact that the rich are getting both relatively and absolutely richer, and the poor are getting relatively (if not absolutely) poorer, in the United States today is abundantly clear to all—although the true extent of this trend defies the imagination. Between the years 1950 and 1970, for each additional dollar made by those in the bottom 90 percent of income earners, those in the top 0.01 percent received an additional $162. In contrast, from 1990 to 2002, for every added dollar made by those in the bottom 90 percent, those in the uppermost 0.01 percent (today around 14,000 households) made an additional $18,000.[4]

Wealth is always far more unevenly divided than income. In 2001 the top 1 percent of wealth holders accounted for 33 percent of all net worth in the United States, twice the total net worth of the bottom 80 percent of the population. Measured in terms of financial wealth (which excludes equity in owner-occupied houses), the top 1 percent in 2001 owned more than four times as much as the bottom 80 percent of the population. Between 1983 and 2001, the top 1 percent grabbed 28 percent of the rise in national income, 33 percent of the total gain in net worth, and 52 percent of the overall growth in financial worth.[5]

Nevertheless, a considerable portion of the population still seems willing to accept substantial differentials in economic rewards on the assumption that these represent returns to merit and that all children have a fighting chance to rise to the top. The United States, the received wisdom tells us, is still the "land of opportunity." The new data on class mobility, however, indicate that this is far from the case and that the barriers separating classes are hardening.

How class advantages are passed on from one generation to the next is of course enormously difficult to determine—if only because class privileges are so various. Class inequality manifests itself in wealth, income, and occupation, but also in education, consumption, and health—and each of these are among the means by which class advantages/disadvantages are transmitted. Class inequalities, Sweezy explained,

are not only or perhaps even primarily a matter of income: [in certain social settings] a considerable range of income differentials would be compatible with all children having substantially equal life chances. More important are a number of other factors which are less well defined, less visible, and impossible to quantify: the advantages of coming from a more "cultured" home environment, differential access to educational opportunities, the possession of "connections" in the circles of those holding positions of power and prestige, and self-confidence which children absorb from their parents—the list could be expanded and elaborated.[6]

Such intangibles are difficult to measure, but in a capitalist society they tend to interact with large differentials in income and property ownership and hence leave their quantitative trace there. It is this constellation of class advantages roughly correlated with income and wealth, though not simply reducible to these elements, that allows the privileged to maintain their positions of economic status and power intergenerationally, even in the context of a society that on the surface appears to have many of the characteristics of a meritocracy. The well-to-do get better education, enjoy better health, have more opportunities to travel, benefit from a wide array of personal services (derived from purchase of the labor services of others), etc.—all of which translates into class advantages passed on to their children.

The fact that strong barriers restricting upward class mobility exist is of course the first point to be considered in class analysis—since without this classes would be non-existent. However, the real historical significance of class goes far beyond this. Class is not simply about the life chances of a given individual or a family; it is the prime mover in the constitution of modern society, governing both the distribution of power and the potential for social change. It therefore permeates all aspects of social existence.

At present there is no well-developed theory of class in all of its aspects, which remains perhaps the single biggest challenge facing the social sciences. Indeed, failure to advance in this area can be seen as symptomatic of the general stagnation of the social sciences over much of the twentieth century. Nevertheless, most Marxist analyses of class take their starting point from Lenin's famous definition of class:

> Classes are large groups of people differing from each other by the place they occupy in a historically determined system of social production, by their relation (in most cases fixed and formulated in law) to the means of production, by their role in the social organization of labour, and, consequently, by the dimensions of the share of social wealth of which they dispose and the mode of acquiring it.[7]

Like all brief definitions of class, this one has its weaknesses, since it is not able to take in the dynamic nature of class relations. As Sweezy argued, a systematic treatment of class and class struggle "needs also to encompass at least the following: the formation of classes in conflict with other classes, the character and degree of their self-consciousness, their internal organizational structures, the ways in which they generate and utilize ideologies to further their interests, and their modes of reproduction and self-perpetuation."[8] If we are speaking of a "ruling class," then the ways in which this class dominates the economy and the state need to be understood. Further, it is crucial to ascertain how class articulates itself in relation to other social relations and forms of oppression, such as race and gender.

An investigation of class thus leads to the analysis of society as a whole, its relationships of power, conflict, and change. Marxist approaches to class are distinctive in the degree to which they adopt the standpoint of *the class struggle*. By focusing on class and class struggle in this way the underlying purpose is clear: not simply to interpret the world but to change it.

2

The Worldwide Class Struggle

Vincent Navarro

A trademark of our times is the dominance of *neoliberalism* in the major economic, political, and social forums of the developed capitalist countries and in
the international agencies they influence—including the International Monetary
Fund, the World Bank, the World Trade Organization, and the technical agencies of the United Nations such as the World Health Organization, Food and
Agricultural Organization, and UNICEF. Starting in the United States during
the Carter administration, neoliberalism expanded its influence through the
Reagan administration and, in the United Kingdom, the Thatcher administration, to become an international ideology. Neoliberalism holds to a theory
(though not necessarily a practice) that posits the following:

1. The state (or what is wrongly referred to in popular parlance as "the govern-
    ment") needs to reduce its interventionism in economic and social activities.

2. Labor and financial markets should be deregulated in order to liberate the
    enormous creative energy of the markets.

3. Commerce and investments should be stimulated by eliminating borders
    and barriers to allow for full mobility of labor, capital, goods, and services.

Following these three tenets, according to neoliberal authors, we have seen
that the worldwide implementation of these practices has led to the development
of a "new" process: a globalization of economic activity that has generated a period of enormous economic growth worldwide, associated with a new era of social

progress. For the first time in history, we are told, we are witnessing a worldwide economy in which states are losing power and are being replaced by a worldwide market centered in multinational corporations, which are the main units of economic activity in the world today.

This celebration of the process of globalization is also evident among some sectors of the Left. Michael Hardt and Antonio Negri, in their widely cited *Empire*, celebrate the great creativity of what they consider to be a new era of capitalism. This new period, they claim, breaks with obsolete state structures and establishes a new international order, which they define as an imperialist order. They further postulate that this new order is maintained without any state dominating or being hegemonic. Thus, they write:

> We want to emphasize that the establishment of empire is a positive step towards the elimination of nostalgic activities based on previous power structures; we reject all political strategies that want to take us back to past situations such as the resurrection of the nation-state in order to protect the population from global capital. We believe that the new imperialist order is better than the previous system in the same way that Marx believed that capitalism was a mode of production and a type of society superior to the mode that it replaced. This point of view held by Marx was based on a healthy despisement of the parochial localism and rigid hierarchies that preceded the capitalist society, as well as on the recognition of the enormous potential for liberation that capitalism had.[1]

Globalization (i.e., the internationalization of economic activity according to neoliberal tenets) becomes, in Hardt and Negri's position, an international system that is stimulating a worldwide activity that operates without any state or states leading or organizing it. Such an admiring and flattering view of globalization and neoliberalism explains the positive reviews that *Empire* has received from Emily Eakin, a book reviewer of the *New York Times,* and other mainstream critics not known for sympathetic reviews of books that claim to derive their theoretical position from Marxism. Actually, Eakin describes *Empire* as the theoretical framework that the world needs to understand its reality.

Hardt and Negri applaud, along with neoliberal authors, the expansion of globalization. Other left-wing authors, however, mourn rather than celebrate this expansion, holding globalization as the cause of the world's growing inequalities and poverty. It is important to stress that even though the authors in this latter group—which includes, for example, Susan George and Eric

Hobsbawm—lament globalization and criticize neoliberal thinking, they still share with neoliberal authors the basic assumption of neoliberalism: that states are losing power in an international order in which the power of multinational corporations has replaced that of states.

The Contradiction Between Theory and Practice in Neoliberalism

Let's be clear right away that neoliberal *theory* is one thing and neoliberal *practice* is another thing entirely. Most members of the Organization for Economic Co-operation and Development (OECD)—including the U.S. federal government—have seen state intervention and state public expenditures *increase* during the last thirty years. My area of scholarship is public policy and I study the nature of state interventions in many parts of the world. I can testify to the expansion of state intervention in most countries in the developed capitalist world. Even in the United States, President Reagan's neoliberalism did not translate into a decline of the federal public sector. Instead, federal public expenditures increased under his mandate, from 21.6 to 23 percent of GNP, as a consequence of a spectacular growth in military expenditures from 4.9 to 6.1 percent of GNP (Congressional Budget Office National Accounts 2003). This growth in public expenditures was financed by an increase in the federal deficit (creating a burgeoning of the federal debt) and an increase in taxes. As the supposedly anti-tax president, Reagan in fact increased taxes for a greater number of people (in peace time) than any other president in U.S. history. And he increased taxes not once, but twice (in 1982 and 1983). In a demonstration of class power, he drastically reduced taxes for the 20 percent of the population with the highest incomes, while raising taxes for the majority of the population.

It is not accurate, therefore, to say that Reagan reduced the role of the state in the United States by reducing the size of the public sector and lowering taxes. What Reagan (and Carter before him) did was dramatically change the nature of state intervention, such that it benefited even more the upper classes and the economic groups (such as military-related corporations) that financed his electoral campaigns. Reagan's policies were indeed class policies that hurt the majority of the nation's working class. Reagan was profoundly antilabor, making cuts in social expenditures at an unprecedented level. It bears repeating that Reagan's policies were not neoliberal: they were Keynesian, based on large public expenditures and large federal deficits.

Also, the federal government intervened actively in the nation's industrial development (mainly, but not exclusively, through the Defense Department). As Caspar Weinberger, secretary of defense in the Reagan administration, once indicated (in response to criticisms by Democrats that the administration had abandoned the manufacturing sector), "Our Administration is the Administration that has a more advanced and extended industrial policy in the western world."[2] He was right. No other Western government had such an extensive industrial policy. Indeed, the U.S. federal state is one of the most interventionist states in the Western world.

There exists very robust scientific evidence that the United States is not a neoliberal society (as it is constantly defined) and that the U.S. state is not reducing its key role in developing the national economy, including in the production and distribution of goods and services by large U.S. corporations. This empirical evidence shows that federal government interventionism (in the economic, political, cultural, and security spheres) has *increased* over the last thirty years. In the economic sphere, for example, protectionism has not declined. It has grown, with higher subsidies for the agricultural, military, aerospace, and biomedical sectors. In the social arena, state interventions to weaken social rights (and most particularly labor rights) have increased enormously (not only under Reagan, but also under Bush Senior, Clinton, and Bush Junior), and surveillance of the citizenry has increased exponentially. Again, there has been no diminution of federal interventionism in the United States, but rather an even more skewed class character to this intervention during the last thirty years.

Neoliberal narratives about the declining role of the state in people's lives are easily falsified by the facts. Indeed, as John Williamson, one of the intellectual architects of neoliberalism, once indicated, "We have to recognize that what the U.S. government promotes abroad, the U.S. government does not follow at home," adding that "the U.S. government promotes policies that are not followed in the U.S."[3] It could not have been said better. In other words, if you want to understand U.S. public policies, look at what the U.S. government does, not what it says. This same situation occurs in the majority of developed capitalist countries. Their states have become more, not less, interventionist. The size of the state (measured by public expenditures per capita) has increased in most of these countries. Again, the empirical information on this point is strong. What has been happening is not a reduction of the state but rather a change in the nature of state intervention—further strengthening its class character.

Deterioration of the World Economic and Social Situation

Contrary to neoliberal dogma, neoliberal public policies have been remarkably unsuccessful at achieving their declared aims: economic efficiency and social well-being.

Table 1. Economic Growth, 1960–2000		
Rate of economic growth in developing countries (except China)	**1960–1980**	**1980–2000**
Annual economic growth	5.5%	2.6%
Annual economic growth per capita	3.2%	0.7%
Rate of economic growth in China		
Annual economic growth	4.5%	9.8%
Annual economic growth per capita	2.5%	8.4%

Source: World Bank, *World Development Indicators,* 2001 CD-ROM; Robert Pollin, *Contours of Descent* (New York: Verso, 2003), 131.

If we compare the period 1980–2000 (when neoliberalism reached its maximum expression)[4] with the immediately preceding period, 1960–1980, we can easily see that 1980–2000 was much less successful than 1960–1980 in most developed and developing capitalist countries. As Table 1 shows, the rate of growth and rate of growth per capita in all developing (non-OECD) countries (excluding China) were much higher in 1960–1980 (5.5 percent and 3.2 percent) than in 1980–2000 (2.6 percent and 0.7 percent). Mark Weisbrot, Dean Baker, and David Rosnick have documented that the improvement in quality-of-life and well-being indicators (infant mortality, rate of school enrollment, life expectancy, and others) increased faster during 1960–1980 than 1980–2000 (when comparing countries at the same level of development at the starting year of each period).[5] And as Table 2 shows, the annual rate of economic growth per capita in the developed capitalist countries was lower in 1981–2000 than in 1961–1980.

the state in which they are based; and (h) promotion of an anti-interventionist discourse in clear conflict with the actual increased state interventionism to promote the interests of the dominant classes and the economic units—the transnationals—that foster their interests. Each of these class-determined public policies requires a state action or intervention that conflicts with the interests of the working and other popular classes.

The Primary Conflict in Today's World: Not Between North and South But Between an Alliance of Dominant Classes of North and South Against Dominated Classes of North and South

It has become part of the conventional wisdom that the primary conflict in the world is between the rich North and the poor South. The North and South, however, have classes with opposing interests that have established alliances at the international level. This situation became clear to me when I was advising President Allende in Chile. The fascist coup led by General Pinochet was not, as was widely reported, a coup imposed by the rich North (the United States) on the poor South (Chile). Those who brutally imposed the Pinochet regime were the dominant classes of Chile (the bourgeoisie, petit bourgeoisie, and upper-middle professional classes), with the support not of the United States (U.S. society is not an aggregate of 240 million imperialists!) but of the Nixon administration, which was, at that time, very unpopular in the United States (having sent the army to put down the coal miners' strike in Appalachia).

A lack of awareness of the existence of classes often leads to condemnation of an entire country, frequently the United States. But, in fact, the U.S. working class is one of the first victims of U.S. imperialism. Some will say that the U.S. working class benefits from imperialism. Gasoline, for example, is relatively cheap in the United States (although increasingly less so). It costs me thirty-five dollars to fill my car in the United States and fifty-two euros to fill the same model in Europe. But, by contrast, public transportation is practically nonexistent in many regions of the United States. The working class of Baltimore, for example, would benefit much more from first-class public transportation (which it does not have) than having to depend on cars, whatever the price of gasoline. And let's not forget that the energy and automobile industry interests have been major agents in opposing and destroying public transportation in the United States. The U.S. working class is a victim of its nation's capitalist and imperialist system. It is not by chance that no other country in the developed capitalist world has such an underdeveloped welfare state as the United States. More than 100,000 people die in the United States every year due to the lack of public health care.

The tendency to look at the distribution of power around the world while ignoring class power within each country is also evident in the frequent denunciations that the international organizations are controlled by the rich countries. It is frequently pointed out, for example, that 10 percent of the world population, living in the richest countries, has 43 percent of the votes in the IMF, but it is not true that the 10 percent of the population living in the so-called rich countries controls the IMF. It is the dominant classes of those rich countries that dominate the IMF, putting forward public policies that hurt the dominated classes of their own countries as well as of other countries. The director of the IMF, for example, is Rodrigo Rato, who while Spain's economy minister in the ultra-right government of José María Aznar (who partnered with Bush and Blair to support the Iraq war) carried out the brutal austerity policies that severely reduced the standard of living of the Spanish popular classes.[7]

Let me also clarify another point. Much has been written about the conflict within the WTO between rich and poor countries. The governments of the rich countries, it is said, heavily subsidize their agriculture while raising protective barriers for industries such as textiles and foods that are vulnerable to products coming from the poor countries. While these obstacles to world trade do indeed adversely affect poor countries, it is wrong to assume that the solution is freer worldwide trade. Even without the barriers, the higher productivity of the rich countries would guarantee their success in world trade. What poor countries need to do is to change from export-oriented economies (the root of their problems) to domestic-oriented growth—a strategy that would require a major redistribution of income and is thus resisted by the dominant classes of those (and of the rich) countries. It is extremely important to realize that most countries already have the resources (including capital) to break with their underdevelopment. Let me quote from an unlikely source: the *New York Times*, on September 12, 1992 (when the population explosion was held to be the cause of world poverty), published a surprisingly candid assessment of the situation in Bangladesh, the poorest country in the world. In this extensive article, Ann Crittenden touched directly on the root of the problem: the patterns of ownership of the production asset—the land:

> The root of the persistent malnutrition in the midst of relative plenty is the unequal distribution of land in Bangladesh. Few people are rich here by Western standards, but severe inequalities do exist and they are reflected in highly skewed land own-

ership. The wealthiest 16% of the rural population controls two thirds of the land and almost 60% of the population holds less than one acre of property.

Crittenden is not hopeful that the solution is technological. Quite the contrary, technology can make things even worse:

> The new agricultural technologies being introduced have tended to favor large farmers, putting them in a better position to buy out their less fortunate neighbors.

Why does this situation persist? The answer is clear:

> Nevertheless, with the government dominated by landowners—about 75% of the members of the Parliament hold land—no one foresees any official support for fundamental changes in the system.

Let me add that in the U.S. State Department's classification of political regimes, Bangladesh is placed in the democratic column. Meanwhile, hunger and underweight are the primary causes of child mortality in Bangladesh. The hungry face of a child in Bangladesh has become a common poster used by many charitable organizations to shame people in developed countries into sending money and food aid to Bangladesh. With what results?

> Food aid officials in Bangladesh privately concede that only a fraction of the millions of tons of food aid sent to Bangladesh has reached the poor and hungry in the villages. The food is given to the Government, which in turn sells it at subsidized prices to the military, the police, and the middle class inhabitants of the cities.

The class structure of Bangladesh and the property relations that determine it are the causes of the enormous poverty. As Ann Crittenden concludes:

> Bangladesh has enough land to provide an adequate diet for every man, woman and child in the country. The agricultural potential of this lush green land is such that even the inevitable population growth of the next 20 years could be fed easily by the resources of Bangladesh alone.

Most recently, Bangladesh has been much in the news as having undergone high economic growth due primarily to its exports in the world market. But that growth has been limited to a small, export-oriented sector of the economy and has left untouched the majority of the population. Malnutrition and hunger, mean-while, have increased.

The States and Class Alliances

In the establishment of class alliances, states play a key role. U.S. foreign poli-cy, for example, is oriented toward supporting the dominant classes of the South (where, incidentally, 20 percent of the world's richest persons live). These alliances include, on many occasions, personal ties among members of the dominant classes. Examples are many—among them, the traditional sup-port of the Bush family for the Middle East feudal regimes; Clinton's support for the United Arab Emirates (UAE), one of the major supporters of the Clinton Library in Little Rock, Arkansas, and a major donor to Clinton in speaking fees (up to a million dollars) and to causes favoring Clinton.[8] The UAE is one of the world's most oppressively brutal regimes. The dominant classes deny citizen-ship to 85 percent of the working population (called "guest workers"). Needless to say, international agencies (heavily influenced by the U.S. and European governments) promote such alliances based on the neoliberal rheto-ric of free markets. Cutting social public expenditures, advocated by the IMF and the World Bank, is part of the neoliberal public policies pushed by the dominant classes of both the North and South at the expense of the well-being and quality of life of the dominated classes throughout the world. In all these examples, the states of the North and the South play a critical role.

Another example of alliances among dominant classes is the current pro-motion of for-profit health insurance by the Bush administration, both to the U.S. population and, increasingly, to the developing world. This is done with the advice and collaboration of conservative governments in Latin America on behalf of their dominant classes, which benefit from private insurance schemes that select clientele and exclude the popular classes. Those popular classes, in the United States and Latin America, profoundly dislike this push toward for-profit health care. (The movie *John Q* relates the hostility against health insurance companies among the U.S. working class.) The fact that the dominant classes in the developed and developing countries share class inter-ests does not mean they see eye-to-eye on everything. Of course not. They have major disagreements and conflicts (just as there are disagreements and conflicts among the different components of the dominant classes in each country). But these disagreements cannot conceal the commonality of their interests as clearly exposed in the neoliberal forums (such as at Davos) and neoliberal instruments that have a hegemonic position (such as *The Economist* and *Financial Times*).

Is There a Dominant State in the World Today?

More than globalization, what we are witnessing in the world today is the *regionalization* of economic activities around a dominant state: North America around the United States, Europe around Germany, and Asia around Japan—and soon China. Thus there is a hierarchy of states within each region. In Europe, for example, the Spanish government is becoming dependent on public policies of the European Union in which the German state predominates. This dependency creates an ambivalent situation. On the one hand, the states of the EU chose to delegate major policies (such as monetary policies) to a higher institution (the European Central Bank, which is dominated by the German Central Bank). But this does not necessarily mean that the Spanish state loses power. "Losing power" means you had more power before, which is not necessarily the case. Spain, for example, is more powerful with the euro as currency than it was with the peseta. Indeed, Spanish president Jose Luis Rodriguez Zapatero would have paid a very high price in his confrontation with Bush (in withdrawing Spanish troops from Iraq) if Spain still had the peseta as its national currency. Sharing sovereignty can increase power. On the other hand, the European government is frequently used by Europe's dominant classes as justification for unpopular policies they want to implement (such as reducing public expenditures as a consequence of the European Stability Pact, which forces countries to maintain a central government deficit below 3 percent of GNP); these policies are presented as coming from European legislation rather than any of the member states, thus diluting the responsibility of each government. Class alliances at the European level are manifested through the operation of EU institutions committed to neoliberal ideology and policies. The "no" vote on the proposed European Constitution was the response of the working classes of some member states to the European institutions that operate as alliances for Europe's dominant classes.

Within the hierarchy of states, some are dominant. The U.S. state has a dominant place that is maintained through a set of alliances with the dominant classes of other states. Neoliberal ideology provides the linkage among these classes. Needless to say, there are conflicts and tensions among them. But these tensions cannot outweigh the commonality of their class interests. Among the practices that unite them are aggressive policies against the working class and left institutions. The 1980–2005 period was characterized by aggressive campaigns against left parties that had been successful in the 1960–1980 period. During the neoliberal period, the alliance of the dominant classes has promoted multi-class religious movements that have used religion as a motivating force to stop socialism or communism. It was the Carter administration that began to support the religious fundamentalists in Afghanistan against the Communist-led government. From Afghanistan to Iraq, Iran, the Palestinian Territories, and many Arab countries, the dominant classes of the United States and Europe, through their governments, funded and supported the religious fundamentalists—often not only out of their own class interests but out of their own religiosity. The "moral majority" in the United States was supposed to become the moral majority worldwide. These profoundly anti-left fundamentalist movements developed their own dynamics, making use of the enormous frustrations of the Arab masses with their oppressive feudal regimes, to facilitate the capture of the state and the installation of regimes with equally oppressive religious theocracies, as has happened in many Arab countries.

But it is wrong to see the support by the dominant classes of the feudal regimes as simply a product of the Cold War. It was much more than that. It was a class response. The best evidence for this is that the support has continued even after the collapse of the Soviet Union. The Cold War was an excuse for carrying on the class struggle at the world level—as its continuation proves. Class war has indeed become an extremely active component of U.S. interventionism. It was the "shock therapy" pushed by Lawrence Summers and Jeffrey Sachs in Russia during the Clinton administration that led to the shortening of life expectancy in Russia, a consequence of the dramatic decline in the standard of living of the Russian popular classes. The increased privatization of major public assets was part of that class war in Russia—as it has been in Iraq.

The chief of the U.S. occupation in Iraq, Paul Bremer, fired half a million government workers, slashed business taxes, gave investors extraordinary new rights, and eliminated all import restrictions for all business except the oil industry. Jeff Faux relates in *The Global Class War* that the only laws from the brutal Iraqi dictatorship that the occupation retained were those that were anti-labor union, including a restrictive collective-bargaining agreement that took away all workers' bonuses and food and housing subsidies.[9] As *The Economist* editorialized, the economic reforms in Iraq are a "capitalist's dream."[10]

Recently, another version of the North-South divide appeared in the writings of one of the most influential thinkers in the United States, the philosopher John Rawls, who divides the countries of the world into "decent" and "non-decent" countries. The decent countries (mostly located in the developed capitalist world) are those that have democratic rights and institutions, and the non-decent countries (mostly located in the developing capitalist world) do not. After dividing the world into these two categories, he concludes that the non-decent countries had better be ignored, although he admits "a moral responsibility to help poor countries that are prevented by poverty from organizing themselves as liberal or decent societies." Such positions and statements testify to an overwhelming ignorance of past and present international relations, as well as of the class relations in each of those countries. Rawls further confuses governments with countries (a confusion that occurs frequently in the assumption that the primary conflict is between North and South). What he calls non-decent countries (characterized by brutal and corrupt dictatorships) have classes; their dominant classes have not been ignored in activities cultivated and supported by the dominant classes of the decent countries, which have also hurt the quality of life and well-being of their own dominated classes. Also, in Rawls's so-called non-decent countries, there are class-based movements that endure enormous sacrifices, carrying out a heroic struggle for change, struggling constantly while handicapped and opposed by the dominant classes of the so-called decent countries. It is remarkable (but predictable) that such an intellectual figure defines the moral compass of these indecent classes.[11] The latest example of this indecency is the reported support by the U.S. and British governments for the King of Nepal, which grows out of their desire to stop a mass revolt led by leftist parties in a third world country.

Inequalities among Countries and Their Social Consequences

That inequalities contribute to a lack of social solidarity and increase social pathology is well documented. Many people, including myself, have documented this reality.[12] The scientific evidence supporting this position is overwhelming. In any given society, the greatest number of deaths would be prevented by reducing social inequalities. Michael Marmot studied the gradient of heart disease mortality among professionals at different authority levels, and he found that the higher the level of authority, the lower the heart disease mortality.[13] And he further showed that this mortality gradient could not be explained by diet, physical exercise, or cholesterol alone; these risk factors explained only a small part of the gradient. The most important factor was the position that people held within the social structure (in which class, gender, and race play key roles) and the social distance between groups, and the differential control that people have over their own lives.

This enormously important scientific finding has many implications; one of them is that the major problem we face is not simply eliminating poverty but rather reducing inequality. The first is impossible to resolve without resolving the second. Another implication is that poverty is not just a matter of resources, as is wrongly assumed in World Bank reports that measure world-wide poverty by quantifying the number of people who live on a dollar a day. The real problem, again, is not absolute resources but the social distance and the different degrees of control over one's own resources. And this holds true in every society.

Let me elaborate. An unskilled, unemployed young black person living in the ghetto area of Baltimore has more resources (he or she is likely to have a car, mobile phone, and TV, and more square feet per household and more kitchen equipment) than a middle-class professional in Ghana, Africa. If the whole world were just a single society, the Baltimore youth would be middle class and the Ghana professional would be poor. And yet, the first has a much shorter life expectancy (forty-five years) than the second (sixty-two years). How can that be, when the first has more resources than the second? The answer is clear. It is far more difficult to be poor in the United States (the sense of distance, frustration, powerlessness, and failure is much greater) than to be middle class in Ghana. The first is far below the median; the second is above the median.

Does the same mechanism operate in inequalities among countries? The answer is, increasingly, yes. And the reason for adding "increasingly" is commu-nication—with ever more globalized information systems and networks, more information is reaching the most remote areas of the world. And the social dis-tance created by inequalities is becoming increasingly apparent, not only with-in but also among countries. Because this distance is more and more perceived as an outcome of exploitation, we are facing an enormous tension, comparable with that of the nineteenth and early twentieth centuries, when class exploita-tion became the driving force for social mobilization. The key element for defining the future is through which channels that mobilization takes place. What we have seen is an enormous mobilization, instigated and guided by an alliance of the dominant classes of the North and the South, aimed at—as men-tioned earlier—stimulating multi-class religious or nationalistic mobilizations that leave key class relations unchanged. We saw this phenomenon at the end of the nineteenth and beginning of the twentieth centuries. Christian democracy in Europe, for example, appears as the dominant classes' response to the threat of socialism and communism. The birth of Islamic fundamentalism was also stimulated for the same purposes.

The left-wing alternative must be centered in alliances among the dominated classes and other dominated groups, with a political movement that must be built upon the process of class struggle that takes place in each country. As Hugo Chávez of Venezuela said, "It cannot be a mere movement of protest and celebration like Woodstock." It is an enormous struggle, an endeavor in which organization and coordination are key, calling for a Fifth International. This is the challenge to the international Left today.

3

The Power of the Rich

William K. Tabb

Two trends dominate today's world political economy. The first is growing inequality. The second is slower economic growth. Both trends have important consequences, which flow from the increased power of capital in a globalized world. The hegemony of the capitalist class is not new, but in any specific conjuncture, how its power is exercised depends on how technological possibilities are deployed, the degree of ideological clarity of the working class (broadly conceptualized), and the political activity of factions of the ruling class itself. In looking at the power of the rich in the United States, I will discuss structural power and also contingent developments of George W. Bush's presidency and make a few remarks on Clinton to show some basic continuities.

William Domhoff, when he famously asked "Who Rules America Now?" noted that class and power are terms that make Americans a little uneasy and that concepts such as "ruling class" and "power elite" (the term popularized by C. Wright Mills) immediately put people on guard. The very idea that a relatively small group might dominate government as well as the economy went against the American grain, Domhoff wrote. We prefer to talk about interest groups. Nonetheless, in his view a cohesive ruling class "has its basis in the large corporations and banks, plays a major role in shaping the social and political climate, and dominates the federal government through a variety or organizations and methods."[1] Domhoff made clear he understood that this class system is an open and changing one and that our political system is a democratic one, that there are opportunities for social mobility, and that ordinary people are not powerless. Class domination in his view did not mean total control but the setting of the terms under which other classes and groups operate. The existence of a ruling class of the very rich does not mean that voting does not matter or that under certain circumstances this elite cannot be constrained. That all seems right to me.

Whereas Domhoff was focused on the social cohesion of this elite and Mills on the various pillars of its rule in the military, corporate, and political spheres, other analysts have stressed the way capitalists in different sectors and industries compete for influence to forward their narrower sector or specific firm interests. This understanding of the competing factions of the ruling class has its classic formation in *Federalist* Number 10, where James Madison wrote, "The most common and durable source of factions has been the various and unequal distribution of property . . . . A landed interest, a manufacturing interest, a mercantile interest, a moneyed interest, with many lesser interests grow up of necessity in civilized nations, and divide them into different classes actuated by different sentiments and views." Debate among classical political economists, for example, Malthus, who stressed the primary role of landowners, and his friend Ricardo, who defended the manufacturers as being the primary class whose interests should come first, took for granted such divisions. It was left to the last of the principal classical economists, Karl Marx, to introduce and champion the third great class existing under capitalism and to suggest that oppressed and exploited as the working class was it was destined to overthrow the class system.

Class power is less acknowledged today, even if its central importance remains evident to those who would look beyond their noses for its influence on how we produce and distribute the social product and on what kind of democracy we have. What is new is the conjunctural specifics of class formation and the exercise of the power of the rich, for, as political philosophers from Aristotle to Harold Laski and C. B. Macpherson have told us, political power is the handmaid of economic power.

Here I focus on the United States in our own time but will bear in mind, as Kevin Phillips has written, that "from the nursery years of the Republic, U.S. government economic decisions in matters of taxation, central bank operations, debt management, banking, trade and tariffs, and financial rescues or bailouts have been keys to expanding, shrinking, or realigning the nation's privately held assets."[2] The specifics of the way the Bush administration and the Republican Congress accelerated the regressive tilt to the rich echo those heard down through our nation's history and today take on resonance analogous to the Gilded Age and the Roaring Twenties, the other periods when conservative ideology and politics held sway and rapid increases in inequalities were produced by deregulation and variants of laissez-faire policy and Social Darwinist thinking. But in all periods, we have had a government of the rich that has acted in the interests of the rich.

Let us discuss the economics of the investment theory of politics through which such power is exercised. Officeholders and aspirants to high office are themselves typically wealthy individuals. One could examine any point in history and find this to be the case. Today "representatives" overwhelmingly come from careers in banking, law, or business and retire from public office to lobby for these and other interests, just as generals go on to second careers as military contractors. To pursue national office requires a personal fortune of one's own, rich friends, or patrons. There are 100,000 people in this country who give virtually all the money spent in political campaigns, and no one wins high office without assembling sufficient financing.

Once in office, elected officials tend to get far richer than they were when they entered politics. They are cut in on various deals. They become unusually successful investors. Empirical investigation reveals that in any given year between 1993 and 1998, senators who played the stock market did remarkably well. It turns out they were prescient in anticipating the market's movements up and down, purchasing a particular stock before it took off like a rocket and dumping stocks just in time. Consider a landmark study in the *Journal of Financial and Quantitative Analysis*, which took eight years to complete because there was no database from which the scholars could work and they had to develop one, gathering and examining data manually. They found that the stock portfolios of a random group composed of tens of thousands of households underperformed the market as a whole by 1.4 percent annually. Corporate insiders beat the market by 6 percent. But the senators (including their spouses and children) beat the market by 12 percent a year.[3] The study reminds one of the findings of U.S. Senate Banking Committee counsel Ferdinand Pecora who in 1933 exposed how J. P. Morgan had reserved shares for certain clients—FDR's secretary of the treasury, the chairmen of both the Republican and Democratic National Committees, and others. It also brings to mind Mark Twain's observation that "if your congressman comes back to your state to run for reelection and is not a millionaire, he is a fool and should be turned out of office."

Lobbyists, of course, also shower funds on those who vote their way. The Center for Public Integrity tells us that in 2003, lobbyists spent $2.4 billion (and they estimated for 2004 at least $4 billion), which was about twice as much as was spent on campaign finance in the same period. Roberta Baskin, the Center's executive director said, "Our report reveals that each year since 1998 the amount spent to *influence* federal lawmakers is double the amount of money spent to *elect* them" (emphasis in original).[4]

Whereas such spending by corporations has usually been pragmatically bipartisan, paying off whoever might advance the material interests in question, from 2000 to 2006, Republicans, who controlled all three branches of the federal government, created the K Street Project. This was an attempt by Republicans—led by Tom DeLay (who has serious legal problems due to corruption and alleged lawbreaking beyond the accepted limits and has resigned his House job)—to force lobbying organizations to hire only Republicans or suffer the consequences.

This drive toward one-party government is thankfully in some trouble because of ineptitude and overreaching. The other major party has been able to use the numerous scandals afflicting Republican officeholders and lobbyists to advance its own prospects. When people ask why the Democrats make a pathetic opposition party, they forget that Democrats must appeal to the rich to fund their campaigns, too, and cannot stray from serving these interests. Bill Clinton was able to win, in significant measure, thanks to investment bankers, high-tech entrepreneurs, and Hollywood money, as well as Democratic core supporters among urban-based constituencies in retail and real estate, and among wealthy non-WASPS, predominantly wealthy Jews. Today as the Bush gang stumbles from one embarrassment to the next, the lack of effective opposition party politics is astounding. The Democrats have chosen the issue of "competence." They campaign on the platform that they can run the system better and hope that this mild promise will attract voters and bring rich individuals and corporations to back them. They do not promise jobs, pensions, health care, or other aspects of personal security for American workers, nor an end to the war in Iraq. They accept corporate globalization and the political priorities of the rich.

Political parties need votes, but they are not simply vote maximizers. Parties are better understood as blocs of investors that back candidates who represent their interests. Public policy is shaped by the interplay and jockeying of these blocs, since most voters are unorganized, often minimally informed, hostile to the political process, and so prone to emotional appeals on issues of only glancing interest to the investor class. Public opinion on issues of interest to this investor class has weak influence on outcomes.

Although there is some muted talk of cleaning up corporate America, it is to these same corporations that politicians must go hat-in-hand for contributions. Those most eager to give and generous in their giving tend to be the individuals and corporations looking for handouts from elected officials or seeking protection from legal trouble, as any look at the contributors who have upped their giving shows. The contradiction is blatant. Politicians may seek popular support by responding to public outrage, but they do not bite the hand that feeds them. Since pro-business policies are necessary, much is off-limits for legislative debate. Seriously regulating corporations or forcing the rich to pay their taxes might please most voters but would effectively de-fund those who propose such an agenda. Such initiatives are not likely unless alternate funds become available from working-class movements and renegade wealthy folks or popular mobilization can make up with activism what it lacks in financial assets.

The idea of citizen sovereignty has much in common with the marketplace ideology of consumer sovereignty, which posits that buyers determine what producers offer. In the idealized market model, consumers have perfect information of what their choices are, the attributes of all alternative products on offer, and the prices charged by all sellers, and there are so many sellers that none can have influence over the market price. Further, it is assumed that individual consumers know what they want and are not influenced by peer pressure or advertising. In this simplistic model, the distribution of income goes unquestioned, even though some consumers have far more dollar votes than others. Public goods and merit goods, which constitute the social wage and contribute substantially to individual standards of living, are ignored if they cannot be sold through the private market —unless people are mobilized to demand what they understand is theirs by right. Government is viewed as inefficient and presumed to need to be made as businesslike as possible in its use of market incentives. A businesslike government is one premised on a capitalist view of limited functions, subservient to the class interests hegemonic in a social formation.

Even as this false understanding of the function of the state is promulgated, the growing share of national income accruing to the rich is fostered by government policies, tax cuts skewed in their direction, and subsidies for favored industries from oil to military contractors to the banking industry and Wall Street more generally. When the market goes down, government pumps it back up. The Federal Reserve guarantees the famous "Greenspan Putt," now perhaps to be known as the Bernanke Bounce, of lower interest rates as needed and promotes speculation by guaranteeing against downturns—since it is ever-ready with bailouts, whether of third world debt to private banks or special treatment for investors.

When Ronald Reagan said, "What I want to see above all is that this remains a country where someone can always get rich," his base understood him to say, "where those already rich can get vastly richer." George W. Bush's "ownership society" expands this idea and builds on the supply-side "analysis" that lower taxes and lower marginal rates provides greater incentives for investors and others to work harder, since you get to keep more of what you earn leading to more growth. The ideology claims that tax cuts cause "us" all to grow rich; that trickle-down economics benefits everyone. Since the result is growing inequality and lower real income for the working class than would be the case under more equitable arrangements, the rich extend honorary memberships. Just as white plantation owners told poor whites in the South that race was what counted, not wealth, a tactic that traveled well to other parts of the country, the ruling class tells the petit bourgeoisie, "We are all capitalists together. Let us protect 'our property.' " The Republican Party has also skillfully mobilized the anger of the petit bourgeoisie faced with harsh competition and resentful of the large corporations and the rich elite. In this vein, in the 2004 campaign George W. Bush criticized John Kerry's proposal to eliminate tax cuts for the wealthy, saying that "the rich in America happen to be small business owners." Further, Bush said that "the very rich people figure out how to dodge taxes anyway."[5]

Meanwhile, when addressing his big contributors, Bush was more inclined to say, as he did fundraising for the 2000 election to a very different gathering, "This is an impressive crowd—the haves and have-mores. Some people call you the elite. I call you my base."[6]

Bush is hardly the first U.S. president to serve this base. But in the years since the demise of Keynesian social policy and the rise to dominance of neoliberal globalization, capital has successfully made greater demands on both labor and the state. Between 1979 and 1989, the proportion of the nation's wealth held by the richest 1 percent of Americans nearly doubled, from 22 to 39 percent. A decade or so later, the discussion was in terms of what was happening to the richest 0.1 percent of the population. In 2002, 145,000 taxpayers, the top one-thousandth of the American people, enjoyed 7.4 percent of the nation's income, a percentage twice their share in 1980. In running for reelection, Bush said that most of the tax cuts of his first term went to low- and middle-income Americans. In fact, more than half (53 percent) will go to the top 10 percent over the first fifteen years of these cuts and more than 15 percent to the top one-thousandth of Americans. The *only* taxpayers whose share of taxes declined in 2001 and 2002 were those in the top 0.01 percent of the distribution. As of 2005, under the Bush tax cuts, the 400 taxpayers with the highest income (the "poorest" of these had an annual income of $87 million) paid income and FICA (Social Security) taxes at the same percentage of their income as those making between $50,000 and $75,000 a year. Another way to look at these growing inequalities is to consider that between 1950 and 1970, for every additional dollar earned by the bottom 90 percent, the top 0.01 percent (one ten-thousandth of Americans) rose by $162. From 1990 to 2002, for each additional dollar earned by the bottom 90 percent, the top 0.01 percent got an extra $18,000.[7]

Since the income of the bottom 90 percent is not growing, U.S. markets can only stimulate demand through the creation of debt, both personal and public. Companies have high profits but are not investing. They are cutting costs to raise profits, since sales are not rising due to inadequate domestic demand. What is happening is that as income becomes more and more unequal, so too does political influence grow for the elite of the super-rich who are increasingly able to recast the state to accommodate their narrow interests. Given the money it takes to be heard on the political scene, their power grows and democracy withers.

Wall Street and the president proclaim that all investors, half of all Americans, benefit from these tax cuts, but this is a calculated lie. Ordinary investors with 401(k) plans, other pension plans, and mutual fund holdings were already tax-exempt. They do not benefit from the change. It was the very rich, including the Wall Street CEOs with their compensation packages running into the tens of millions a year, who save hundreds of thousands, and for some, a million dollars or more a year in such tax cuts. Data on the effects of extending capital gains and dividend tax breaks are available from the careful and well-respected Citizens for Tax Justice based on an Institute on Taxation and Economic Policy tax model. It turns out that the vast majority of Americans would receive nothing from an extension of these special tax rates. Seventy-eight percent would get no tax cut, and an additional 10 percent would get less than $100. Most (53 percent) of the benefit would go to the richest 1 percent of Americans.

How do the rich get such favored treatment? The answer is to be found in the logic of the investment theory of politics. Groups like the Committee for Growth raise huge amounts from the super-rich with the purpose of intimidating politicians who would deny them more and more tax cuts. Grover Norquist, leader of the well-funded Americans for Tax Reform, whose aim is to shrink government down to the size where he can "drown it in a bathtub," has extracted a pledge never to raise taxes out of countless politicians as the price of support from the anti-tax forces.

In the era of national Keynesianism, domestic demand was important to economic growth and profitability. Under the regime of global neoliberalism, the goal of lowering costs everywhere is in the interest of both national capital and smaller entrepreneurs. The latter hated the government redistributional programs that lowered the cost of job loss and made workers uppity—they are always interested in putting greater pressure on the working class. Internationalized capital, which had earlier accommodated the welfare state and trade unions in the interests of domestic peace, can now threaten labor, which is immobile and at a greater disadvantage, with disinvestment. Its greater mobility gives it increased power over the state as well. With this major reuniting of factional interests, the Republicans gain strength while New Democrats look for ways to follow New Labour in jettisoning trade union influence. In such a context the basic rule of investor politics comes home to roost.

As Thomas Ferguson writes, "On issues affecting the vital interests that major investors have in common, no party competition will take place."[8] It is not that the issues of interest to these investors will be the only ones discussed. The point is for the candidate favoring the vital interests of the investors to win. This leads to candidates giving prominence to all manner of issues, from gay marriage to abortion, which may not be of central concern to investors but are calculated to ensure victory, and to mud-slinging and negative advertising based on false and malicious claims. The point is winning so that investor objectives can be legislated. The big campaign givers are those whose wealth depends on the government, such as military contractors, or those who want to change government regulations, like the securities and energy sectors, as well as everyone from tobacco to those on the receiving end of asbestos lawsuits. Some individual contributors are driven by ideology. The wealthy individual contributors overwhelmingly support Republicans, and the most ideologically right wing invest heavily in pursuing extremist politics. This group, which has shown itself willing to back radical right candidates opposing more moderate Republicans in primaries, has the money and clout to intimidate.

Whereas rich investors know well what is in their interest, and devote serious resources to influence outcomes, ordinary voters often lack incentives to be informed. Many are influenced by the repetition of the messages paid for by the rich that "taxation is bad, tax cuts are good," and some learn to parrot the ideology adopting anti-government positions. Some are convinced that the government taxes hardworking people and gives money to "welfare." Some, though they understand that the state favors the rich, conclude "government" is the enemy and so oppose taxation, helping the wealthy escape both the taxation and regulation that could be imposed by popular movements contesting for greater leverage over the state.

Given the resources and interests of this elite, they are more than willing to help along the careers of those who will be useful to them. One need look no further than the example of George W. Bush to see this process in action. Bush was able to enter the oil business thanks to money extended by rich individuals interested in helping him along. He pretty much failed in the oil business but was repeatedly bailed out. His insider sale of Harken Energy has gotten some attention because it was the source of his first serious income. In 1989 he invested $606,000 as part of a syndicate that bought the Texas Rangers baseball team, borrowing the money and repaying the loan with the proceeds from selling Harken stock before the company collapsed, a classic insider trading arrangement. The city of Arlington then was kind enough to build the Rangers a new stadium with public funds. His popularity as a public owner of the team, family connections, and associated good PR allowed Bush to run for governor of Texas "on the theme of self-reliance rather than reliance on government," as Paul Krugman recounts in his telling of Bush's career successes. The Rangers were sold for triple the price paid. Bush's share came to $2.3 million, but his partners voluntarily gave up some of their shares so Bush received 12 percent of the gain or $14.9 million—a $12 million gift to a sitting governor.

The buyer of the Rangers was a man named Tom Hicks. This last detail may seem arcane, but bear with me a moment. Quoting again from Krugman:

> The University of Texas, though a state institution, has a large endowment. As governor, Mr. Bush changed the rules governing the endowment, eliminating the requirements to disclose "all details concerning the investments made and income realized," and to have "a well-recognized performance measurement service" assess investment results. That is, the government officials no longer had to tell the public what they were doing with public money, or to allow an independent performance assessment. Then Mr. Bush "privatized" (his term) $9 billion in university assets, transferring them to a nonprofit corporation known as Utimco that could make investment decisions behind closed doors.[9]

In effect, the money was put under the control of Utimco's chairman, Tom Hicks, allowing millions of dollars to be invested in private funds managed by Hicks's business associates and major Republican Party donors who received large fees for making bad investments. This is not just a matter of corrupt dealings but a tale of how the rich profit from influence over officeholders and how they groom our country's leaders, who may not themselves have their own fortune, even when as in the case of George W. Bush they come from an elite family.

As to the normal workings of the system, we do not need to review the circumstances surrounding Tom DeLay and Jack Abramoff. Rather, the individual abuses call attention to the structural power of the rich and the systemic corruption of politics in the presence of great inequalities of wealth. This is the continuing issue. Bush is interesting for the naked openness with which he uses his office and his success in doing so. As *The Economist* has written, "George Bush's relationship with his business supporters could hardly be more straightforward. Business people give him huge piles of money. In return he cuts their taxes and shreds red tape."[10] But again this is not only about George Bush. A decade ago, David Sanger of the *New York Times* wrote, "Ever since Bill Clinton came to office, he has done more for the Fortune 500 than virtually any president in this century."[11] In the summer of 1995, the *Chicago Sun Times* disclosed that in a letter signed by the Democratic Party co-chairs (Christopher Dodd and Donald Fowler) a menu of meal-deals was offered: a $100,000 contributor would get two meals with President Clinton, two meals with Vice President Gore, a slot on a foreign trade mission with DNC leaders, a daily fax report, and an assigned DNC staff member to assist with "personal requests." Other lesser inducements were offered for $50,000, $10,000, and $1,000.

Clinton, a New Democrat, was pro-business (of course), pro-trade, and anti-union. Since many Silicon Valley entrepreneurs the Democrats counted on were pro-choice and pro-environment, he was these things also. The Clinton White House and the New Democrats in Congress supported the high-tech agenda of more visas for high-tech workers, tax credits for R&D, support for trade with China, a moratorium on Internet taxes, and so on. However, as *Mother Jones* reported, Vice President Gore's post-convention "populism" drove techies to the Republicans, who finally raised almost as much from this sector as the Democrats.[12]

Wall Street was crucial to Clinton. The Republicans noted this and made privatization of Social Security a lead issue, and in so doing they reaped Wall Street's gratitude. Many point out that Bush failed in his efforts to privatize Social Security. True. But Wall Street rewarded the effort. Sixty-seven names on the *Mother Jones* list of the 400 biggest contributors are security brokers and investment managers who poured money into Republican coffers. They would benefit by the fees earned from all of the new monies in the proposed private retirement accounts. The push to set up private accounts for retirement, and indeed for health care, are ideologically appealing to the Republican anti-government base and to the companies that would directly benefit from selling and managing these accounts. It is also a brilliant economic wedge issue, attacking the Democrats at what has been one of their popular strengths. For the Democrats, support from labor unions, which most strongly oppose Social Security privatization, is important. For New Democrats to walk away from such core commitments of the traditional party is difficult.

In 2000, Bush's strong backers were Sunbelt, especially Texan, oil and contractor contributors and cronies of the governor. By 2004, big bucks were coming especially heavily from Wall Street, which on one occasion, June 23, 2004, offered up $4 million in one night. E. Stanley O'Neal, the chairman, CEO, and president of Merrill Lynch, and Stephen Lessing, managing director of Lehman Brothers, were two of the first "Rangers" and the top bundlers of $200,000 or more. Other leading Wall Street figures were "Pioneers," who bundled $100,000 or more. This support represented a change from 2000, when two weeks before he was sworn in, Bush held a business leader forum in Texas with dozens of CEOs but none from Wall Street. In a 2002 economic summit in Waco the same was true. By 2003, Wall Street had surpassed all other groups in contributing to Bush. The administration thereafter was a more enthusiastic advocate of "pro-investor policies" that cut in Wall Street for favored treatment. Such a shift was inevitable. In the statistical tables of the *Economic Report of the President 2006* (Table B-91: Corporate Profits by Industry, 1959–2005), in 2003, for corporate profits for domestic industries, the financial sector enjoyed $313 billion in profit compared to $534 for all non-financial sector firms, a remarkable change from the days when one thought of finance as lubricating manufacturing (a sector that earned only $119 billion in profits in 2003). Profits accruing from corporate activities in the rest of the world were $176 billion, and by the third quarter 2005 these were $223 billion. Imperialist demands on host governments assisted such penetration and promoted greater profits for U.S.-based transnationals.

Let me conclude by putting some of these aspects together. The investor theory is clear enough in its predictions that issues of interest to the majority of citizens will be ignored if the rich contributor class does not want them considered. Likewise, issues of interest to the rich will be put forward and reinforced in media discussion even though they lack popular support. The legislation that follows—the focus here is on tax policy—seems to confirm a correlation between investments and government policies favoring investors. The rise of income inequality, though it has many causes, has been powered by federal taxation policies of bought politicians and ruling-class representatives who hold control of the federal government. Lastly, simply voting for Democrats may not essentially change what needs to be changed. Only when elected officials face a well-organized and mobilized popular opposition do they pause in simply voting for what the rich want.

4

Some Economics of Class

Michael Perelman

How much more will be required before the U.S. public awakes from its political slumber? Tepid action in the workplace, the voting booth, and the streets have allowed the right wing to steamroll revolutionary changes that have remade the entire sociopolitical structure of the United States. Since the election of Franklin Roosevelt in 1932, every Democratic administration with the exception of Lyndon Johnson's has been more conservative—often far more conservative—than the previous Democratic administration. Similarly, every elected Republican administration, with the single exception of George Herbert Walker Bush's, has been more conservative than the previous Republican administration. The deterioration in the distribution of income is a symptom of a far larger problem. Perhaps formulating the situation in the United States might help people understand their class interests as well as reveal who has benefited from the right-wing revolution.

Critics of Marx have long taken pleasure in claiming that the rise of the middle class in the United States and other advanced capitalist economies disproves Marx's "predictions" of the course of capitalism. In recent decades, however, the distribution of income in the United States is coming to resemble that of many poor Latin American economies, with a shrinking middle class and an obscene share of wealth going to the richest members of society.

Although proponents of the U.S. model pretend that recent economic trends represent a success, in truth they are signs of capitalism's failure. Once capitalism began to falter in the late 1960s, the ruling class in the United States was unable to gain ground by ordinary business practices. So, the ruling class pursued a two-fold strategy: attacking workers' rights while pursuing tax cuts, deregulation, and government subsidies. In effect, when forces integral to the normal functioning of capitalism began to depress the rate of profit, the ruling class adopted measures to change the balance of power in a way that would shift wealth and income in its direction.

Between 1970 and 2003, the Gross Domestic Product (GDP) adjusted for inflation almost tripled, from $3.7 trillion to $10.8 trillion.[1] Because the population also increased by about 35 percent during that same period, per capita income more than doubled. However, not everyone's income rose. Hourly wage earners certainly did not benefit from the economic growth. According to government statistics, hourly wages corrected for inflation peaked in 1972 at $8.99 measured in 1982 dollars. By 2003, hourly wages had fallen to $8.29, although they rose modestly using a different measure of inflation.[2]

Economists Thomas Piketty from the French research institute CEPREMAP and Emmanuel Saez of the University of California at Berkeley assembled detailed information about the distribution of income using data from the Internal Revenue Service. They defined income in current 2000 dollars as annual gross income reported on tax returns, excluding capital gains and all government transfers (such as Social Security, unemployment benefits, welfare payments, etc.) and before individual income taxes and employees' payroll taxes. For the bottom 90 percent of the population, the average income stood at $27,041 in 1970, then peaked in 1973—at the same time as hourly wages—at $28,540. This figure bottomed out in 1993 at $23,892. By 2002, average income for this group stood at $25,862, about 4.5 percent below where it stood in 1970.[3]

This estimate does not mean that everybody in the bottom 90 percent fell behind, but that the losses among the vast majority of these people were sufficient to counterbalance the gains of the more fortunate members of the bottom 90 percent. So probably 80 percent of the population was worse off in 2002 than in 1970.

At the top, matters were quite different. Piketty and Saez found that in 1970 the top ten corporate CEOs earned about forty-nine times as much as the average wage earner. By 2000, the ratio had reached the astronomical level of 2,173 to 1. The rate of growth of executive pay has also outstripped the rate of growth of profits. For example, between the periods 1993–1995 and 2001–2003, the ratio of total compensation to the top five executives of public companies to those companies' total earnings increased from 4.8 percent to 10.3 percent.[4]

Despite the decline in the average well-being of people in the bottom 90 percent of the population because it grew by approximately 30 percent, this group probably still received about 30 percent of the increase in the GDP. In addition, the GDP does not exactly equal the income figures of the Internal Revenue Service, but the figures are close enough to conclude that the top 10 percent of the population received the lion's share of all economic growth between 1970 and 2000.

You can quibble with the Piketty and Saez estimates about the distribution of income. Including transfers, such as Social Security, and by using a different estimate of inflation, the incomes of the bottom 90 percent of the population appear to have grown by about 20 percent between 1970 and 2002—a mere 0.6 percent per year. However, looking at the situation from another perspective, this data may be far too conservative in estimating how much the poor have fallen behind and the rich have prospered. First of all, the data exclude capital gains, which represent a major share of the income going to the very rich. In addition, as Richard Titmuss observed in 1962, efforts by the rich to avoid taxes makes the distribution of income appear far more equal than it actually is.[5]

Academic economics has done little to investigate the extent of this distortion, although David Cay Johnston's outstanding book *Perfectly Legal*, which describes the contribution of the tax system to inequality, forcefully demonstrates how the law permits the rich to use ingenious means to hide their wealth and income in order to avoid paying taxes.[6] Many of the tax avoidance schemes are perfectly legal, even though they may violate the spirit of the law; others, what economist Max Sawicky calls do-it-yourself tax cuts, are not.[7]

For example, in a globalized economy, hiding money offshore is not particularly difficult. One recent study estimated that the world's richest individuals have placed about $11.5 trillion worth of assets in offshore tax havens, mainly to avoid taxes. This amount is roughly equal to the GDP of the United States. Of course, citizens of the United States are not responsible for the entire $11.5 trillion, but then the report does not take account of the assets that corporations stash in tax havens.[8] Although the Internal Revenue Service occasionally convicts an unsophisticated offender, this practice is relatively safe.

In addition, taxpayers underestimate their tax liabilities by inflating the cost basis of assets on which they take capital gains. One estimate puts the extent of this inflation at about one-quarter trillion dollars.[9] This practice obviously serves to benefit the richest taxpayers, although it does not affect the Saez and Piketty results, which exclude capital gains.

Of the estimated 16 percent of the legal tax obligation that goes unpaid, according to the latest data from the IRS, we can rest assured that the vast majority comes from the wealthiest members of society. The clever tactics of tax avoidance prevent the IRS data from capturing a good deal of the wealth and income of the top 10 percent of the population. In short, as hotel magnate Leona Helmsley famously said, "Only the little people pay taxes." The government facilitates shenanigans, such as those used by Helmsley, by steadily increasing the complexity of the tax code while reducing the resources for enforcement. Helmsley served eighteen months in jail for her financial transgressions, but not because of diligence on the part of the government. She refused to pay money due to contractors. The resulting civil suit incidentally exposed her tax fraud.

The IRS also reinforces inequities between rich and poor by devoting a disproportionate share of its scrutiny to those without substantial resources, especially poor people who declare an "earned income tax credit."[10]

Over and above tax-related distortions of the distribution of income, the wealthy have access to resources that do not count as income. Consider Johnston's description of the personal use of corporate jets:

> When William Agee was running the engineering firm Morrison-Knudsen into bankruptcy, he replaced its one corporate jet, already paid off, with two new ones and boasted about how the way he financed them polished up the company's financial reports. His wife, Mary Cunnigham Agee, used the extra jet as her personal air taxi to hop around the United States and Europe. When F. Ross Johnson ran the cigarette-and-food company RJR Nabisco, which had a fleet of at least a dozen corporate jets, he once had his dog flown home, listed on the manifest as "G. Shepherd." And Kenneth Lay let his daughter take one of Enron's jets to fly across the Atlantic with her bed, which was too large to go as baggage on a commercial flight.[11]

Here again, Johnston understates the situation. Consider this fuller description of the RJR Nabisco case:

> After the arrival of two new Gulfstreams, Johnson ordered a pair of top-of-the-line G4s, at a cool $21 million apiece. For the hangar, Johnson gave aviation head Linda Galvin an unlimited budget and implicit instructions to exceed it. When it was finished, RJR Nabisco had the Taj Mahal of corporate hangars, dwarfing that of Coca-Cola's next door. The cost hadn't gone into the hangar itself, but into an adjacent three-story building of tinted glass, surrounded by $250,000 in landscaping, complete with a Japanese garden. Inside a visitor walked into a stunning three-story atrium. The floors were Italian marble, the walls and floors lined in inlaid mahogany. More than $600,000 in new furniture was spread throughout, topped off by $100,000 in *objets d'art*, including an antique Chinese ceremonial

robe spread in a glass case and a magnificent Chinese platter and urn. In one corner of the ornate bathroom stood a stuffed chair, as if one might grow fatigued
walking from one end to the other. Among the building's other features: a walk-
in wine cooler; a "visiting pilots' room," with television and stereo; and a "flight-
planning room," packed with state-of-the-art computers to track executives'
whereabouts and their future transportation wishes. All this was necessary to
keep track of RJR's thirty-six corporate pilots and ten planes, widely known as
the RJR Air Force.[12]

David Yermack of New York University's Stern School of Business produced
a paper with the delightful title "Flights of Fancy: Corporate Jets, CEO
Perquisites, and Inferior Shareholder Returns," in which he investigated the relationship between this particular luxury and corporate efficiency. He found that
the cost for CEOs who belong to golf clubs far from their company's headquar-
ters is two-thirds higher, on average, than for CEOs who have disclosed air travel
but are not long-distance golf club members.[13]

Based on Yermack's paper, a *Wall Street Journal* article titled "JetGreen"
described corporate jets "as airborne limousines to fly CEOs and other executives to golf dates or to vacation homes where they have golf club memberships."[14]
To add insult to injury, the government subsidizes corporate jets. For example,
the government waves the hefty landing fees that commercial aircraft must pay in
order to support the air traffic control system. The value of these subsidies
amounts to billions of dollars.[15] A significant amount of these subsidies benefits
the private lives of corporate executives.

High-level corporate executives enjoy many other perquisites besides free
travel, including the provision of luxury boxes at sports stadia, chefs, lawn care,
and a multitude of other benefits that ordinary people would have to pay for on
their own, if only they could afford them. *New York Times* business columnist
Gretchen Morgenson described the excesses of Donald J. Tyson, former chairman of Tyson Foods, ranging from the personal use of corporate jets to house-
keeping and lawn care. Echoing Leona Helmsley, she appropriately titled her article "Only the Little People Pay for Lawn Care."[16]

The Piketty and Saez data also overestimate the welfare of the poor, especially
if one considers that ordinary people must increasingly work more hours to get
what they earn. For example, between 1970 and 2002, annual hours worked per
capita rose 20 percent in the United States while falling in most other advanced
economies.[17] Besides, for ordinary workers, benefits such as pensions and health
care are in rapid decline. Finally, the reported income of the poorer segments of

society does not take account of the many expenses that poor people pay. The data ignore the late fees that banks and other corporations charge, along with usurious interest rates and various other costs that fall mostly on the least fortunate. Even though the government disregards these factors in assembling its statistics about wealth and income, they can be significant. In 2004, banks, thrifts, and credit unions collected a record $37.8 billion in service charges on accounts, more than double what they got in 1994, according to the Federal Deposit Insurance Corporation and the National Credit Union Administration. Banks are also raising fees for late payments, low balances, and over-the-limit charges to as much as $39 per violation. Some banks even charge for speaking with a service representative. These fees predominantly fall on the poor.[18]

Even among the richest 10 percent of the population, the unseemly distribution of income is increasingly skewing toward the richest of the rich. In 1970, the top 0.01 percent of taxpayers had less than 0.53 percent of total income. By the year 2000, their share had soared to 3.06 percent. In other words, the income of these 13,400 taxpayers exploded from being fifty-three times the national average to an almost unbelievable 306 times, slightly less than it was in the peak year of 1928, right before the Great Depression. These 13,400 richest families in the United States had about the same income as the poorest 25 percent of the households in the country.[19] Of course, membership in this elite group was not unchanging, but it was probably relatively stable. Certainly, few of these fortunate people ever fell into the bottom 25 percent.

Ownership of wealth is even more concentrated than income. With the bursting of the dot-com bubble, wealth inequality had temporarily fallen a bit, as it usually does during an economic decline. Even so, by 2001, the top 1 percent of households owned 40 percent of the financial wealth in the United States.[20] Had the calculation of the wealth holdings of the richest 1 percent been made while the stock market had still been expanding the number would have been even more extreme than the reported 40 percent. I have no doubt that inequality will continue its upward climb in the absence of a new recession or a rapid change in the political climate.

At the same time, ordinary people are rapidly losing their pensions and medical benefits, while government programs upon which they depend, such as Medicare and Medicaid, are becoming less generous. Robert K. Merton, the sociologist and father of a Nobel Prize–winning economist, writing in the context of the accumulation of scientific prestige by the elite, called attention to the "Matthew effect," alluding to the biblical passage: "For to everyone who has will more be given, and he will have abundance but from him who has not even what he has will be taken away."[21] Today we are witnessing an economic Matthew effect beyond what anybody could have imagined only a few decades earlier.

Whether the Piketty and Saez estimates are overstated or too conservative, I leave for others to decide. No matter which estimate you prefer, nobody can deny that the business offensive has certainly paid off handsomely. Since the election of George W. Bush in 2000, the transfer of wealth and income has accelerated at an alarming rate.

Even that arch-free-marketeer, former Federal Reserve chairman Alan Greenspan, was moved to express concern about the extent of inequality in the United States today, admitting to Senator Jack Reed, "I think that the effective increase in the concentration of incomes here, which is implicit in this, is not desirable in a democratic society."[22] Admittedly, one might question the chairman's sincerity considering his preferred remedies. For example, in response to a question about Social Security from Senator Schumer at a hearing before the same Senate committee a few months later, Greenspan responded, "I've been concerned about the concentration of income and wealth in this nation . . . and this [the privatization of Social Security], in my judgment, is one way in which you can address this particular question."[23] Here is a more genuine expression of concern from Warren Buffett, perennially the second-richest person in the world regarding the excessive tax cuts:

> Corporate income taxes in fiscal 2003 accounted for 7.4 percent of all federal tax receipts, down from a postwar peak of 32 percent in 1952. With one exception (1983), last year's percentage is the lowest recorded since data was first published in 1934 . . . . Tax breaks for corporations (and their investors, particularly large ones) were a major part of the Administration's 2002 and 2003 initiatives. If class warfare is being waged in America, my class is clearly winning.[24]

Buffett's figures actually overstate the corporate tax contribution. In fact, the Federal Reserve System—the purpose of which is supposed to be the public welfare, not profits—paid 16 percent of all corporate income taxes in 2002. Of those real corporations, many of the largest pay no taxes whatsoever. A fair number of these large corporations even pay negative taxes.

One study of 275 profitable Fortune 500 corporations with total U.S. profits of $1.1 trillion over the three-year period of 2001 through 2003, found that 82 of these corporations:

> . . . paid zero or less in federal income taxes in at least one year from 2001 to 2003. Many of them enjoyed multiple no-tax years. In the years they paid no income tax,

these companies reported $102 billion in pretax U.S. profits. But instead of paying $35.6 billion in income taxes as the statutory 35 percent corporate tax rate seems to require, these companies generated so many excess tax breaks that they received outright tax rebate checks from the U.S. Treasury, totaling $12.6 billion. These companies' "negative tax rates" meant that they made more after taxes than before taxes in those no-tax years.[25]

Twenty-eight of these companies had a negative tax rate over the entire three-year period. The report continues, suggesting that the inequities are getting worse year by year:

In 2003 alone, 46 companies paid zero or less in federal income taxes. These 46 companies, almost one out of six of the companies in the study, reported U.S. pretax profits in 2003 of $42.6 billion, yet received tax rebates totaling $5.4 billion. In 2002, almost as many companies, 42, paid no tax, reporting $43.5 billion in pretax profits, but $4.9 billion in tax rebates. From 2001 to 2003, the number of no-tax companies jumped from 33 to 46, an increase of 40 percent.[26]

Putting this erosion of corporate taxes into perspective, the authors conclude:

Corporate taxes paid for more than a quarter of federal outlays in the 1950s and a fifth in the 1960s. They began to decline during the Nixon administration, yet even by the second half of the 1990s, corporate taxes still covered 11 percent of the cost of federal programs. But in fiscal 2002 and 2003, corporate taxes paid for a mere 6 percent of our government's expenses.[27]

A follow-up study showed that the erosion of taxes on the state level was even more extreme.[28]

Gaining a perspective on the extent of the effect of cuts in personal income taxes may be easier. In 2005, President Bush was campaigning to make his tax cuts permanent. If he succeeds, the benefits for the top 1 percent of the population over the following seventy-five years will amount to an estimated $2.9 trillion.[29] In other words, the tax cuts for this small segment of the population over this period would equal about one-quarter of the current annual GDP of the United States.

The lethal combination of tax cuts for the rich and the growing burdens on the poor threaten to annihilate what is left of social mobility. In the words of Thomas Piketty, mentioned earlier for his startling work on income inequality:

These new high-income tax cuts, together with all the previous tax cuts (including the repeal of the estate tax), will eventually contribute to rebuild a class of ren-
tiers in the U.S., whereby a small group of wealthy but untalented children controls vast segments of the U.S. economy and penniless, talented children simply
can't compete . . . . If such a tax policy is maintained, there is a decent probabili-
ty that the U.S. will look like Old Europe prior to 1914 in a couple of generations.[30]

I do not mean to imply that the right wing is totally indifferent about people
not carrying their share of the tax burden. Without betraying a trace of irony, a
famous *Wall Street Journal* editorial wailed about "the non-taxpaying class,"
complaining about the "lucky duckies."[31]

The lucky duckies in question were those people who were too poor to make
enough to pay taxes, not the affluent beneficiaries of the right-wing revolution.
And what a revolution it was! Even if we correct for population growth and transfer payments, ignoring all the reasons why the gains of the wealthy may be an
understatement, we can safely say that the right-wing revolution still represents
the largest transfer of wealth and income in the history of the world—far larger
than what occurred during either the Russian or Chinese revolutions. After all,
neither China nor Russia had an economy that came anywhere near $7 trillion,
the amount by which the annual U.S. GDP grew between 1970 and 2002.

In terms of wealth, the differences are far more extreme because creating an
annual income flow requires a much greater level of wealth, comparable to the difference between the annual rent of a house and its purchase price. Government
policies continue to promote an even more extreme redistribution of wealth and
income to the rich. Most economists manage to turn a blind eye or to make an
effort to explain those policies as necessary to create jobs or to make the economy more productive. The short-term victory in capturing virtually all of the
growth of wealth and income while shedding tax obligations may seem like cause
for jubilation—at least within some circles—but this victory may turn out to be
hollow, even for those at the top of the pyramid. The right-wing revolution is
ruthlessly pursuing policies that are undermining education, health care, and virtually every other public institution that supports the economy in an effort to
extract more surplus value from ordinary people. In the process, the right wing is
undermining the very foundation of the economy.

5

Harder Times: Undocumented Workers and the U.S. Informal Economy

Richard D. Vogel

Many of the informal economies operating in the world today are the offspring of globalization and need to be understood as such. The economic and social prospects for people engaged in informal employment—sometimes referred to as "precarious" and "off-the-books" employment—as well as their families and communities, are substantially inferior to those associated with formal employment, and the current boom of informal economic activity bodes ill for all working people.

Referred to variously as "underground," "shadow," "invisible," and "black" (as in black market) economies, many informal economies have developed around the economic survival activities of workers who have been excluded from the formal economy of their nation or region and exploited by entrepreneurs willing to take advantage of their desperation. Initially considered phenomena of the third world and developing nations, informal economies are now expanding rapidly in the free market nations of the Western world, including the United States.

Work in the informal economy contrasts sharply with formal employment: wages and working conditions are substandard; there are no guaranteed minimum or maximum hours of work, paid holidays, or vacations; gender, ethnic, and racial discrimination are uncontrolled and systematically exploited; no mandatory health or safety regulations protect workers from injury or death on the job; and workers are denied the traditional benefits of employment—workman's compensation; health, unemployment, and life insurance and pensions. Needless to say, few workers join the informal labor force voluntarily—the vast majority are recruited primarily through economic desperation unmitigated by even a minimal social safety net.

Worker participation in the informal economy is a complex phenomenon. While immigrant workers play a significant role in the informal U.S. economy, native workers also participate. These workers in the informal sector include widely divergent groups, from professionals who do unreported jobs on the side and craft workers who exchange work in kind to marginalized native workers who, because of cutbacks in welfare programs, must accept any work they can find.

The informal sector of the U.S. economy is growing as the working population expands and employment opportunities in the formal economy do not keep pace. Not only are workers being displaced as companies move their operations off-shore in search of lower labor costs, but an increasing number of U.S. corporate start-ups are overseas ventures. These current trends contribute to the exclusion of both new and veteran workers from the formal economy.

Los Angeles: A Definitive Case Study

Although no comprehensive national studies of the informal U.S. economy have been published to date, a study of work in the informal economy of the City of Los Angeles by the Economic Roundtable, a nonprofit public policy research organization, titled *Hopeful Workers, Marginal Jobs: LA's Off-the-Books Labor Force,* offers an in-depth look at a local informal economy.[1] Since this recently reported case study of Los Angeles's informal economy presents the most refined estimates of informal employment and its impact, it deserves special attention.

Chart 1 provides a detailed study of informal employment. The CPS line in Chart 1 is based on employment status reported by Current Population Survey respondents residing in Los Angeles County. The ES–202 line in Chart 1, based on California Employment Development Department records, is specific to California. It represents all wage and salary employment reported by Los Angeles County employers in their payroll tax submissions to the state. The gap between the two lines in Chart 1 can be considered a good indicator of informal economic activity.

This chart reveals a widening gap between worker and employer reported employment signaling an ongoing informalization of the Los Angeles County economy that has continued unabated through boom and bust for the last eighteen years.

The most remarkable data come from the period following the economic recession of 2001. The data indicate that as late as 2004 economic recovery was still out of sight. In spite of that, the informal economy held relatively steady during this period while the formal economy continued in serious decline. The 2005 data, not included in the Economic Roundtable study, indicates a continuation of the same trend. The conclusion of the Economic Roundtable researchers, that

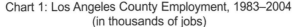

Chart 1: Los Angeles County Employment, 1983–2004
(in thousands of jobs)

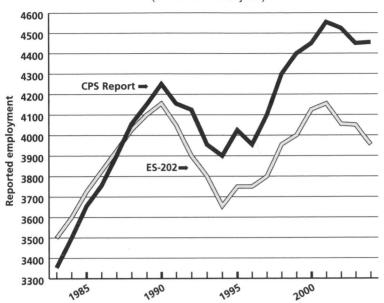

the economic stagnation of Southern California triggered by the recession of 2001 would have been worse without the ameliorating effects of the informal economy appears to be fully warranted.

In addition to documenting the general trends of informal economic activity, the Economic Roundtable study also offers credible estimates of the actual size of the informal economy in Los Angeles County. These researchers calculated low-range, mid-range, and high-range estimates for the number of county workers in the informal labor force and, after careful consideration, settled on the mid-range estimate of 679,000 workers in 2004. This number represented a substantial 15 percent of Los Angeles County's labor force in that same year.

The Economic Roundtable researchers used this number to determine the cost of informal employment to the public social safety net in Los Angeles County. Determining that the average annual wage for off-the-books jobs was slightly over $12,000 in 2004, they calculated that the informal economy produced an $8.1 billion payroll. This unreported and untaxed payroll short-changed the public sector in Los Angeles County by the following amounts:

- $1 billion in Social Security taxes (paid by both employers and workers)
- $236 million in Medicare taxes (paid by both employers and workers)

- $96 million in California State Disability Insurance payments (paid by workers)
- $220 million in Unemployment Insurance payments (paid by employers)
- $513 million in Workers Compensation Insurance payments (paid by employers)

These losses add up to over $2 billion in unpaid payroll benefits and insurance that are needed to fund a minimal social safety net for workers. The payroll tax shortfall is continuing and resistance on the part of California taxpayers to underwrite public relief measures has resulted in the widespread deterioration of social services for informal workers and their families across the state.

Though the Economic Roundtable study is focused primarily on work in the informal economy, researchers point out that informal workers in Los Angeles County spend an estimated $4.1 billion per year that should generate $440 million in sales tax revenue. However, these workers purchase many goods and services from informal retailers and service providers who do not collect sales taxes and submit them to the state, further eroding support for the public sector.

The social and political crises of the region are being fueled by the expanding informal economy in Southern California based on the widespread exploitation of undocumented Mexican and Central American workers. This state of affairs has elevated the issue of illegal immigration in California (and, of course, the nation) to center stage.

The Exploitation of Undocumented Workers

Fundamental to understanding the informal economy in Los Angeles is the issue of the exploitation of undocumented workers. Although it is true that many native workers and legal immigrants participate in Los Angeles's informal economy, undocumented immigrants represent the majority of the off-the-books workers. At the same time, though many individuals, both natives and immigrants, participate in both economies, these dual roles should not be allowed to obscure the dominant role of undocumented immigrant workers in Los Angeles's informal economy.

The Economic Roundtable study substantiates the dominant role of undocumented workers in Los Angeles County when it addresses the question of how many workers in the informal economy are undocumented immigrants and which industries employ them. Based on U.S Immigration and Naturalization Service (INS) and Census 2000 data, the Economic Roundtable estimates that undocumented immigrant workers make up 61 percent of the informal labor force in Los Angeles County and 65 percent in the city. Census 2000 data also establishes that though there are sizable numbers of Asian and Middle Eastern immigrants in Southern California, the vast majority of the immigrants residing and working there are from Latin America.

The proportion of undocumented workers in the informal economy of Los Angeles is remarkable, but where these workers are employed is also surprising. The top twenty industries employing undocumented immigrants in Los Angeles County are ranked in Chart 2. The picture of the informal labor force presented here contrasts sharply with popular perceptions of immigrant workers based on glimpses of day laborers soliciting on street corners, domestic workers waiting at bus stops, and landscape crews packed into pickup trucks. Derived from INS and Census 2000 data, this chart indicates that a wide array of industries in Los Angeles County systematically exploit undocumented immigrant labor. The Economic Roundtable study reveals that the majority of informal workers labor regularly and out of public view in factories, mills, restaurants, warehouses, workshops, nursing homes, office buildings, and private homes. In actual numbers, the

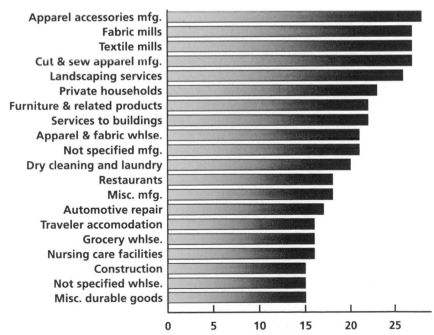

Chart 2: Estimated Percent of Undocumented Workers, Top 20 Industries, Los Angeles County, 2000

researchers estimate that these top twenty industries in Los Angeles County alone employ over 180,000 undocumented workers.

Most of these undocumented workers are obviously not casual day laborers. The nature of the majority of the jobs listed in Chart 2 entails stable relationships between employers and workers and requires extensive community networks to recruit and support those workers.

The Super-Exploitation of Undocumented Immigrant Women

Although the earnings of immigrant workers in the informal economy are inferior to that of native workers across the board, they do not represent the rock bottom of exploitation. The Economic Roundtable's breakdown of earnings by gender reveals the super-exploitation of undocumented women workers in the Los Angeles informal economy.

Since this exploitation takes place almost exclusively out of sight, it all but escapes public attention. However, the Economic Roundtable documents significant employment of undocumented women workers in the top twenty industries that employ the most informal workers. Generally, women tend to work in homes, personal service jobs, and light manufacturing, traditionally low-paying jobs, while men hold the majority of the jobs in transportation, construction, and other relatively higher-paying blue-collar jobs.

Economic Roundtable researchers highlight undocumented women's super-exploitation in the Los Angeles informal economy when they compare wages by gender in specific job categories for the year 1999. For example, in the category of services to buildings, where the gender shares of jobs were exactly equal, men averaged $13,308 while women made an average of $6,869 (51 percent of the earnings of men). Even in private households, beauty salons, department stores, and health care services, jobs clearly dominated by women workers, men were paid more. While women held 75 percent of the jobs in these categories, they earned only 66 percent of the wages of men doing the same work. Overall, the average wage for undocumented women workers in the informal economy of Los Angeles County was $7,630 compared to $16,553 for men. That amounts to only 46 percent of undocumented men's annual earnings.

The economic basis of Los Angeles's informal economy can be summed up succinctly: undocumented women workers make less than one-half (46 percent) of what undocumented men workers make, and the average wage of all undocumented workers is less than one-half (41 percent) that of native workers in the same job categories in the formal economy. Even these glaring inequalities under-estimate the super-exploitation of informal laborers because they do not account for the other employment benefits that workers in the formal economy receive, which range from 27 to 30 percent of their total employment compensation.

National Trends

The Economic Roundtable study indicates that the informal sector of the Los Angeles economy, which depends on the exploitation of undocumented workers, has become an integral part of the area's economy. The implications of this suggest that the trends of the national informal economy deserve careful reconsideration.

The informal economies of Los Angeles and Los Angeles County are unique. The proximity of Southern California to Mexico and the ready access to Mexican and Central American labor have historically shaped the economy, social structure, and culture of the area. That Los Angeles remains the primary destination of Mexican immigrants, both legal and undocumented, is a matter of public record.

Chart 3 is based on the important Immigration and Naturalization Service, Office of Policy and Planning study, *Estimates of the Unauthorized Immigrant Population Resident in the United States: 1990–2000.*[2] The INS statistics verify the concentration of undocumented immigrants in California but also reveal that Texas, New York, and Illinois (primarily New York City and Chicago) have considerable concentrations. All of these areas also have sizable established informal economies.

The big surprises in the INS study are the recent trends of worker immigration from Mexico and Central America to other destinations in the United States. These national trends are recorded in chart 4, based on the same INS study as chart 3. This shows that six of the top ten states that experienced the highest growth rate of undocumented immigrants during the last decade of the twentieth century are in the southeastern United States with three states in mid-America not far behind. The phenomenal increase in immigration is to the southeast and the booming metropolitan areas where new construction and service-oriented businesses have created a huge demand for low-cost labor. During the period 1990–2000, the number of undocumented immigrants doubled from 3.5 to 7 million for the United States overall. Current estimates indicate that those immigration trends have accelerated and the nation's total is now between 11.5 and 12 million.[3]

The present patterns of illegal undocumented worker immigration in the United States signal a rapid expansion of the national informal economy. The practice of

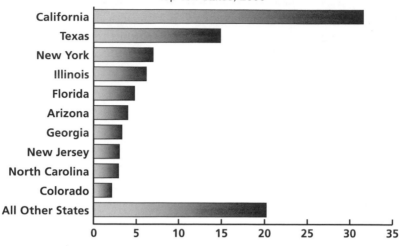

Chart 3: Estimated Percent of Total Undocumented Immigrants,
Top Ten States, 2000

basing the informal economy on the exploitation of undocumented workers, well established in California and Texas, is rapidly spreading across the nation. The Pew Hispanic Center estimates that in March 2005, 7.2 million of the 12 million undocumented immigrants in the United States were working, making up about 4.9 percent of the total work force. Applying the same correction factor to this Pew assessment that the Economic Roundtable researchers applied to employment data in the Current Population Survey for Los Angeles County suggests that 8 to 10 percent of all workers might be employed in the informal economy nationwide.

This emerging informal economy signals perennial hard times for undocumented workers and a continuing war of attrition against the U.S. working class at large.

Harder Times, U.S. Style

Global economic theory discusses informal economies in terms of "restructuring." This neoclassical and neoliberal theory maintains that all the workers of the world are competing with one another in a zero-sum game. Informal economies arise when the workers in one economic region of the world lose out to the workers in another region and the formal economy of the loser region contracts or collapses. According to this theory, informal economies arise to fill the resulting economic vacuum, and the mechanism of the free market will determine the outcome.

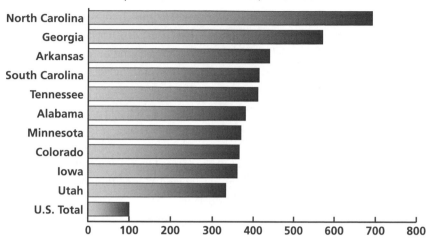

Chart 4: Percent Change in Undocumented Immigrants, Top 10 States and U.S. Total, 1990–2000

Neoliberal economists argue that displaced immigrant workers, primarily from Mexico and Central America, migrate to the United States and compete with native workers for scarce jobs in a post-industrial economy, as dictated by the "invisible hand" of the free market. The ideological cover story for public consumption, meanwhile, is that immigrant workers take the jobs that native workers refuse.

But it is *political economics*, not free markets, that shape global, national, and local economies. The movement of industrial and service production offshore to take advantage of cheap labor requires the compliance, or outright cooperation, of both home and foreign governments and is therefore a quintessentially political act. Also political is the widespread subversion of immigration and labor law for the sake of profits. These political machinations—not some mythical "invisible hand"—are the engines of the informal economy in the United States.

The burgeoning informal economy in the United States is introducing new elements into familiar historical patterns of exploitation. Although the U.S. economy has traditionally been fueled by immigrant labor, the current dependence on undocumented labor is unprecedented. Although the masses of Western and Eastern Europeans who immigrated to do America's dirty work in the past were rewarded with citizenship for their sacrifices, there is no indication that the current Mexican and Central American workers can expect the same. Naturalization is not part of the deal. Dirty and poorly paid work in the contemporary informal economy is not an initiation into the mainstream U.S. working class. The current wave of undocumented immigrants who work in the informal economy today are more likely than not to stay in the informal U.S. economy—as long as they are needed.

The U.S economy is indebted to undocumented immigrant workers, but there is no indication that the debt is going to be paid. The proposed "guest worker" programs currently being debated in Congress are nothing more than reruns of the Bracero Program that lasted from 1942 to 1964, and the debts owed to workers from that program are still outstanding. The contemporary strategy is to use Mexican and Central American workers displaced by NAFTA as long as possible. If, or when, they are no longer needed, they can be repatriated. It happened to their compatriots who were uprooted from their homes and communities and driven across the border at the onset of the Great Depression and again during the paramilitary deportation campaign designated "Operation Wetback" in the recession that followed the Second World War.

The current boom in the informal economy bodes no better for native workers in both the informal and formal sectors of the U.S. economy. Real wages, benefits, and standards of living continue to decline for all workers and the labor movement is stalled. Realizing the American Dream through hard work in a promising job is becoming a remote possibility rather than an accessible opportunity. And there's nothing like the naked specter of wage slavery in the informal economy and the ghettoization of the poor to keep the expectations of all workers in check. The revolution of rising expectations that gripped workers and minorities in the 1960s has been overshadowed by the prospect of pauperization.

Until the labor movement develops the solidarity necessary to confront the current assault of capitalism, the expanding informal economies of the world will continue to impoverish the lives of all working people. The call to all workers of the world to unite has never been more urgent than it is today.

6

The Retreat from Race and Class

David Roediger

As the twentieth century started, indeed at almost exactly the same moment that W. E. B. Du Bois predicted that the "color line" would be its great divide, Eugene Victor Debs announced that the socialist movement he led in the United States could and should offer "nothing special" to African Americans. "The class struggle," Debs added, "is colorless." As the century unfolded, the white Marxist Left, schooled by struggles for colonial freedom and by the self-activity of people of color in the centers of empire, increasingly saw the wisdom of Du Bois's insight and tried hard to consider how knowledge of the color line could illuminate, energize, and express class struggles. We would increasingly turn to other passages from Debs, including one expressing a historical insight he could already articulate in the early twentieth century but that his color blindness kept him from acting upon: "That the white heel is still on the black neck is simply proof that the world is not yet civilized. The history of the Negro in the United States is a history of crime without a parallel."

As the twenty-first century starts, the idea of a colorless struggle for human progress is unfortunately back with a vengeance. Such is of course the case on the Right in the United States, where what the legal scholar Neil Gotanda and others have called "color-blind racism" has underpinned attacks on affirmative action and even on the collection of the race-based statistics necessary to show patterns of discrimination. The high-sounding, ostensibly freedom-loving names given to such well-funded campaigns—"civil rights initiatives" to undermine affirmative action and "racial privacy acts" for amassing basic knowledge regarding the impact of race—have contributed mightily to attempts to recapture the moral high ground by those contending that a society in which white family wealth is about ten times that of black family wealth is nonetheless a color-blind one.

Nor are such instances confined to the United States. With the blood scarcely dry from white Australian riots against Arab beachgoers, that country's neoliberal leader John Howard reacted to press headlines screaming "Race Hate" and "Race War" by loudly proclaiming that he heads a color-blind society. When the French interior minister Nicolas Sarkozy, leader of the ruling party and leading candidate to replace Jacques Chirac as president, recently suffered criticism on race issues, he quickly planned a trip to Martinique to emphasize how little race allegedly matters in the French colonial world. Sarkozy stood out as especially harsh in his response to the rebellions of Islamic youth in France against police violence. He failed to join the president and prime minister in belatedly distancing themselves from a recently passed law requiring that French textbooks "recognize in particular the positive role of the French presence overseas, notably in North Africa." But an escape to color blindness still seemed possible.

Yet, Sarkozy was so thoroughly not welcomed by Martinique's great politician, poet, and theorist of liberation, Aimé Césaire, and others that the publicity stunt had to be canceled. Nonetheless, within France the pernicious role of long-established "color blindness" operates so strongly that Sarkozy can remain a top presidential contender. The legislative Left did not originally raise any serious protest against passage of the pro-colonialist textbook legislation, and the nation adheres to the same basic no-counting-by-race policies that racial privacy acts seek to establish in the United States. Ironically, Sarkozy himself has recently called for limited *"discrimination positive"* (affirmative action), using it as the carrot, operating in tandem with deportations and immigration restriction, to quell rebellions in France. But to put any "positive" measures into practice remains a problem. As *The Economist* recently put it, the French minister for equality remains practically alone at the top of the government in advocating finding a way to "measure the presence of the children of immigration" in political structures, the bureaucracy, and the labor force.

Against Race But Not for Class: Raceless Liberalism and Social Theory

What is distressingly new is the extent to which indictments of antiracism, and even attacks on the use of race as a concept, come now from liberalism and from the Left. Electorally, one hallmark of efforts by the Democratic Leadership Council to move the Democratic Party still further to the Right has been an attempt to distance the party from concrete appeals to, and identification with, people of color. Thus the constituencies most aware of both race and class inequities are marginalized in the name of appeals for "universal" programs. Meanwhile existing universal social programs, such as "welfare-as-we-know-it," have been subjected to withering (and anything but color-blind) bipartisan attacks. The Left was capable a decade ago of dissecting such a shell game, most trenchantly in Stephen Steinberg's 1994 *New Politics* article on the "liberal retreat from race," and in what will presumably be Christopher Hitchens's last serious book, his 1999 dismantling of Clintonism, *No One Left to Lie To.*

At a time when no real political alternatives are offered by Democratic candidates who confine their tepid appeals for racial justice to the King holiday and to talks in black churches, the intellecutual Left also seems to be abandoning race. Thus the brilliance of Paul Gilroy is turned to writing *Against Race,* and Antonia Darder joins Rodolfo D. Torres in producing the triumphal *After Race.* Orlando Patterson holds forth under the title "Race Over," and Loïc Wacquant and the late activist/sociologist Pierre Bourdieu brand analysis of race as an axis of inequality in Brazil as a pernicious export from a U.S. social science establishment that is as "cunning" as it is "imperialist."

These works are much more, and in some ways much less, than a return to Debs's "colorless" ideas. They lack the same focus on, and confidence in, socialist transformation and are often in dialogue less with class struggle than with cultural studies ideas about the importance of "hybridity" and the pitfalls of "essentialism." In the best-known cases they do not specifically try to recenter class by removing a fixation on race. When they do make such an attempt at class analysis, as in the work of Adolph Reed Jr., they cannot yet deliver results. On the whole they reflect the ways that increases in immigration, intermarriage, and cross-racial adoptions have destabilized discussions of race-as-usual. Ironically, the very success, largely under United Nations and nongovernmental organization auspices, of organizing around race globally has also laid bare the stark differences in national patterns of racialized inequality and the blurred borders between racial, religious, language, and national oppressions.

But though retreats from race are at least understandable in part in view of the difficult and changing political tasks we face, they are in their most sweeping forms no more an answer when they come from the Left than when they come from the Right and center. The context in which they emerge, the stature of voices contributing to them, and the ways that they fit into various tempting electoral

shortcuts informing left strategies nonetheless demand that they be taken seriously. To do so requires us to look at the varieties of left critiques of race thinking,
with the goal being not so much to show their incompatibility with each other
than to identify various changes and threats to which they inadequately respond.
The most celebrated advocates of "race is over" and "against race" positions—
Gilroy, Patterson, and Bourdieu and Wacquant—do not directly raise the issues
of race and class central to this article, but their influence and arguments must be
at least briefly discussed if we are to situate and critique the more explicitly class-
conscious writings of Darder, Torres, and Reed.

Gilroy's *Against Race* begins with an extraordinarily dense and challenging
discussion of the connections between the very idea of "race" and what Gilroy
terms "raciology," the nexus of murderous practice, policy, and science born out
of seeing race. Race, Gilroy holds, is a "relatively recent and absolutely modern
invention" and its scientific credentialing cannot be considered apart from its
bloody implication in "evil, brutality and terror." In a new world ostensibly
beyond white supremacist science, and one in which black bodies are marketed
as desirable and even superhuman rather than only as degraded, Gilroy sees both
new dangers and the possibility for a "novel and ambitious abolitionist project,"
this time doing away with race itself. "Renouncing 'race' " becomes not only the
key to "bring[ing] political culture back to life" but also the only proper "ethical"
response for confronting the wrongs done under the banners of raciology.
Acknowledging that for "many racialized populations, 'race' and the hard-won,
oppositional identities it supports are not to be lightly or prematurely given up,"
Gilroy proposes a long campaign designed to show that "action against racial
hierarchies can proceed more effectively when it has been purged of any lingering
respect for the idea of 'race.' " In the book's early stages, a critique of racist science and a recognition of the need to add up the costs of ignoring gender and
class divisions by some black nationalist movements seem to have Gilroy reject-
ing race but endorsing a more mature antiracism.

But by the book's end, despite asides suggesting that he will not too harshly
judge those who hesitate to abandon the politics of antiracist solidarity in favor of
a "heterocultural, post-anthropological, and cosmopolitan yet-to-come," Gilroy
has undercut much of the grounds of antiracism. Declaring the very "mood" of
projects attacking white supremacy to be hopelessly passé as we leave Du Bois's
"century of the color line behind," he also strongly dissents from any firm connection of racism to power or to white supremacy. *Against Race* poses the choice in
approaches as being between an outmoded concern for "Africa's antiquity" and an
appropriate commitment to "our planet's future." Gilroy writes, "To be against

racism, against white supremacism, was once to be bonded to the future. This no longer seems to be the case." The monumental but incomplete and fragile achievements of black internationalism, so searchingly explored in their contradictions in Gerald Horne's recent *Race War*, are reduced to scattered instances of precocious appreciation for the "planetary." The utopian dimensions that Robin D. G. Kelley shows to be essential to struggles against white supremacy and capitalism become for Gilroy moments to be captured by reading history against the grain, and through a lens that can reduce Frantz Fanon to "that prototypical black-European" noteworthy in large measure for his "indiscreetly anti-Marxist spirit."

Like Gilroy, the sometimes-on-the-Left Harvard sociologist Orlando Patterson explicitly pronounces Du Bois's remarks on the color line to be well past their sell-by date. "Race Over," was the headline for Patterson's projections in *The New Republic* in 2000. The article uses the premise that Du Bois may have been "half-right" regarding the color line in the twentieth century, but Patterson insists that any attempt to continue to apply Du Bois's formulation would be "altogether wrong." For Patterson the problems with twenty-first-century race thinking are less political and ethical than they are simply demographic, a view scarcely different from the endless accounts in the mainstream press predicting that the United States will become a white-minority nation in the not-too-distant future. By 2050, the United States "will have problems aplenty [but] no racial problem whatsoever," Patterson tells his readers. By then, "the social virus of race will have gone the way of smallpox." This retreat from race will allegedly fall into regional patterns, the details of which call the predictions of racelessness somewhat into question. On the West Coast, "cultural and somatic mixing" will produce a population mainly "Eurasian but with a growing Latin element." In the Northeast and Midwest, deindustrialized zones of misery will contain the white, African American, and Latino poor, bound together by "social resentment" and a "lumpen-proletarian hip-hop culture," and isolated from the gated communities of the prosperous. In the Southeast, the "Old Confederacy" race divisions will continue—"race over" does not in fact apply there—but somehow this will make no difference in the national picture.

At almost every turn the raceless predictions coexist for Patterson with appeals to old-style raciology. "Murderous racial gang fights" remain a fact of 2050 life, and new technologies to change race are deployed. But an even more glaring contradiction obtrudes when Patterson adds other set of prognostications in a *New York Times* article, now distancing himself from the view of demographers that whites will become a minority in the United States in the twenty-first century. Arguing that "nearly half of the Hispanic population is white in every social sense," Patterson forecasts that "the non-Hispanic white population will . . . possibly even grow as a portion of the population." Patterson may be right that children of marriages between a non-Hispanic white and a Hispanic will identify as (and be identified as) "white," but the jarring contrast between the two articles suggests just how slapdash the race-is-over position remains. Race disappears and whiteness reigns.

Wacquant and Bourdieu's "On the Cunning of Imperialist Reason," published in *Theory, Culture and Society* in 1999, best shows how appreciation for the ways in which racial oppression differs across national boundaries can fuel an argument for jettisoning, or at least quarantining, the use of race in social theory and political strategy. The article foregrounds with surprising stridency Karl Marx's argument that the ruling ideas of an age are produced by those who dominate. However, the authors put Marx's insight into the service of an attack on the discussions of racial inequality that have recently led to adoption of forms of affirmative action in Brazil. They argue that new attention to race in that country is a result of elite ideas shipped south from the United States. Wacquant and Bourdieu pinpoint the "cultural imperialism" of U.S. scholars as the source of attempts to flatten varied regimes of race and class oppression, flattening that they see as producing a misreading both of history and of current political possibilities. Focusing on the case of Brazil, Bourdieu and Wacquant contend that U.S.-inspired, U.S.-funded, and U.S.-produced research works to impose a "rigid black/white social division," offering the rest of the world a "poisonous" export. Such imperialism insinuates itself, in Bourdieu and Wacquant's view, despite the fact that its arguments are "contrary to the image Brazilians have of their own nation." It does so by trading on a perverse and unspecified combination of antiracist rhetoric and neoliberal financing for scholarship.

However, a number of acute responses, especially from the Brazilianists Michael Hanchard and John French, have criticized Bourdieu and Wacquant's contention that race is somehow a peculiarly U.S. concept, one that would have to be exported because it could not be homegrown in Brazil. The critical responses show that in neither the United States nor Brazil is race regularly deployed, as Bourdieu and Wacquant charge, for purposes of accusation rather than analysis, and that what they call the "neutralization of historical context" is a charge that might be turned back on their own reductive understanding of Brazil. Most important, the critics show that the scholars accused of spreading "imperialist reason" and rigid caricatures of the Brazilian social system actually continue a long line of argument *within Brazil* which recognizes that the historical context of displacement of indigenous people, empires, slave-trading, and slavery produced very different, but not incomparable, racial systems in Brazil and in the United States. When Hanchard draws on the work of cultural theorists Robert Stam and Ella Shohat to show that the analysis produced by Wacquant and Bourdieu is not without its own universalistic views of race (and presumed color blindness), founded in French imperialism, the argument that we need a fuller and more complex discussion of race and empire rather than an end to debate is squarely put on the table.

Does Moving Away from Race Move Us Toward Class?

The very first words in Darder and Torres's *After Race* attempt to improve on Du Bois's dictum regarding the color line: "We echo his statement but with a radical twist. The problem of the twenty-first century is the problem of 'race'—an ideology that has served well to obscure and disguise class interests behind the smokescreens of multiculturalism, diversity, difference, and more recently, whiteness." *After Race* centrally holds that race is a biological myth at long last invalidated by science, but now dangerously re-created because scholars persist in using the term. Such scholars thereby decisively aid the rise of culturally based neoracisms and even the recrudescence of biological racism. On this view, the "idea of race" itself, not capitalism, is somehow the "lynchpin of racism."

Like the early sections of Gilroy's *Against Race*, the work of Darder and Torres holds out the hope that retreating from the invocation of race will actually empower a more effective struggle against racialized hierarchies. Indeed, they approve of Barbara Fields's uncharitable contention that "liberal, leftist, or progressive" writers dwell on the "homier and more tractable notion" of race to avoid being "unsettled" by talking about racism. However, as in Gilroy's case, the emphasis on racism is not sustained, and neither race nor racism function as categories of analysis—that is, they cannot be the reasons for people acting as they do, but must themselves be explained.

Insofar as Fields, Darder, Torres, and others contend that inattention to class distorts inquiry into all inequalities in the United States, they are exactly right. However, the strategy of banking on the retreat from race to solve that problem is a highly dubious one. It leads to an extremely embattled tone and to ignoring the most exciting work building on materialist insights. From Cheryl Harris's brilliant studies of whiteness as property to Eduardo Bonilla-Silva's research on racial systems, to somewhat older South African scholarship on racial capitalism, to Lisa Lowe's important observations on race, universality, and labor at the start of *Immigrant Acts*, much work seeks to revive the class question by bringing racism and class together more systematically. But you would not know it from *After Race*.

Indeed, at critical junctures the book is so eager to be against race that it departs dramatically from historical materialism and thus cannot be effective for understanding class. Darder and Torres praise the liberal sociologist William Julius Wilson, for example, for supposedly demonstrating that "the significance of class has increased and is now far more salient than 'race' in determining the life chances of African Americans." This either/or, class-not-race position leads *After Race* to ignore the devastating counterarguments that Melvin Oliver, Thomas Shapiro, and others have made for Wilson's work and to subordinate to an endnote their own appreciation that Wilson's work is about as distant from Marxism as is possible. That endnote promises a different approach, focusing "with specificity [on] the dialectic between the means of production and the process of racialization," but so far Darder and Torres have not produced anything like such an analysis. *After Race* emphasizes theological matters, not slavery, settler colonialism, and the primitive accumulation of capital in accounting for the origins of racialized groups. Such a view is very much consonant with the book's emphasis on plural "racisms"—including the tendency to "inferiorize" whites—and its marginalization of any systematic discussion of white supremacy.

This same inattention to white supremacy makes it almost impossible for *After Race* to contribute to pressing discussions of how to build Latino-black working-class unity. The book's puzzling title—clearly race was no more "real" in 1670 than in 2004—makes sense in terms of the book's structure, one that culminates in chapters on Asian American and Latino experiences and emphasizes that the "browning of America" will shake old certainties regarding racism. The danger here lies in making the possibility of abandoning race contingent on the Latino population exceeding that of African Americans. This would leave us passing out of a relatively unproductive period of political mobilization based on race, during which blacks predominated, and into a promising raceless one in which Latinos do. But there is then no sustained analysis of African Americans, of African American studies, or of the tradition of black Marxism, as would seem to be necessary to calibrate such an argument. Moreover, that African Americans can practice "racism" is a consistent refrain of the study, which persistently lays all manner of mischief at the door of the civil rights and the Black Power movements. The former movement, we learn, emphasized a "liberal, rights-centered political agenda [that] undermined the development of a coherent working-class movement in the United States." Here the reflexive move away from seeing racism as having critical explanatory weight lets white supremacist trade unionism off the hook and leads to the missing of the centrality of jobs, union organizing, welfare rights, poor people's campaigns, and point-of-production organizing—of class—to the civil rights and Black Power movements. Missing class, it becomes possible to charge that Black Power narrowly "seiz[ed] the moment in the name of antiracism and 'black autonomy,' " and that it somehow shut off debate over the consequences of using "the language of 'race' to do battle with racism." At its worst this line of argument allows Darder and Torres to loosely link a Black Power movement animated by anticolonialism and anticapitalism to the Nation of Islam's extravagant pronouncements on "white devils."

Whereas Darder and Torres allow that "racism" is still a problem worth addressing, the recent writings of the radical political scientist Adolph Reed Jr. are done even with that. Sounding more like the "colorless" Debs than any major left commentator on race and class in recent memory, he argues, "Exposing racism [is] the political equivalent of an appendix: a useless vestige of an earlier evolutionary moment that's usually innocuous but can flare up and become harmful." Reed's two late-2005 articles, "Class-ifying the Hurricane" and "The Real Divide," are the signature pieces of the Left's retreat from race. They appeared in relatively popular Left-liberal venues, *The Nation* and *The Progressive* respectively, and represent attempts by a prominent activist in the movement to build a labor party in the United States to speak broadly and frankly. Moreover, Reed's scholarship has offered significant opposition to liberalism's retreat from race during the Clinton era, especially in his collection *Without Justice for All*.

"Class-ifying the Hurricane" appeared while the horrific impact of Katrina in Reed's former hometown of New Orleans was fresh in readers' minds, just after many had noted the racist reporting that contrasted black "looters" with white survivors shown doing precisely the same foraging. It noted "manifest racial disparities in vulnerability, treatment, and outcome" of the experience of natural disaster. And then it turned on a dime to excoriate the "abstract, moralizing patter about how and whether race matters." Even so, in this first of his two paired essays Reed's retreat from race could be read as simply a strategic one. "For roughly a generation it seemed responsible to expect that defining inequalities in racial terms would provide some remedial response from the federal government," he writes. "But for some time race's force in national politics has been as a vehicle for reassuring whites that that 'public' equals some combination of 'black,' 'poor,' and 'loser.' " Katrina laid bare both race and class injustices, but partly because of the *growing* strength of racism an effective response to it would have to be strictly "class-ified," according to Reed.

"The Real Divide" repeated, expanded, and made more bitter the arguments in *The Nation* article. Reed continued to mention, in a labored construction, that he was "not claiming that systemic inequalities in the United States are not significantly racialized." Indeed, "any sane or honest person" would have to acknowledge the overwhelming evidence of "racial disparities [that] largely emerge from a history of discrimination and racial injustice." Nonetheless, Reed followed up these generalizations by categorically declaring that "as a political strategy exposing racism is wrongheaded and at best an utter waste of time." The focus on racism is for Reed a dodge designed to make "upper-status liberals" feel morally superior as they vote for the deeply compromised Democratic Party and ignore the "real divide" of class. In one of the few bits of the article offering ostensible, if incredibly narrow and misguided, class analysis, exposing racism is said to serve "the material interests of those who would be race relations technicians." As in "Classi-fying the Hurricane" the arguments are partly that racism, being "too imprecise" and too abstract, lacks power as an analytical tool. However, the point Reed develops more is that among whites the very "discussion of race" reinforces "the idea that cutting public spending is justifiably aimed at weaning a lazy black underclass off the dole." The "racism charge," on this view, is easily defeated by Republican appeals to "scurrilous racial stereotypes" and therefore should be jettisoned.

Gilroy's *Against Race* at least acknowledges that a call for giving up on race-based traditions of struggle asks a lot of social movements rooted in communities of color. In law, for example, exposing racism is often the sole strategy available to protect, after a fashion, the rights of many of the poorest workers in the United States. Reed's view that elite liberalism is the source of movements to expose and combat racism—a view much facilitated by his outspoken dismissal of the reparations movement—forestalls consideration of the dynamics of concrete struggles around race and class, leaving the call for a retreat from race itself as something of an abstraction.

Fortunately, there is no reason to decide whether to organize and to analyze around either racism or class oppression, one to the exclusion of the other. The case of New Orleans, which moved Reed to present us with such a choice, offers good examples of why we should reject it. Compare, for example, Reed's thumbs up/thumbs down approach to race and class with the left activist and writer Mike Davis's accounts of post-Katrina New Orleans. Davis raised a series of questions three months into the rebuilding process in New Orleans and perfectly captured the continuing color line and more:

> Why is there so much high-level talk about abandoning the Ninth Ward as unin-
> habitable when no one is proposing to turn equally inundated Lakeview back into
> a swamp? Is it because Lakeview is a wealthy white community? And/or is it
> because the 30,000 reliably Democratic Black votes in the Ninth Ward hold the
> balance of power in Louisiana politics?

To what extent, Davis wondered, did "ethnic cleansing" and rebuilding coincide? Davis's accounts have also been especially acute on the ways in which elites, including the black political elite in New Orleans, have played on, and indeed created, black-Latino tensions during the rebuilding process. How are we to conceptualize these tensions, and to struggle to overcome them, without discussing both race and class, as well as white supremacy?

In recent antiwar demonstrations the most fascinating sign has read: "No Iraqi has ever left me to die on a roof." Its words recall haunting post-Katrina images and also bring to mind the celebrated antiwar dictum attributed to Muhammad Ali: "No Vietnamese ever called me 'nigger.'" The latter line was perhaps the quintessential late twentieth-century example of Du Bois's insight, ignored by U.S.-centered readings of his words in *The Souls of Black Folk*, regarding how the color line in the United States existed in systems of racialized global inequality. We should allow that the twenty-first-century "No Iraqi" sign's variant of the earlier slogan is considerably more complex and expansive. Poor whites, and indeed the large numbers of Vietnamese resettled in the gulf region and abandoned in Katrina's considerable wake, could conceivably march under the "No Iraqi" sign. In that sense the sign, and the reality of New Orleans, speak powerfully to the most profound insight in Reed's recent work, namely that poor, mostly black, New Orleanians suffer from a plight that is "a more extreme version of the precarious position of millions of Americans today, as more and more lose health care, bankruptcy protection, secure employment, affordable housing, civil liberties, and access to education." To combat such misery will require race and class analysis, as well as antiracist and anticapitalist organization.

As Reed's articles appeared, the *New York Times* ran an article titled "For Blacks, A Dream in Decline." It revealed that after a 1980s peak in which one black worker in four was a union member, the figure today approaches one in seven. In the last year, African American workers accounted for a whopping 55 percent of the drop in union membership by 304,000 nationally, although they represent just one unionized worker in six. The *Times* article quoted William Julius Wilson himself as urgently calling on the unions to address the issue. "They haven't done so yet," he lamented. Union leaders, according to the article, "resist viewing what is happening in racial terms." One prominent labor leader quoted on the decline of black membership sounded for all the world like Eugene V. Debs: "We see it as a class issue rather than a race issue." It is both, and the retreat from race and class will get us closer to addressing neither.

7

Hard Truth in the Big Easy: Race and Class in New Orleans, Pre- and Post-Katrina

Kristen Lavelle and Joe Feagin

In the wake of disastrous Hurricane Katrina in 2005, debate quickly surfaced over race, poverty, and the United States government's responsibility to its citizens. Many people weighed in on the question of whether the effects of the country's biggest natural disaster had more to do with race or class. In an impromptu, much-discussed moment on national television, rapper-producer Kanye West blurted out, "George Bush doesn't care about black people," putting a celebrity voice to what appeared obvious to many African Americans. To many, the disproportionate impact Hurricane Katrina had on thousands of black New Orleanians was shameful but no big surprise, merely joining a long history of mistreatment and neglect by the government toward its citizens of color. Other Americans reacted to the hurricane from a different perspective, dismissing the race explanation and citing socioeconomic class as the key factor in the storm's immediate effects and in relief efforts. After all, those families most able to afford homes in flood-protected areas and who had resources to evacuate suffered much less than poorer families. Who was right? Did the natural disaster reveal an enduring anti-black race problem, or did it merely expose economic inequities? We begin to answer these questions fully by offering essential historical background on race and class in New Orleans. Additionally, we consider white America's reaction to the disaster and what this illuminates about race relations in the contemporary

United States. We also discuss the uncertain future of one of America's most cherished cities, the "Big Easy."

Many social analysts contributed to the "race or class" question. Those claiming race as the bigger issue were criticized for wanting to appear righteous and for wasting time attacking a government that is unmoved by accusations of racism.[1] Michael Eric Dyson claimed that the argument for class over race was used to deflect attention away from race and to discourage a deeper discussion about the ways in which race and class intertwine.[2] We agree with Dyson; the separation of race from class was an artificial differentiation from the onset, because the vast majority of those left behind in New Orleans were poor *and* black. In New Orleans, race and class have become deeply intertwined social constructions because of the long history of well-institutionalized racism in the United States.[3] Since the 1700s, the New Orleans white elite, with the support of the white citizenry, has worked to racialize the class system and to class-situate racial distinctions, first and foremost, to *maintain white supremacy and white privilege*. And, importantly, New Orleans is no exceptional case of historical racism but rather is one manifestation of pervasive, white-racist, American policies and practices.

In a September 2005 address to the nation from the streets of New Orleans, even conservative president George W. Bush stated that "deep, persistent poverty" in the southern city "has roots in a history of racial discrimination, which cut off generations from the opportunity of America," and he declared a "duty to confront this poverty with bold action."[4] Straight from the president's mouth, America heard for one brief moment that the contemporary racialization of poverty is directly connected to a long history of unjust impoverishment of black Americans and unjust enrichment of white Americans. And, although the Bush administration's policies have shown no commitment to rectify a racist class structure, there is much validity in his short statements. To illustrate the roots of race and class in New Orleans, we now discuss the historical structuring of New Orleans from the booming antebellum metropolis to the contemporary city hard hit by Hurricane Katrina.

Race and Class in Antebellum New Orleans

A central historical question: Why are there so many African Americans in southern Louisiana and nearby coastal areas today? The clear answer is that in the late 1700s and early 1800s many powerful white slaveholders, including the brutal president Andrew Jackson, intentionally sought to make the Gulf Coast a major region for profitable slave plantations. White powerholders selected race as the characteristic that would determine who would do the labor (enslaved blacks) and who would profit from the labor (whites), and this wealth for whites has accumulated since slavery to the present day.

The descendants of those enslaved—forced to move to the Gulf Coast states by powerful white men—are many of the impoverished African Americans who bore the brunt of Hurricane Katrina.

Sugar plantations, commercial shipping, and enslaved labor distinguished the economy of lower Louisiana during the antebellum period. The sugar boom of the 1700s and 1800s increased demand for slave labor and turned New Orleans into one of two principal slave markets for North America.[5] Purchase and sale of slaves tightly linked New Orleans to the larger southern economy. During the antebellum period, tens of millions of dollars were pumped into the southern economy through the trade in enslaved human beings. Slave trading was a daily, bloody, and highly visible public affair of New Orleans life. Each year, thousands from across the South passed through New Orleans slave pens, arriving and departing via boat or driven on foot, in chains.[6]

The free labor of African Americans was integral to sugar and other agricultural production, as well as to the development of city utilities and facilities. The New Orleans City Council established a chain gang in 1805, where black prisoners worked side by side with enslaved laborers to develop public works projects. Civic improvement was carried out by jailed and enslaved African Americans who kept up levees, erected public buildings, cleaned streets, and expanded the city's boundaries. Vast amounts of uncompensated black labor modernized the city, ushering in a new era of prominence to New Orleans.[7]

Slave trade and labor brought great prosperity to New Orleans whites, but slavery was not merely an economic arrangement. We must acknowledge the humanity of the forgotten millions forced through the New Orleans slave markets. The city symbolized countless *social deaths* for those torn from families, communities, and histories. Once sold through those slave markets, few would ever see or hear from family and friends again.[8] Yet their stolen labor generated hundreds of *billions* (in current dollars) in wealth for a great many whites in various higher classes in the region. Thus white supremacy facilitated a powerful slavery system that inextricably connected race and class—whites to wealth and African Americans to poverty.

The trade in, and labor of, enslaved black Americans helped turn the former swampland of New Orleans into the fourth-largest city in the United States by 1840, with over 100,000 people. Black Americans made up 40 percent of the population; over 23,000 were enslaved, and nearly 20,000 were free people of color.[9] At the beginning of the Civil War, most free people of color were of mixed race and light skinned, whereas most of those enslaved were darker skinned.[10] Many of the light-skinned claimed French or Spanish ancestry and often referred to themselves not as black or African American but as Creole.[11] The American "one drop of blood" standard would have considered these two groups of people to be collectively "black." However, largely because their combined numbers were substantial, New Orleans whites aggressively furthered the notion of free blacks being a distinct "third caste"—not as contemptible as slaves but not as respectable as whites—in order to control these two sizable groups of color. Stringent color-class lines were accented to ensure that free blacks and slaves— the lighter skinned and darker skinned—remained at odds, and a free person was barred by law from mingling with the enslaved.[12]

Many of the numerous free black Creoles held reputable professions, which diversified the city's racial-economic landscape. Free people of color had some entitlements that distinguished their legal and financial status above that of those enslaved, such as their own private schools and the rights to marry and pass wealth to heirs.[13] Gradations in skin tone came to be associated with class status in New Orleans on a level unparalleled in most other parts of the United States. Certainly many of those with very light skin passed into white society in order to prevent being targeted by racial discrimination. Indeed, many Louisiana area families, both those considered "white" and "black" by outsiders, hide relatives' passing from blackness to whiteness to the present day.

Despite having some entitlements over enslaved blacks, free people of color were still effectively separated from whites. And, though intimate relations and marital partnerships between free blacks and whites were not unheard of in this time period, firm segregation was enforced locally in New Orleans well before the advent of post-Reconstruction Jim Crow laws. Theaters, hospitals, streetcars, restaurants, hotels, and cemeteries either kept their facilities segregated or excluded people of color altogether.[14] Free blacks were expected to defer to whites in everyday interactions, were usually not allowed to vote, could not legally marry whites, were required to give service to the white community by working as city police and slave patrollers, and could not expect to receive justice from police or courts.[15] Skin color was the primary marker of economic class and social status for people of color, so much so that hundreds of darker-skinned free blacks with no chance of passing into white society emigrated to Haiti and Mexico in the mid-1800s.

Thus in New Orleans the rift between whites and blacks was strict but not impenetrable for those people of color with very light skin and financial resources. Furthermore, the relationship between light-skinned and dark-skinned African Americans was a complex one: There was tension over the social and economic privileges that whites allowed to those with light skin color, as well as kinship over shared struggles as people of color in a white supremacist society.

Moreover, the proliferation of light-skinned African Americans (most of the free blacks as well as many of the enslaved) in New Orleans and across the South in large part indicated a long history of white men's sexual assaults on black girls and women. This vulnerable situation for women of color was no secret in the antebellum period and was acknowledged by a Louisiana court in 1851 when it stated that "the female slave is peculiarly exposed to the seductions of an unprincipled master."[16] However, rape of enslaved women was more than an act of a few "unprincipled masters," for over one-quarter of enslaved New Orleanians in 1860 (*thousands* of individuals) were officially counted as biracial, or "mulatto."[17] Free black women were also susceptible to the sexual advances of white men, with some entering into concubine-like relationships with members of the white elite, often for financial stability.[18] By the time Reconstruction began, more New Orleanians in both the "white" and the "black" populations had ancestry in the other racial group than residents of any other U.S. city.[19] Race and class have thus *never* been separate issues in New Orleans but are inextricably intertwined and, importantly, were created by practices of white racism.

Twentieth-Century New Orleans

After slavery, during the short period of Reconstruction from the late 1860s to the 1880s, newly emancipated African Americans saw some improvement in their access to national and local politics, public accommodations, and education. However, most still faced harsh conditions, a type of "near slavery" without the chains. The morbidity and mortality rates for all African Americans was extremely high compared to whites, and life expectancies were ten years lower, despite variations in class status. A few black professionals in New Orleans were able to advance economically, but most African Americans were severely hindered from doing so by recurring depressions in New Orleans' economy and pervasive racial discrimination. Unemployment was endemic and ensured that the few labor unions formed by black workers were weak.[20]

By 1890, formal "separate but equal" segregation statutes were written into Louisiana state law, and, in the century following the end of Reconstruction,

New Orleans continued to be dominated by whites. White New Orleanians began to drastically restructure the city's residential landscape in this century. White flight from Orleans Parish (City of New Orleans) to surrounding suburbs began after the Second World War.[21] Postwar prosperity facilitated the draining of the Jefferson Parish swamp, land soon converted to suburbs, and new neighborhoods quickly filled with middle-class and working-class whites, most moving in from Orleans Parish. Most blacks were barred from moving there by economic constraints and blatant discrimination by white realtors and were forced to remain in the fast-deteriorating neighborhoods inside the city limits.[22]

During Reconstruction in New Orleans, many African Americans supported the creation of integrated schools, but most whites were vehemently opposed and even projected their own white supremacist desire for segregation onto African Americans. For example, a mass meeting of white New Orleanians declared in September 1875 that "the compulsory admixture of children of all races, color and condition in the schools, in the same rooms and on the same benches, is opposed to the principles of humanity, repugnant to the instincts of both races, and is not required by any provision of the laws or constitution of this State."[23] Local white-owned newspapers were staunch defenders of segregation and white supremacy and frequently referred to African Americans collectively as "niggers," "darkies," and "sambos." In 1874 the New Orleans *Bulletin* boldly stated: "The white race rules the world—the white race rules America—and the white race will rule Louisiana—and the white race shall rule New Orleans." Newspapers even incited whites to outright violence as a means of maintaining the subordination of all blacks, no matter their class position.[24] After emancipation, class differences remained between the former free blacks and the newly freed former slaves, but whites furthered a strong anti-black ideology that characterized all people of color as decidedly beneath them.

Throughout the twentieth century, economic and social distance persisted between whites and African Americans, as well as between light-skinned Creoles and darker-skinned African Americans. These rifts were very apparent in the school systems—white private, black private, and primarily black public systems. From the beginning of the public education system in the late-1800s, southern Louisiana public schools were underfunded. Many white Catholics and affluent white Protestants sent their children to parochial schools and preferred not to pay public school taxes. This white private school system functioned as a gatekeeper for admission to the city's ruling elite. Separate private schools also served mostly light-skinned people of color who could afford the tuition. The *Brown v. Board of Education* (1954) integration order solidified the plight of underfunded and disproportionately black New Orleans' public schools. National media outlets broadcasted images of angry white mobs in New Orleans reacting with violence to federal-ordered desegregation in the late 1950s. Affluent whites who had children in Orleans Parish public schools transferred the students to private institutions or joined in white flight by moving to white suburban neighborhoods.[25] Ironically, white segregationists' fear that New Orleans' public schools would be ruined by integration turned into a structural reality because of their own actions.

Racial equality and integration have been hotly contested throughout New Orleans' history, and the role of organized white violence in stopping it has been commonplace. For example, in 1874, Canal Street, still one of the city's main thoroughfares, was the site of what has been deemed the largest street fight in U.S. history. In the "Battle of Liberty Place" 3,500 armed, white supremacist White League members attacked and ousted the newly elected Republican and black-led government. Federal troops were able to restore order, but the white supremacists ultimately prevailed three years later, when the national "Compromise of 1877" allowed Klan-type *terrorist groups* to restore the former slaveholding oligarchy back to power across much of the South.[26] Throughout the South, white terrorist groups typically had the full support of the white elite and political officeholders. In 1891, the all-white New Orleans City Council ordered a monument erected on Canal Street commemorating the "Liberty Place" attack. The monument became highly controversial as the city's black constituency grew over the following century and the first two African American mayors were elected (1978 and 1986), who each worked to have it removed permanently. Instead of removal, a weak compromise was reached with white supremacists and preservationists, and the monument was preserved and relocated to a less visible spot merely one block away.[27] White supremacy trumped equality-and-justice values once again in New Orleans, as the city's whites maintained their economic, political, and symbolic dominance.

In a city where many (especially white) residents have been so proud of the supposedly "good racial relations," it is significant that New Orleans' demographic shifts and violent white resistance to black progress in the 1900s mirrored other racially tumultuous cities. In terms of well-institutionalized, white-on-black racism, New Orleans has consistently shown itself to be a *typical* Southern city, despite having a significant population of mixed-race people of part-African ancestry unfettered by poverty and educated in elite private schools.

Contemporary Pre-Katrina New Orleans

For well over a century, New Orleans had one of the highest proportions of African Americans of all large cities, and until recent years it had been one of the most geographically integrated cities. However, by 2000, consistent white flight, disinvestment in public schooling, and the out-migration of decent-paying jobs led to the city becoming more segregated than ever. The inequities between rich and poor were as extreme as at any time since slavery.[28] Two-thirds of pre-Katrina New Orleans was black while just 28 percent was white. It was the sixth-poorest large U.S. city, with more than one in four residents living below the official poverty line.[29] Four in ten black families were in poverty, the highest rate for black urbanites nationwide. Graver still was the fact that a majority of the poor scraped by on incomes of *less than half* the official poverty level.[30]

A history of anti-black discrimination coupled with the current status of the city economy were to blame for the high levels of black poverty in New Orleans. The economy of the New Orleans area had long been substantially grounded in oil, petrochemical, and fishing industries, but became more tourist-oriented after the oil bust of the 1980s and the related economic downturn. Tax revenues plummeted and unemployment increased, which adversely affected working-class African Americans more than whites. By 1990, unemployment among black men was 11 percent—more than double the rate for whites—and those who were able to keep jobs were often poorly paid.[31] Thirteen percent of residents (compared with 9 percent nationwide) were employed in the relatively low-wage food and accommodations industry.[32] Industries that pay above-average wages, such as shipping and oil and gas extraction, accounted for relatively little employment when Hurricane Katrina hit in summer 2005.[33]

Furthermore, the city's public schools were in horrific condition, even in comparison to the rest of Louisiana, which ranks third lowest for teacher salaries in the country. The public school system served poor whites better than poor blacks; poor white children were less likely to attend schools in areas of concentrated poverty. High school dropout rates were very high, and over half of black ninth graders were projected not to graduate in four years. Upon finishing or dropping out of school, many young African American men wound up at Angola Prison, a correctional facility located, ironically, on a former slave plantation where black inmates still perform manual farm labor like their enslaved ancestors—and where many eventually die.[34]

Numerous analysts have argued that, among New Orleans whites, racial attitudes and practices have been milder and less overtly racist than in the rest of the South because of the Creole heritage and the easygoing feelings of the original

French and Spanish residents toward racial mixtures and interaction. Yet this imagery is full of white fictions and misrepresentations. Economic and political power in New Orleans, except for a brief period during Reconstruction, has *always* been held by the white elite and a handful of their *chosen* lighter-skinned black colleagues. In the 1970s, blacks were nearly half the city population, yet held less than 5 percent of the highest leadership positions.[35] Those people of color who did gain political leadership posts were disproportionately light skinned and Creole. For example, all New Orleans' mayors of color have been Creole, and none especially dark skinned. Nevertheless, they have all been called "African American" and are implicitly considered to be representative of the majority black population. Instead, they are members of the somewhat in-between racial-class group in New Orleans, the (usually better educated) group that whites have deemed superior to the dark-skinned blacks but inferior to whites since the 1700s. And, again, despite the gains of a select few light-skinned New Orleanians of part-African ancestry, the elite circle of white power has been very difficult to crack well into this century. In fact, in the 1990s, civil rights activists fought to desegregate the secretive Mardi Gras krewes and social clubs, into which a few black millionaires were finally, and reluctantly, admitted.[36] In New Orleans, wealth *and* a legacy of anti-black racism still appear to rule, hand in hand.

The Future of New Orleans

The social and economic circumstances of New Orleans' poor (who were primarily black) and African American (who were disproportionately very poor) residents were a "disaster" well before devastating Hurricane Katrina made landfall on August 29, 2005. After one day of intense wind and rising water, major levees were breached, and parts of the city lay under deep water. Regardless of a city-wide mandatory evacuation notice before the storm made landfall, thousands of residents remained in the flooded city. As commentators scrambled to offer explanations, much of the reaction consisted of aggressive finger pointing, with most initially directed at local and state governments or at the residents themselves. Many (mostly white) commentators and onlookers used a racial framing and placed blame on residents' character or intelligence for not heeding the evacuation order, but economic conditions, rooted in a long history of racial oppression, were the major determinants in whether people were able to evacuate. Comparisons between poor whites and poor blacks in New Orleans received little publicity but clearly showed that poor whites were *much* better off overall.

For example, only 17 percent of poor whites lacked access to a car, against nearly 60 percent of poor blacks.[37] The black evacuees frequently said they did not
leave prior to the hurricane because they lacked resources, yet few white officials
or media pundits gave credence to their claims.[38]

New Orleans' 2004 population was estimated by the U.S. Census Bureau at
444,000, having already shown a steady decline since its 1960 peak at over
625,000. As of 2007, New Orleans' population stands at *less than half* the pre-hur-
ricane level, and savvy analysts are expressing doubt that the population will ever
return to its pre-Katrina levels.[39] The Bring New Orleans Back Commission pre-
dicts that, by 2009, just over half of the city's population will have returned, and
even fewer from its disadvantaged population.[40] The New Orleans area has had the
most extreme demographic shift of any other Gulf Coast region affected by any
recent hurricane, and, moreover, the Katrina hurricane is not the major cause for the
seemingly enduring population shifts in New Orleans. Rather, preexisting economic problems appear to be the main hindrance to pumping life back into the city.[41]

Many New Orleanians, understandably, were greatly disappointed that
George W. Bush's 2007 State of the Union address gave no mention of a federal
commitment to continued hurricane relief. For, less than a year and a half had
passed since he acknowledged a "duty to confront" the poverty in New Orleans
with "bold action." In actuality, much of the structural rebuilding and recovery
has been carried out by volunteer groups and residents themselves; *thousands* of
New Orleans homes have been cleaned and made ready for rehabilitation by the
dedicated work of volunteers. But government efforts still have yet to provide a
public hospital for New Orleans and a fully functional school system.
Furthermore, the government is making plans to demolish, rather than reopen,
lightly damaged New Orleans public housing developments.[42]

Early on, analysts predicted, often with approving comments, that a smaller,
whiter, more affluent New Orleans would be created in the future—with thousands
of poor black residents who survived the flooding staying dispersed across the
country. This has been the result thus far, in the year and a half following the hurricane. In the available statistics on racial demographics, which include the larger
metropolitan area, the black population of greater New Orleans has declined from
36 percent to 21 percent, with mostly whites filling the gap. The signs are obvious.
Such a large proportion of the black population is gone that some radio stations
have switched from funk and rap to soft rock.[43] This shift is largely due to the better economic situation of New Orleans' white residents versus the poor African
American residents.[44] Many former residents of the city will never return, simply
because they do not have the resources to do so. A February 2006 Gallup poll

found that 53 percent of black residents reported they lost everything, compared with *only 19 percent of whites*.[45] Notably, these numbers are likely even higher, especially for the poor black constituency, because the poll only contacted residents with an active New Orleans telephone number. Other polls indicate that the desire of residents to return to their home city is strong, but the majority were renters who know they will be severely limited in their housing choices if they try to move back.[46]

The 2006 Bring New Orleans Back report claimed that the "heart of the matter" regarding city revitalization was to rebuild neighborhoods, to bring people back, and to attract new residents, claiming, "The Committee wants everyone to return and new people to come."[47] However, behind its welcoming words to former residents are *no* strong assistance measures to ensure their return and help them rebuild. Instead, the report puts the onus on poor people to return and become financially stable in a depressed New Orleans' economy, which the governing elite who wrote the report knows is unlikely to happen. Joseph Canizaro, wealthy developer and head of the Bring New Orleans Back Commission's urban planning committee, nonchalantly stated: "As a practical matter, these poor folks don't have the resources to go back to our city just like they didn't have the resources to get out of our city. So we won't get all those folks back. That's just a fact."[48] This unemotional, matter-of-fact statement completely overlooks the primary role whites have had throughout history in *creating* great poverty and oppression for black New Orleanians.

What virtually all analyses on New Orleans and Hurricane Katrina have neglected is a full historical context for the racial inequities exposed by the storm. Some have pointed to the unique "rootedness" of city residents, a distinction that sets the city apart from other more transient large urban areas, because a very large proportion of born-and-raised New Orleanians live their entire lives there.[49] Consequently, it is important to recognize that many, perhaps the majority, of the poor inner-city evacuees whose desperate faces filled television screens in the weeks following the flood are the descendants of antebellum enslaved Louisianans. Their inherited legacy of the past few centuries was not one of fabled "American equal opportunity," but one of enslavement, exclusion, blatant discrimination, and dramatically inadequate resources.

Alienating Racist Relations

Many, primarily white, Americans have been unable or unwilling to relate to or empathize with these relatively poor black New Orleanians. This social distance became apparent at the onset of the disaster. During a trip to a Houston arena shelter, Barbara Bush, the former First Lady, made a comment that reflected a lack of empathy for the hardest-hit hurricane victims and the stark social distance separating whites from blacks generally: "So many of the people in the arena here, you know, were underprivileged anyway, so this—this [she chuckles slightly] is working very well for them."[50] Such out-of-touch white women and men somehow believed that the poor, African American evacuees, without even the resources to afford a hotel room, were *better off* after the hurricane than before. This kind of flippant reaction to suffering by thousands reveals the deeper dynamic of *alienating* racist relations, in which a white-racist framing and ideology deny any white agency in creating black poverty and impede empathy, understanding, and solidarity across the U.S. color line.

Additionally, in the wake of what was likely the most traumatic event in their lives, African American hurricane victims faced racism in their personal treatment from aid workers and volunteers. Interviews with forty-six evacuees at Houston's Reliant Park shelter revealed that being black was central to evacuation experiences; several reported suffering racial discrimination by members of the primarily white police and aid staffs. Significantly fewer reported having experienced class discrimination, that is, discrimination because of their poverty status.[51] Additionally, scores of people across the country who graciously offered evacuees free or low-cost shelter on emergency housing websites often *blatantly excluded* African Americans from their offers. One white woman, upon questioning, said it was not a matter of white racism but, rather, whites would be the most comfortable in her home and she would not have known what kind of soap to provide for black evacuees.[52]

Therefore, not only were poor African American residents of New Orleans affected disproportionately by the hurricane directly, but they were also disproportionately ill-assisted and unempathized with by primarily white would-be helpers. Additionally, over 1,450 people died in Louisiana as a result of Katrina, most from flooding in New Orleans.[53] A comprehensive *social death* looms large once again for the African American population of this slavery-origin region. The loss of families, homes, and communities on such a large scale is reminiscent of the great human devastation that the antebellum New Orleans slave markets brought to African Americans.

As the months proceed, awareness of and sympathies for the displaced poor, black New Orleanians wane, especially in the white majority population. The 2006 Houston Area Survey showed the sentiment of Houston residents toward the 150,000 Louisiana evacuees (the largest of any U.S. city) to have grown quite negative. Nearly half of Houstonians surveyed in early 2006 thought that the influx of evacuees had been a "bad thing" for Houston. White Republican Representative John Culbertson of Houston referred to New Orleans evacuees as "deadbeats" and summed up his mostly white and wealthy constituency's feelings: "If they can work, but won't work, ship 'em back. If they cause problems in the schools, if they commit a crime, there ought to be a one-strike rule—ship 'em back."[54] This irrational and insensitive attitude reveals the old white-racist framing of society and, again, harkens back to the slave trade—for in this view the evacuees are dehumanized, mere bodies to be judged and then transported as those in power see fit. Nor does he seem to recognize that there is no home place *there* for those he so cavalierly dismisses.

Many mainstream media accounts portrayed poor African Americans who did not evacuate New Orleans as deviant or criminal from the onset of the natural disaster. Many media-fueled notions—such as rampant looting, shooting at rescuers, and countless rapes in the convention center—turned out to be white fabrications, unsubstantiated, and false. Still, months after the hurricane, many media outlets continue to vilify the displaced and to characterize them generally as deviants and criminals. *City Journal*, which claims to be "the nation's premier urban-policy magazine," printed an early 2006 article titled "Katrina Refugees Shoot Up Houston" that refers to a "uniquely vicious New Orleans underclass culture of drugs, guns, and violent death," explaining that "it's bad news for cities like Houston, which inevitably must struggle with the overspill of New Orleans' pre-Katrina plague of violence."[55] Sweeping generalizations about a "criminal element" from New Orleans simply do not apply to the vast majority of evacuees. For example, Houston has experienced major economic benefits because of the new residents, yet this gets little regional or national media attention. In the first few months, New Orleans transplants contributed to double-digit sales tax revenue increases, spurred the housing market, and brought $150 million in loans from the U.S. Small Business Administration.[56]

The grossly overstated, inaccurate generalizations of black deviance and criminality stem from the white-racist framing that views the prevalence of inner-city poverty to be of African Americans' own creation and to link to a genetic or cultural pathology of shiftless, ruthless, gang violence. These characterizations are built out of whites' racist fears that imagine a large cadre of black men dedicated to committing crimes, especially crimes of violence, against a supposedly civilized (white) society. (Ironically, this takes place within a society whose white leadership has been responsible for more overseas invasions and wars than any other in modern world history.) These images deny the long history of institutionalized and violent oppression by whites at various class levels that has excluded African Americans from equal opportunity and placed them in these dire situations of poverty without access to better housing, living-wage jobs, and high-quality schools. Additionally, these images reject the very real humanity and nuanced complexity of New Orleans black residents, disturbingly mirroring crazed white notions of black inferiority and criminality that have proliferated in white imaginations for centuries.

The positive attributes of the flood-washed communities have been completely overlooked in nearly all popular analysis of the Katrina disaster. Statistics on such negative things as crime, drug use, unemployment, and high school dropouts reveal very little about positive things, like the strength of multigenerational extended families, communal child care, and community activism. Compared to other American cities, New Orleanians are very attached to their city and neighborhoods.[57] Whether economically impoverished or not, New Orleans neighborhoods offered a vital support network and a strong sense of community for residents. Comprising the labor of the economy and the lifeblood of the city, this core of moderate-income and poor black citizens fostered a pride and thriving spirit unique to the Big Easy that welcomed 10 million tourists each year.

Conclusion: The Need for Empathy

Even now, powerful tools from the white-racist framing of society are used to justify racial inequality and perpetuate the still fundamental *racist relations* of the United States. Under the watchful eyes of white elites, New Orleans and the United States generally have developed structurally over fifteen generations to maintain these alienated and alienating racist relations in major societal institutions. In this manner, white elites, as well as rank-and-file whites, have kept a large proportion of our African American citizens in unjust poverty—with chronically underfunded schools, diminished job opportunities, and limited affordable housing choices. This unjust impoverishment operates within a continuing framework of well-institutionalized racism, which provides a majority of whites with the current and significant benefits and privileges coming from many generations of unjust enrichment. In the history of most U.S. cities and rural areas, whites have imposed racial oppression so long and so often that it has long been a foundational and undergirding reality, routinely shaping *both* the racial dynamics *and* the class dynamics of U.S. society. In the U.S. case, "race" and "class" are often two sides of the same coin.

Because whiteness and white dominance have been *normalized* for so long now in the United States, it is understandable that media and even scholarly commentators often miss or downplay the racist foundations of contemporary class inequalities. Without a critical historical lens and an understanding of current forms of white-on-black oppression, it is a simple move to apply equality-and-justice American ideals to something like Hurricane Katrina. Doing so allows one to conclude that racial characteristics have nothing to do with anything unpleasant affecting impoverished people of color today, for our society is committed to freedom and equal rights. However, these conclusions are also inexcusable. The racist history of the United States in addition to current forms of discrimination, *despite* long-standing *principles* of equality, is well documented. The hurricane was merely one unexpected, sudden disaster that exposed another centuries-long, unremitting disaster—anti-black racism. It is past time we offered up more than well-intentioned words about "a duty to confront a history of racial discrimination, which cut off generations from the opportunity of America." Institutionally created problems require institutional solutions, and the United States has a responsibility to remedy *now* the problems it has constructed for African Americans—and the privileges which have been bestowed upon whites— for four centuries.

Yet another problem with the "it's not racism" perspective is that it requires the further silencing of people of color's voices. The Katrina catastrophe, at least for a short while, forced white America to hear and listen to some of those impassioned and insightful black voices. The white majority has rarely attended to the racism-honed perspectives of African Americans. These Americans often expressed views, albeit in the language of everyday survival, similar to those we develop here. In the future, only by attending carefully to history and the perspectives of Americans of color can the United States expect to see improvement in the direction of real democracy. Attending well to all people's viewpoints will enable us to see that the survival of the United States, and indeed of humanity, requires us to see and act beyond the boundaries of our own racial group and social class interests. Just before his assassination by a white man, Dr. Martin Luther King, Jr. wrote that all human beings live in a "great world house," in which we must find a way to move beyond individual selfishness and group dominance: "From the time immemorial human beings have lived by the principle that 'self-preservation is the first law of life.' But this is a false assumption. I would say that other-preservation is the first law of life precisely because we cannot preserve self without being concerned about preserving other selves."[58]

8

Will the Real Black Middle Class Please Stand Up?

Sabiyha Prince

Long before Bill Cosby publicly picked on the vulnerable and before black neocons began portraying themselves as the sole proponents of personal responsibility among African Americans, diversity of thought, action, and experience ruled the day in the fictional place called "Black America." Class has been one of the more consequential forces contributing to dissimilarity within African American communities.

Despite its influence, there is a lot of confusion about the impact of class inequality in American life. In this essay I share meaningful patterns of cultural variance in everyday life among black middle-class people. I highlight common patterns, occurrences, and ideas that affect relations between community and kin and have implications for policymakers. Readers should not interpret my focus on this middle stratum as an attempt to minimize the grave impact of economic differences between black professionals and African Americans who did not graduate from college, and in some cases, high school. Class differentiation, intraracial or otherwise, leads to unequal access to income, wealth, health care, travel opportunities, strategic information, job prestige, and other key resources. It is a harsh form of inequality to endure and when it traverses race, gender, and other standpoints in the social hierarchy, the resulting conditions and experiences can be even more severe.

On the national level, children are not taught about class in public school curricula. Mainstream media attention regarding class inequality has been sorely inadequate. In terms of low-income populations, few portrayals on television are not cartoonish or stereotypical. While powerful economic interests increasingly rely on cheap and exploited labor, policymakers cater to President Bush's "haves" with lucrative tax cuts and other incentives. Performance industry conglomerates push images of the rich, famous, and artificially beautiful upon us like a dangerous drug. It would seem that the United States is headed for a nervous breakdown under the psychic weight of our cultural contradictions regarding class, but we have been here before and continue unabated without any sign of change.

When African Americans are added to this equation, the potential for confusion quadruples, for even less attention has been given to class diversity among this population. When such discrepancies are acknowledged, it often occurs in a simplistic or misleading fashion that is further exacerbated by the preexisting and wide-ranging impact of racist representations on the minds of non-African Americans—and even blacks themselves.

A brief review of the literature on the black middle class is a case in point.[1] From E. Franklin Frazier's *The Black Bourgeoisie* (1957) to William Julius Wilson's *The Declining Significance of Race* (1978), seminal sociological studies have flattened out this stratum into an uppity, disconnected group of wannabes or a collective of accomplished individuals who have fled their old, urban neighborhoods and become inaccessible to those who need them most—typically expressed as "blacks trapped in the inner city." These characterizations are true in bits and pieces, but reality is more gray than these dichotomies allow for.

Other "truisms" generally taken for granted include the idea that middle-class values are something real and tangible. This has been linked to an emphasis on middle-class role models as significant forces for leading disadvantaged black kids out of their disadvantaged situations. In this formulation, low-income or working-class community workers and members are devalued by omission. Perhaps the same goes for the white middle class and poor, but low-income white people are so infrequently discussed in mainstream media and public discourse that it is difficult to be sure.

Historical studies show that African American professionals first emerged as a solid grouping during the turn of the twentieth century as a result of black migrants settling in urban centers across the United States. New York, Philadelphia, Washington, D.C., Atlanta, Cleveland, and many other cities were the places where African American professionals began serving the needs of the segregated, urban populations as physicians, businesspeople, teachers, journalists, and other occupations. This is not to say that there was no economic diversity among blacks before this, for even during enslavement captive workers had "enjoyed" varied levels of prestige, primarily among their peers, based on the type of work they did. Individual dexterity with particular skills could enhance status. Engaging in work that came with access to strategic information, resources, and work-related autonomy (the latter offered by such male-dominated occupations as the carriage driver) also helped.

Bart Landry says in *The New Black Middle Class* that after slavery ended, there was no black middle class as we conceptualize it today.[2] Instead, there emerged an African American elite that consisted of a small number of blacks, many of whom were born from relations between black women and white men. Only a few of these men and women obtained a college education. Larger numbers earned their status by working in prominent white households as domestic servants and others parlayed this work into entrepreneurial ventures such as catering, which was particularly lucrative in Philadelphia and New York City during the late 1800s. As more African Americans began migrating north and settling in cities, numerous additional income-generating opportunities were presented, and what Landry calls the old black middle class began to take shape.

In addition to urban segregation, the other development that played a pivotal role in facilitating the emergence of an African American middle class historically was the civil rights movement. Patricia Hill-Collins notes that, similar to what occurred to European Americans with the GI Bill, the doors to upward mobility for African Americans were thrown open through the legislation and social programs of the 1960s and 1970s.[3]

The findings I present here are supported in part by data from my own anthropological research in New York City that began in 1993 and continues on a smaller scale today. For three consecutive years I visited the homes and jobs of African Americans who lived and worked in Central and West Harlem, collecting data through participant observation, informational interviews, and oral histories. Members of the African American middle class were the specific focus of my doctoral dissertation, and I have published journal articles that explore class differentiation based on my ethnographic exploration into the lives of college-educated, black professional Harlemites.[4] I wanted to know what was unique or class-specific about their experience, particularly when compared to people from black working-class or white socioeconomic groupings.

This study led me to the subtopic of within-group differentiation, although I did not enter the field with a keen sense of how this issue would play out in Harlem. Even so, to pause for a moment of reflexivity and self-disclosure, the ideas presented here are not solely the product of scholarly methodologies. In this era where the top-down disregard of science has turned global warming into a

quaint idea and evolution into the musings of the godless, the lessons of empiricism are of ever increasing importance. But, as Collins and others so aptly teach,
there are additional epistemologies that shape our perceptions and understandings and one of these relates to the role of standpoint.[5]

I write as an anthropologist and African American female who has traveled
across the United States, lived in various cities along the Northeast Corridor, and
traveled to Canada, Mexico, Brazil, Guatemala, Belize, the Caribbean, Europe, and
West Africa. My working life as both an academic and an activist, in the anti-
apartheid, environmental justice, and antiwar movements—much of this with my
direct action mentor and friend, the late human rights organizer Damu Smith—has
exposed me to an array of struggles and experiences. Social justice work is rewarding beyond measure, and an added bonus is the way these efforts can widen one's
circle of friends and considerably enhance one's personal epistemology.

Beyond the process of bringing formal training and life experience to the professional habit of cultural deciphering, it was my field experience that caused so
many analytical lights to go off in my head about the impact of class differentiation in black communities. It was in the early 1990s when I began, and the
changes that now define the Harlem of the twenty-first century were just in their
embryonic stages. Perhaps I was driven by my earlier desire to become a historian
—the collection of oral histories always excited me just as much as participant
observation, if not more. While in the field, I had the sense I was really on to
something when I met with middle-class Harlemites who had lived in the area for
thirty and forty years, some even longer.

One person who fit that description was Mr. Elijah Campbell, an elderly man
who was born in the Striver's Row home in which he lived at that time.[6] During
one visit his wife showed me a photograph of him as an infant, sitting in a baby
carriage in front of his family's row house. I also visited the home of Janice
Douchette, a senior-level manager in Health and Human Services, and the workplace of Dr. Cynthia John, an octogenarian who, as of 1995, was still seeing
patients in her Harlem medical office. These college-educated elders had seen
Harlem through good times and bad, and the way they moved about the community and utilized its resources stood in stark contrast to the new crop of professionals who had then only begun to call the area home.

Generation became an important analytical and intersecting variable that gave
shape and texture to this African American middle class. Researchers have shown
that, across racial lines, people's views on social conditions often grow more conservative as they grow older. This finding panned out in startling ways during my
field research, as African American elders of various class backgrounds were

much more likely to adhere to what sounds a lot like blaming the victim and stereotypical views toward the poor. Of course, it was a pattern that did not apply to each and every senior I met, but when it came to views about class, age significantly affected perspective and habits.

In the Harlem case, it only made sense that people who had lived there for decades would share a greater sense of comfort and familiarity with the place. It was not surprising that those who fit this description would probably be older persons who were born before the Second World War. As I spent increasing amounts of time hanging around and talking with folks in Central and West Harlem, some interesting overlaps became apparent.

I had come to know quite a few working-class homeowners—many of whom were also elders who had lived in the area for decades. Making their acquaintance made it clear that the rigid association of homeownership with being middle class needed a bit of revamping. Working-class homeowners had a long history in Harlem, but, with the tremendous increase in housing costs (some property values have increased over 200 percent during a four-year period), I also encountered plenty of middle-class African Americans who were not in a position to purchase property.

Based on the most recent census data, 17.4 percent of African Americans earn upward of $75,000 annually, and 16.3 percent make between $50,000 and $75,000. These numbers are not particularly revealing without a breakdown of such specifics as where income earners reside and what the salaries and costs of living associated with these areas are. Statistics always leave one pondering what they translate to in terms of the quality of everyday life. Behind the numbers are people who may earn equivalent incomes but who also have varied tastes and live lives as divergent as the natural terrain of their dissimilar regions. Compared with Louisiana, for example, an area known for high rates of obesity, black professionals who live in Colorado and California jog and ski, in keeping with the recreational habits of the general populace in those areas. These practices have implications for morbidity and mortality but they also speak to notions of race and authenticity.

Sports like squash and even recreational activities like scuba diving and camping are not readily associated with African Americans, although a lot of black folks enjoy these kinds of things. What Tiger Woods and the Williams sisters have been able to do for golf and tennis respectively has yet to be repeated in sports like ice skating and skiing. With the medals earned by Chicagoan Shani Davis for speed skating during the 2006 Winter Olympics in Turin, perhaps African American accomplishment in other sports associated with middle-class whites will not be far behind. As it presently stands, Woods, Venus, Serena, and Davis remain groundbreaking exceptions forging new paradigms for being black, active, and healthy in these times.

What social observers have come to grips with is that culture is overlapping, malleable, contradictory, and, with this particular example, given shape and meaning by the specifics of environment. Famed anthropologist Eric Wolf once described culture as something human beings produce and display as they interact with and respond to their surroundings, both social and natural. The Southeast, where thousands of African Americans have relocated from northern cities, presents a good example of the need for geographic specificity. Carol Stack wrote about the trend of reverse migration of descendants of black migrants who came north before and during the Second World War period in *A Call to Home*.[7] Demographers note that New York City alone has lost hundreds of thousands of African American residents since the 1980s. Working-class African Americans are a significant portion of these migrating populations, but black middle-class folks are among the transplants as well.

I am acquainted with two relative newcomers, former New Yorkers, who left the big city in search of less noise and competition in a relatively large Southern city. Both have purchased homes in the suburbs of Atlanta, and though their properties are sizable, they are also much more affordable than what is currently on the market in Manhattan or Brooklyn, the areas where they formerly worked and lived. These men have achieved something that is out of reach for many of their counterparts in New York and they did it without loans, gifts, or inheritances from elder kin.

One man, Dan Slaughter, shared a story with me that demonstrated some of the adjustments that accompany regional relocation. Slaughter never knew that moving from East New York in Brooklyn to Atlanta had lulled him into a sense of complacency about his personal safety, but his relaxed demeanor attracted the wrong kind of attention during one particular return visit to the Apple. While riding on the subway late one evening, he had to quickly resuscitate his alert, "don't tread on me pose" upon noticing he was being eyeballed by a potential predator. Slaughter consciously straightened his back and glared at the individual, who eventually averted his gaze.

These types of "silent dances" between Slaughter and what may or may not have been a bad guy occur everyday in our cities and have been known to result in what law enforcement officials and journalists call "flash-point killings" of young, black males. In addition to the psychological impact, the stress these scenarios generate can also compromise physical health, and class mobility is not necessarily a preventive barrier. African Americans jokingly talk about the "black tax," a toll paid to the altar of a white privilege that most white people are blissfully unaware of. In its many forms, it exists because of the legacy of racism and now, particularly in the urban centers, because of deindustrialization, welfare reform, corporate globalization, and, for some, the absence of hope. The cost is highest for the economically vulnerable, but there are impacts on segments of middle-class African Americans as well and can be included as a differentiating factor within this stratum.[8]

I met numerous black professionals who were not in a position to purchase a home or even live in the sections of Harlem where the streets are lined with elegant, refurbished townhouses. Like their counterparts in other racial/ethnic groups across the country, segments of the African American middle class are not realizing the American dream. And race puts an additional spin on these processes. In *Living with Racism* Joe Feagin and Melvin Sikes noted that everyday, racial inequality affects the black middle class in their capacities as employees, consumers, hospital patients, and car drivers. Sociologist Mary Pattillo wrote in *Black Picket Fences* that African American professionals are more likely than whites of the same background to live near low-income census tracts.[9] Racism shapes an African American middle-class standpoint that is most unlike that of the mainstream (read white) middle class.

In another pattern of within-class differentiation, there are many black professionals who keep close contact with low-income and working-class African Americans. The suburban Maryland home of Kathy Savoy, a woman who sees no contradiction in loving life among the deer, fox, rabbits, and strip malls, and treasuring growing up in West Philadelphia, has been a way station of support for working-class kin for decades. My ethnography, *Constructing Belonging*, explored how this same general phenomenon was evident in Harlem.[10]

Although approximately half of the more than one hundred people I spoke with didn't interact closely with low-income African Americans, for others, strong relationships were established and maintained with the poor through personal kin networks, neighborhood connections, and/or the wage work the black middle class engaged in. The job connection was particularly keen for those who were employed by the city or state as teachers, social workers, or community advocates funded by government grants or programs. These individuals constituted 26 percent of my long-term project participants, and observing and talking with them motivated me to utilize a public/private sector dichotomy as a key analytical tool while making sense of my field data.

The corporate executives I met differed in lifestyle, age, and income when compared with those who worked for the city and the state. Public sector employees tended to be older, long-term residents who had lived in Harlem for twenty years or more, unlike the younger black professionals who had only been in the area for two or three years. As I indicated before, long-term Harlemites also used the resources of the community and had more interaction with nonprofessional workers.

This was an important finding because residents of black low-income communities are frequently criticized for not doing more to improve conditions in their neighborhoods. One mainstream solution has been to devote critical resources to establishing "mixed income" housing in low-income communities. This is justified as an effort to generate more community involvement and uplift residents through an influx of more educated, savvy, and active homeowners who will take pride in their neighborhoods and institute improvements. Embedded within these views are codes that invite and buttress gentrification. When implemented, the result is the appearance of uplift, but the reality is that the poor have simply moved to other, perhaps less visible, locations.

Plenty of middle-strata African Americans are not afraid of the black poor or hell-bent on avoiding them at all costs. Along similar lines, the radical wing of the black middle class played an important role in the revolution of the 1960s. Today, this segment of African American professionals has expanded to include contemporary, college-educated activists and progressive and/or socialist scholars who consciously carry the mantle of their forebears W. E. B. Du Bois, Paul Robeson, Martin Luther King, Jr., Angela Davis, Kwame Toure (Stokley Carmichael), and others.[11] Some have spoken out vociferously against the war in Iraq with the tacit support of African Americans, who poll as overwhelmingly opposed to United States involvement in this conflict. When black professionals are grumblingly characterized as "bourgeoisie," we should unpack these gross generalizations and be reminded of those among the privileged who have fought the good fight against inequality in the United States while other African Americans of all socioeconomic positions were less comfortable speaking out and organizing against oppression.

More recently, social scientists have written about the incongruous value systems of African American poor and upwardly mobile Americans. In a March 26, 2006, op-ed piece in the *New York Times* Harvard-sociologist Orlando Patterson responded to a March 20 editorial in that paper by Erik Eckholm, which presented the dramatic findings of a handful of new studies on the worsening economic conditions faced by black men in the United States.[12]

Patterson's response to the editorial was that African American culture may be at fault and that poor values that have been embraced by African American men today, particularly the youth. Although there is some undeniable truth in what he describes as dire issues, what is problematic is that the young men he describes sound as if they exist in some magically disconnected subculture. Moreover, though Patterson used the paper's editorial page to criticize other social scientists for having no solutions he did not offer any himself. The end result said little of consequence except remind us that culture is changing and not completely disruptive of agency. Unfortunately, his piece reads as a validation of the "culture of poverty" theoretical formulation, and doesn't advance our understanding of cultural specifics in the process.

As a way of reinforcing the broad view of the black experience, I would argue that there are larger, frequently unnoticed and undocumented indicators of cultural gulfs existing within the black middle class itself. In addition to the already discussed variances of income and place of residence, three additional areas reflect salient divergences that affect lifestyle and social relations. These factors can also become a cause for tension among African American populations.

One involves the issue of religious belief systems. Although the ancestors of African Americans arrived on these shores with a number of cosmological views, Christianity has been associated with African American culture from the beginnings in this country. A solid majority of black folks in the United States embrace the religion that worships the Father, the Son, and the Holy Ghost, but there is an additional smaller group that does not: they may be Muslim, Buddhist, Black Hebrew, or practitioners of West African traditions. There is another, even smaller, group within this who are annoyed with religion and views their Jesus-loving counterparts with a bit of contempt. This type of diversity is the cause for some awkward moments when "nonbelievers" are asked what church we go to and our children experience some degree of ostracism when it is learned that their parents are not good church-going folks.

One of the reasons for the disconnect is the social conservatism that progressive African Americans feel compelled to shun. Although I have a strong black identity, I have little in common with the people motivated to place anti-gay marriage bumper stickers on the rear of their cars. Whether it is African American views on immigration, gays, abortion, or interracial dating and marriage, contrasting and reactionary positions can divide in ways that are sometimes irreparable.

There are other fragments that space will not allow me to discuss at length. Some of them are structurally related, like the African American professionals with incarcerated members in their kin networks. Since the rates of arrest and incarceration are disproportionately higher among African Americans, upward mobility does not shield one from knowing criminals or even being profiled as a lawbreaker. There is also the specter of black professionals who actually engage in illegal activities. Like the educated professionals of other racial-ethnic groups, they do so by procuring and consuming controlled substances and other illegal goods or engaging in these forms of commerce to supplement their incomes. It is important to note that although blacks are frequently stereotyped as criminals on television, in film, and via the news media, African American lawbreakers have, historically, not been privileged to rack up the illegal earnings of Republican lobbyist Jack Abramoff, Enron's Ken Lay, or California Representative Duke Cunningham.

Finally, marital status is another factor that separates African American professional workers. As marriage rates for blacks slip, within-class variation can be significant when single, college-educated, and professionally employed women are folded into the equation. The impact on social relations can be based on economic factors when gendered wage equity issues are raised or perhaps the lack of companionship is the key consideration. What happens to heterosexual women faced with what some perceive as a void in their lives? Whether the problem is rooted in the economic or the interpersonal, the result can be drastic, and since African American upward mobility has historically been strongly linked to two-parent incomes and nuclear family formation, "nontraditional" families may face added scrutiny in middle-class milieus. When black social conservatism bumps up against these emerging and alternative family forms, moreover, it is easy to see that conflict can ensue.

How do these nuances get ignored and why is the mainstream public so utterly misinformed about African American cultural diversity? In an era where "liberal" Hollywood pats itself on the back for offering up shrill and racist drivel like *Crash* as a profound cinematic statement, alternative representations exist but are harder to find amid this nauseating flurry of self-congratulation. The branches and contours of African American culture and the battles occurring within our communities and kin networks are lived everyday and depicted and discussed among black folks in book clubs, church meetings, classrooms, magazines, novels, and film scripts, on websites like The Black Commentator, and around dining room tables. Black folks from all economic backgrounds are talking about the state of that fictional place called "black America."

Are they asking if the black middle class lost its mind, as Michael Eric Dyson did in his exposé on the life, work, and philosophy of comedian, actor, and performance industry magnate Bill Cosby?[13] If I could respond to Dyson's questions I would have to preface my answer by pointing out that Cosby's now infamous reflections shared during the NAACP's gala celebration of the fiftieth anniversary of the landmark *Brown v. Board of Education* decision did not uniformly represent the views of African American professional workers. It is also not insignificant to mention that Bill Cosby is not middle class but a member of a small elite cadre of African American entertainers and capitalists. I would not deny that there are black people who share the view that the poor are to blame for their predicament. What is notable about this is that low-income and working-class African Americans were heard among those shouting in agreement with the Cos as well. It is a generational and/or individual standpoint, not middle-class bias, that is at the root of these perspectives on poor black citizens.

What is most significant in this discussion is that poverty has disproportionately plagued African Americans for centuries. Through the mass media, the entertainment industry, and political propaganda, the black poor have become repositories for all that is bad and wrong, and dumped on, as have been the poor of other racial ethnic groupings to varying extents.

The black middle class has been chastised for not doing enough to help the black poor while they are characterized as a stratum that has "made it" amid the riffraff of the faceless and nameless poor. Black professionals are unevenly deemed the good citizens who have worked hard and played by the rules, but the reality is that the African American poor have given birth to the so-called middle class. They have nurtured and mightily sacrificed so that their children, nephews, granddaughters, and fictive kin could achieve; and it is the principles and ethics of the working people—manual labors, domestic servants, cleaning persons, food-service providers, and factory workers—historically, rather than some vague notion of middle-class values, that has helped position and motivate African American professionals to achieve.

Intraracial cultural variables generate impacts for African Americans at work, within their households, and in their larger residential communities. Recognition of these intricacies—including the material and structural, as well as the mundane and the entertaining—is needed because they have implications for social policy and the building of coalitions in contemporary social movements. Effective advocacy for and resistance alongside African American communities makes it incumbent upon policymakers, scholars, and activists from all backgrounds to familiarize themselves with the complexities and contradictions of African American culture and the history of black people in the United States. These endeavors will help foster sustainable social transformation in the United States and around the world.

9

Back to Class: Reflections on the Dialectics of Class and Identity

Martha E. Gimenez

It is no secret that wealth and income inequality in the United States has deepened; plenty of online sources and the mass media provide abundant information about it and pundits comment on its implications. Those on the Right stress the role of entrepreneurship, unique individual skills, and the market in making some people rich, the role of parents and culture in keeping people poor, and the importance of education to push people up the income ladder. In their view, the United States is a meritocracy, where upward mobility is a possibility open to anyone willing to make the effort. Liberals, in contrast, worry about the poor, especially single mothers and minorities. They fret about de-industrialization, immigration, and civil rights. They perceive the threat to democracy that is inherent in the concentration of wealth and power in very few hands.

Between 1972 and 2001, "income at the 99th percentile rose 87 percent; income at the 99.9th percentile rose 181 percent; and income at the 99.99th percentile rose 497 percent."[1] In 2001, the upper class, that is, the top 1 percent of households, "owned 33.4 percent of the wealth and the next 19 percent (the managerial, professional, and small business stratum) had 51 percent," so 84 percent of the privately owned wealth is in the hands of 20 percent of the population.[2] Despite the rise in productivity in the last three years, real wages declined between 2003 and 2006 and the share of GDP of wages and salaries, 45.3 percent, is the lowest on record, whereas the share of corporate profits is the highest since the 1960s.[3] Wages and salaries are stagnating, over 45 million people lack health insurance, and 2.5 percent of the 75.6 million hourly workers in 2005 earned at or below the minimum wage of $5.15 an hour.[4] Salaries, perks, and bonuses of top administrators and CEOs are the highest in the world, but corporations cancel pension plans, layoff thousands of workers, and downsize and outsource jobs with impunity and without eliciting mass protests, workforce unrest, teach-ins at major universities, or government intervention at any level. Indeed, the government has been busy cutting capital gains and estate taxes, thus increasing the concentration of wealth ownership in private hands.

There are many complex reasons for the lack of resistance to policies and corporate practices that restore the era of the robber barons and undermine the quality of life and economic well-being of the vast majority of the population, particularly the working classes.[5] In this paper, I will argue that identity politics, legitimized by academic discourse and strengthened by distortions about class in the media, and in political and public discourse, has greatly contributed to channeling political and intellectual energies toward limited and, ultimately, self-defeating goals.[6] Most people lack clarity about the meaning of class and its importance in their lives; instead they see their experiences, problems, and potential solutions through the lens of politically constructed identities (gender, racial, ethnic, etc.). Identity today is the ideological lens through which class conflicts and the effects of unfettered class power are refracted, understood, and fought. In the current academic, political, and cultural climate, social theories, state policies, and political discourses and practices have severed, in people's consciousness, the connections between experiences of oppression and exclusion, and the material conditions of those experiences. Consequently, identity politics has developed not just as separate from class politics but as the more realistic and legitimate kind of politics. In this essay, I will argue that it is important to transcend their opposition by theorizing the connections between class and the experiences that gave rise to identity politics. Only when class is brought back, not just in academic studies but in political discourse and commonsense understanding of social reality, will working people, regardless of their identities or the color of their collars, gain a deeper knowledge of the material conditions determining their problems and the reasons for the contradictory implications of hard-won civil rights victories.

Class, Status, and Identity Politics: The Social Theory Perspective

I will start with a short detour into the class theories of Marx and Weber, whose views continue to be relevant to understanding the foundations of inequality in capitalist societies. In his analysis of the capitalist mode of production, Marx used a dichotomous concept of class, identifying two classes: the capitalist class—the owners of the means of production—and the proletariat or working class, which owns only the capacity to work (labor power). Historically, there were complex gradations of social rank (peasants, lords, apprentices, serfs) but capitalism "simplified class antagonisms." [7] Classes, for Marx, are not income groups but necessary relations among people mediated by their relationship to the means of production. The relationship between capitalists and workers is necessary (each class presupposes the other) and exploitative (capitalists appropriate the surplus produced by workers); it is also a relationship of domination, for capitalists are placed in a position of economic, political, and social power over the working class. This dichotomous and relational concept of class characterizes capitalism as a mode of production. Empirically, as Marx was well aware, in concrete social formations (e.g., the United States), classes are not found in "pure form" but fragmented by the technical and social division of labor into "middle and intermediate strata."[8]

Weber's concept of class is individualistic; it is not centered on exploitation but on the effect of individuals' class situation or relative position in the market upon their life chances (their economic and social opportunities). Classes, for Weber, are aggregates of individuals who share the same class situation because they bring similar resources to the market; for example, ownership of property of a given kind or different skills.[9] Ownership of property gives market power to owners over non-owners (those who must sell services, labor, and goods in order to survive), so " 'property' and 'lack of property' are . . . the basic categories of all class situations."[10] These categories are, in turn, extremely differentiated according to the quantity and kind of property (financial, commercial, landowning capital, small business ownership), and the type of skills individuals bring to the market (skilled and unskilled manual labor, teaching credentials, professional degrees, administrative and managerial skills).

In addition to their "class situation," individuals are also placed in a "status situation," which refers to that aspect in individuals' lives "determined by a specific, positive or negative, social estimation of honor . . . connected with any quality shared with a plurality."[11] Status qualifications tend to be noneconomic; they are based on political and cultural considerations like gender, ethnicity, race, religion, and education. Status groups are characterized by a specific "style of life" that keeps marriage, friendships, and social interaction within group boundaries, and is displayed in patterns of behavior and consumption associated with the group. Although "property as such is not always recognized as a status qualification ... in the long run it is, and with extraordinary regularity."[12] This means that ultimately the hierarchy between status groups is, to some extent, determined by their economic standing.

Weber theorized about class at the level of the market, which Marx characterizes as "the Eden of the innate rights of man [where] alone rule Freedom, Equality, Property and Bentham," where capitalists and workers meet as individuals, free and equal under the law, buying and selling commodities in the pursuit of their private interests.[13] However, underlying "fair" market exchanges among individuals are ongoing unequal relations among classes: there is no equality in the context of production, for capitalists control working conditions, the labor process, the length of the workday, and the product produced by labor.[14] Furthermore, class power is exerted over the working class as a whole, through state policies favoring capitalists' interests, or through employers' decisions, which affect workers and the communities where workers live.

Class, Status, and Identity in the Social Consciousness

Most people in the United States know little or nothing about Marx's and Weber's views about class and inequality, nor about the importance of social class "from womb to tomb."[15] Their lives, however, are embedded in the class relations, market exchanges, and status groups that Marx and Weber identified as key dimensions of inequality in capitalist social formations. In the late nineteenth and first half of the twentieth century, U.S. workers were militant and aware of their interests as workers. [16] Today most workers, blue or white collar, are mainly concerned with economic survival and do not share a sense of themselves as a class with common anticapitalist grievances. Their spontaneous consciousness is largely individualistic; if they see themselves as part of a larger whole, for example a community or a kindred group, it is not in terms of class but identity or "status honor" that this collectivity is ideologically constructed.

Weber theorized inequality at the level of market exchanges, competition, consumption, and status distinctions, that is, at the level of appearances.[17] It is at this level that people spontaneously become conscious of their place in the structures of inequality that produce and reproduce those appearances and shape their lives.[18] Most people in the United States today, seem to be "Weberians" from birth, understanding class differences mainly in terms of "lifestyles" made possible by their socioeconomic status (their income, education, and occupation), and membership in status groups such as gender, race, and ethnicity. Some of these groups carry a "negative social estimation of honor"—racism, sexism, xenophobia, and so forth. These groups are identified through all encompassing political/ideological labels—minority groups, ethnic pluralities, identity politics, diversity—and specific categories such as Latinos, women of color, African Americans, etc.

The ideological currents shaping the misrecognition of class today are exceedingly complex and result from the conflation, in people's experiences and consciousness, of the effects of class location with the effects of status membership. The outcome of this conflation is the genderization, racialization, and ethnicization of class, and the perception of the effects of class as if they were solely the effects of status oppression. For example, the patterns of economic exclusion and oppression resulting in the relegation of racial and ethnic minorities to the lower layers of the working classes lead to the invisibility of white poverty and near poverty, and the use of race or ethnicity as codes for poverty and lower socioeconomic status.[19] This is why "many Americans have displaced their resentment resulting from what Sennett and Cobb called the 'hidden injuries' of class, to patriotism ... nationalism ... racism and sexism."[20] Notions such as the "feminization of poverty" highlight gender as the main cause of disproportionate female poverty, ignoring class and socioeconomic status differences among women, while overlooking or minimizing the class location of poor and working women.[21]

The conflation of class and status culturalizes the effects of class in gender, racial, and ethnic terms in the eyes of both the dominant and subordinate classes and status groups.[22] From the standpoint of the dominant groups, the culture of minority groups and the cultural patterns into which women are socialized accounts for their poverty, patterns of employment, and lower socioeconomic status. From the standpoint of the economically excluded and oppressed, their culture is something to be proud of and gender and/or racial/ethnic discrimination accounts for their place in the social and occupational structures. In this process, class is erased from consciousness and the effects of class location. For example, unemployment, low levels of education, poverty, low income, participation in the illegal (underground) economy, and employment in race/ethnic and gender segregated labor markets are transformed into the properties or characteristics attributed to the individuals presumed to hold those status-based identities, evidenced in their behavior and the "choices" they make. When class divisions are taken into consideration, it becomes clear that many of the problems afflicting women and people of color are not due entirely to their "identity" but to their class position. Not all women are "a man away from poverty"; only working-class women, mainly those who are single mothers and/or grew up in poor families, and middle-class women entirely dependent on their wages or salaries for the economic survival of themselves and their families, are at a risk of falling into poverty.[23] It is equally mis-leading to generalize about male power; all men are not wealthy or powerful. Most male workers are wage or salary earners vulnerable to outsourcing and downsizing, fully dependent on wages or salaries to support themselves and their families.

Identity politics rests on the assumption that status groups have been oppressed because of the identity of its members, an identity that those in power have vilified while those struggling to vindicate their rights have sought to reaffirm and claim as a source of pride and a basis for political struggle. But the assumption of a shared identity is belied by the heterogeneity of these groups, for they are divided by class, socioeconomic status, national origin, citizenship status, and many other important divisions, and in terms of the historically specific processes resulting in their presence in the United States.[24]

Once historical considerations are taken into account, the complex nature of racial/ethnic identities comes into view, because the comprehensive labels currently used to identify the main groups—blacks/African Americans, Hispanics/Latinos, and Asian Americans—include populations from different historical origins. These include: 1) those whose ancestors have been here for generations, have been subject to slavery, economic exploitation, and oppression, and who participated in important political struggles for civil rights, education, and employment; and 2) immigrants, documented and undocumented, who bring in different skills and resources, ranging from unskilled, manual, and service workers, to middle- and upper-middle-class professional and technical workers, small business owners, and capitalists.[25] What, then, determines identity?

Is it solely skin color? Racialized national origins? Spanish surname? What about the immigrants' original identity? Who are the subjects of identity politics? The subject of feminist theory and politics turned out to be white middle-class American women. Through the critiques of working-class women and women of color that subject was shattered into a variety of female subjects with conflicting political interests. Eventually, feminist theory changed its focus to gender, another category fragmented into multiple genders, and a seemingly unbridgeable chasm developed between academic feminism and the flesh-and-blood women organizing and struggling around concrete issues.

Is something similar likely to happen in the context of racial and ethnic identity politics? Writing in the context of the Anita Hill/Clarence Thomas controversy, Manning Marable differentiates between a *racial* (defined on the basis of physical characteristics) meaning of blackness, forced upon Africans by Europeans, and a *cultural* (defined in terms of the "traditions, rituals, values, and belief systems of African-American people . . . a sense of ethnic consciousness and pride in our heritage of resistance against racism") meaning, collectively constructed through centuries of struggle.[26] Marable points out that this cultural meaning of blackness was largely shared by black Americans until the class structure of the black population changed, as educational and occupational opportunities opened up in the aftermath of the civil rights movement. Middle- and upper-middle-class blacks and their children, especially those who did not participate in struggles against Jim Crow, no longer share that culture and cannot be expected to support the interests of African Americans as a group. Although Clarence Thomas is racially black, his appointment cannot be viewed as a "victory for black people as a group," Marable concludes. This distinction between a racial and a cultural meaning of black identity highlights the cultural nature of identity politics as well as the ideological effects of culture in obscuring the class basis for the distinction between cultural and racial blackness. The cultural meaning of blackness emerged from the struggles of slaves, former slaves, and their descendants who were kept—because of Jim Crow—in the lower levels of the working class. It is a form of class consciousness forged through painful and protracted struggles and perceived, as it could not be otherwise, through the prism of race. This is why it is possible to argue that working-class and poor blacks and the middle- and upper-middle-class blacks who politically support their interests are black in a cultural sense, whereas prosperous blacks—entrepreneurs, businessmen, professionals appointed to prominent economic and political positions—are black in a racial sense only, meaning that they are unlikely to support the interests of working-class and poor blacks. Class differences yield different racial identities, and it is important to keep this insight in mind to decode the meaning of cultural differences in all minority or identity groups, for similar issues could be identified among Latinos and Asian Americans.

Many of the issues that bring a sense of solidarity and common interest to members of racial and ethnic minorities are working-class issues: neighborhood blight, underfunded schools, lack of adequate and affordable housing, health care, lack of job training, sources of employment, unemployment, and so forth. It may be argued that, though it is true that such issues concern all working-class people, regardless of color, these problems are more serious for non-white members of the working class and it is only through the lens of identity that their situation can be best understood. The problem is that the politically feasible measures to deal with gender, racial, and ethnic discrimination (enforcement of civil rights legislation, affirmative action, etc.) are insufficient to deal with the effects of class location and class relations, which require, among other things, economic investments, job training programs, better schools, and a change in the material conditions where the poor and near-poor live.[27]

The past struggles against racism, sexism, and economic inequality sought to undermine the significance of gender, race, and ethnicity in creating barriers to full citizenship, educational opportunities, and employment. The barriers were abolished politically and legally, not materially. Civil rights laws forbid discrimination on the basis of race, religion, national origin, gender, and other distinctions which have not, in practice, been eradicated but continue to have effects on people's lives: "Far from abolishing these *factual* distinctions, the state presupposes them in order to exist." [28] The attainment of civil rights is indeed important, a necessary but not a sufficient condition to abolish the discrimination, oppression, and economic inequality facing most women and members of racial/ethnic minorities. Their problems and differential ability to surmount them, however, are not exclusively the effect of discrimination; they are also caused by their class location—in the lower strata of the working class. To bring class into the analysis is difficult. Social theory and research about these issues, and identity politics— developed as the abstract negations of class reductionisms and economic determinisms, the perpetrators of which are never identified—have became mired in the juggling act of examining the interactions and intersections between race, gender, and class. This perspective reduces class either to the empiricism of socioeconomic status indexes (i.e., some combination of individuals' income, education, and occupation) or to another identity, without incorporating into the analysis the capitalist processes, at both the national and global level, that affect the most vulnerable segments of the working class. As Antonia Darder and Rodolfo D. Torres point out, "The result of theoretical interventions based on identity politics has been the conspicuous absence of a systematic analysis of class relations and critique of capitalism in much of the work on Latino, African-American, Native American and Asian populations." [29]

Given that public and even social science discourse reduce class and socioeconomic differences to "demographics" (that is, to individuals' characteristics on a par with religion, age, sex, and census-defined races and ethnicities), and that labor is consistently treated by the media and politicians as a "special interest," most people are likely to understand their lives in the cultural ideological terms in which they are constantly interpellated. [30] These terms exclude their class location and make it difficult or impossible to name; class, now reduced to another identity, calls to mind not its constitutive relations of economic exploitation, oppression, and exclusion but the evils of "class-ism," namely, stereotypes that "oppress" people on the basis of their class. The ideas of the ruling class are indeed the ruling ideas, and they are particularly effective when the media, academics, and activists cooperate in the production and dissemination of these ideas.[31] In the absence of political parties representing working-class interests, and in the context of exceedingly low levels of unionization, people become conscious of economic, social conflicts, and change in ideological terms;[32] "Class issues are given other names: crime, especially drugs; teenage pregnancy and suicide; homelessness and hunger ... unemployment," and, I may add, racism, sexism, and other "isms." [33]

The culturalization of politics, reflected in the new political and academic language about "diversity,"[34] reinforces the "social amnesia"[35] prevalent today. The celebration of cultural diversity for its own sake, policies about diversity training and multiculturalism (presumably intended to help people understand and respect other people's identities and cultures), recruitment policies designed to increase the diversity of student bodies, teaching staff, and the workforce, through the inclusion of members of "diverse" populations (a euphemism for women and non-whites) in educational institutions and in the workplace, seem to have replaced, to a large extent, earlier concerns with the economic inequality and social discrimination affecting women and racial/ethnic minorities.[36] Walter Benn Michaels argues that "the respect for difference [should not be allowed] to take the place of ... commitment to economic justice."[37] Like affirmative action, policies aiming to increase institutional diversity unwittingly end up benefiting middle-and upper-middle-class women and members of racial and ethnic minorities, many of whom may be foreign-born or first-generation Americans. They will indeed bring cultural diversity to the places where they study and they work, but such a goal is very different from the goals of the 1960s social movements.

Conclusion

It may seem that transcending the opposition between class and identity politics, between the "politics of redistribution" and the "politics of recognition" is an impossible task.[38] Class and identity, however, are not mutually exclusive but part of the network of relationships that shape people's experiences. Class struggles and identity-based struggles are intertwined: class relations presuppose cultural understandings, and cultural and political recognitions are a means toward economic and political justice.[39] Dialectically, experience is a unity of opposites; it is both personal and social and, as such, it is partial, mystifying, thoroughly social, shaped by historical forces individuals may know little or nothing about, and lived under the spell of ideological interpellations among which identity politics are currently perhaps the most compelling.[40] The ideologies of identity politics interpellate individuals as who they *always already* are—as members of a specific group, as the bearers of a given identity.[41] As indicated earlier, macro-level economic and social processes such as immigration, changing census categories used to identify minority populations, and changes in class and social stratification undermine the stability of identity-based groups, thus leading to the emergence of conflicting claims about membership and competing notions of cultural, racial, historical, or pan-ethnic identity. The recent questions raised about Senator Obama's identity are a case in point; they focus on his ancestry and the appropriateness of his self-identification as an African American while no references are made to his class and socioeconomic status. Would critics be equally concerned about his identity if he came from a working-class background, had little or no education, and had risen to political prominence solely on the basis of his charisma? As Manning Marable pointed out, "The problem with the prism of race is that it simultaneously clarifies and distorts reality . . . it often clouds the concrete reality of class, and blurs the actual structure of power and privilege."[42] The overriding concerns with identity and diversity have pushed class into the "political unconscious" from which it can emerge only as a form of cultural difference, as long as a serious consideration of the meaning of class and its unavoidable effects on experience and forms of consciousness continues to be avoided as a form of reductionism or determinism, or as a kind of illegitimate, "un-American" political discourse.

What is needed at this critical time, then, is a return to class, unmediated by the distortions of cultural/ideological understandings of its effects. This entails, among other things, a clear understanding of how the class structure imposes actual limitations on identity politics. What is it that proponents of identity politics could realistically accomplish if they were completely successful in terms of economic redistribution and political recognition? A proportional representation, for women and racial/ethnic minorities, in the occupational structure and income distribution? An end to the disproportional poverty of working-class women and members of racial and ethnic minorities? Are such goals feasible, given the structural constraints inherent in capitalist social formations, particularly at this time when no country is immune to the leveling effects of globalization?

As important as these practical considerations are, it is crucial to engage in a rethinking of identities in light of the class and socioeconomic differences they cloak. It is time, then, to historicize and contextualize the present by bringing up a new kind of "hyphenated identities," the kind that will sharpen understanding about the actual location of people in capitalist society and has the potential to undermine the mystification entailed in reducing people to their gender, age, ethnicity, and race. It is time for academics, journalists, and activists to change from the prism of identity to a prism of class that incorporates and historicizes identity. Such a transition entails bringing up the social-class location and the socioeconomic status, when necessary, of the ideologies, groups, and populations about which data is presented. Identifying—in our research, writing, and speaking—the class of the group about which data, information, and problems are discussed (working-class white women, middle-class black men, poor white homeless men, the poverty of working-class children, and so forth) is an important start in the protracted process of bringing into public consciousness first, the realization that class, gender, race, ethnicity, and other social relations that shape our lives are not materially separate, like billiard balls bouncing off each other, but key dimensions of everyone's life; and second, that the crucial question to ask of others is not "who are you?"[43] but "which side are you on?"

10

Women and Class:
What Has Happened in Forty Years?

Stephanie Luce and Mark Brenner

Forty years ago this past summer, a group of women and men came together to form the National Organization for Women (NOW). NOW's mission was to fight for gender equality through education and litigation. Though not the only group fighting for women's rights, it quickly became one of the best known and largest. Today, NOW has over a half million members and over five hundred chapters throughout the country. NOW was founded at a time when women were entering the paid labor force in increasing numbers. NOW had its critics: many said it ignored race and class, others said it was too focused on liberal feminist legal strategies like passing the Equal Rights Amendment. Numerous other organizations representing working-class women and women of color developed, including the Coalition of Labor Union Women; 9to5: The National Organization of Working Women; and the Combahee River Collective. Together with myriad other groups these organizations helped build the women's movement of the 1960s and 1970s.

It would be difficult to pinpoint how much of the success of this movement was a result of direct organizing or legal efforts, but what is clear is that the 1960s through 1980s saw major changes in the status of working women. Legal barriers to gender-based employment and pay discrimination were eliminated. By 1970, occupational segregation by gender began to fall substantially for the first time since at least the turn of the century.[1] The gender wage gap narrowed, with women earning 59 cents an hour to every dollar earned by a man in 1964, but 77 cents per hour in 2005.[2] The percentage of women in the labor force with a college degree went up from 11.2 percent in 1970 to 32.8 percent in 2005, rising at basically twice the rate for men.[3] And yet, certain things didn't change much at all: women continued to carry the major responsibility for household labor, child rearing and other kinds of care work, and women were still more likely to live in poverty than men.

Meanwhile other trends that had been improving began to stagnate or reverse in the 1990s, such as the degree of occupational integration between men and women. Occupational segregation between white women and black women increased in the 1990s, and wage inequality between women with high school degrees or less and women with advanced education began to rise. An employment gap between young white and black women began to appear for the first time.

What explains these trends? We argue that while some of them can be explained by economic changes such as a rise in the service sector and offshoring of manufacturing jobs, much is explained by social movements of the period. The women's movement of the 1960s and 1970s, along with the civil rights movement, laid the groundwork for significant and real gains for some segments of the working class. However, these movements did not operate in a vacuum. They had internal disagreements over how to shape their demands, and they also had to respond to counterattack and eventual backlash.

This produced a situation where some women have achieved considerable gains while others have not. Although there were differences between women in the 1950s and 1960s, there were more similarities between them than there are today. After forty years of the women's movement, the gains of some women have led to a greater class divide among women workers. This challenges us to consider what working-class women can do to reverse this trend, and whether it would be possible—or advisable—to build a cross-class women's movement today.

What Has Changed for Women Workers Over the Past Forty Years?

In order to understand the conditions for working women today and the potential for a new women's movement, we need to understand what has really changed over the past forty years, and what the consequences are of those changes.

As is well-known by now, one of the largest changes has been the significant increase in the overall labor force participation of women, but especially of married women and women with young children. According to the Bureau of Labor Statistics, only about one-third of all women participated in the paid labor force in

1950, but almost 60 percent did by 2005. Married women increased their participation from 24 to 61 percent in that same period.[4] Of women with children under
age six, 39 percent worked in 1975, and 63 percent did in 2005.[5] Major changes
took place between 1950 and 1990, with women's labor force participation leveling off since then. We have even seen a slight decrease in participation rates among
white married women with infants in the late 1990s and early 2000s, but that
appears to be primarily because of the recession and difficulty in finding work.[6]

Historians are quick to point out that there are notable differences in the trends
by race, as black women have always had higher labor force participation rates than
white women, and tended to work more years in their lifetime whereas white
women took time out for child rearing. However, the general trends of increased
participation hold for white and black women. Unfortunately, we do not have adequate historical data on female participation rates for Asian and Latina women.

In addition to increasing labor force participation rates, there have been major
changes in the gender makeup of certain occupations. By 2005, women accounted for half of all managerial, professional, and related occupations, and this was
the occupational category that saw the greatest growth for women in both
absolute and relative terms.[7]

Who are the women who have benefited from these changes? In academic and
public policy circles a lot of attention has been given to the benefits accruing to
women with a college degree. It is true that this segment of the workforce has seen
enormous gains. Whereas the average woman in this category earned $16.40 an
hour in 1973 (in 2005 dollars), she earned $21.30 an hour in 2005, a 30 percent
increase.[8] By comparison, men with a college degree only experienced a 17 percent increase in wages over the same period. Women with advanced degrees have
seen a 25 percent increase in their average hourly wage during this period. Many
of these women have gained economic independence, allowing them to delay
marriage or avoid it altogether, enter occupations formerly closed to them, and
gain status and authority in their careers. Indeed, work by Erik Olin Wright and
Rachel Dwyer finds that whereas gender was the most significant factor explaining how much someone earned in the *new* jobs created in the 1960s, race had
become more important by the 1990s.[9]

Clearly, the upward mobility of white female workers with significant education is one of the remarkable changes of the past forty years, and the gains for this
group of women are not to be discounted. Still, the way that their success is commonly portrayed misses important parts of the story. First, there are the significant
barriers that still remain for many women due to the "glass ceiling," or other
forms of discrimination that still exist in the labor market. Professional women

who struggle to balance both job and family suffer a penalty in a work world that has changed very little in response to this reality. Second, there are the crucial factors of class and race that are left out by the story of successful professional women. The majority of women are still working class, languishing in low-wage, insecure jobs with little prestige and stability and no benefits.

What Hasn't Changed?

As of 2005, the median hourly wage for all women workers was $12.50. For a single mother with two children working full-time this represents about 153 percent of the federal poverty line for a family of three. Close to 60 percent of all black women and 67 percent of all Latina women earn hourly wages below this amount. Although women now comprise the majority of college students, this still represents only a minority of all women. In 2005 only 27 percent of all women aged 25 or older had a college degree. For black women in this age group, only 19 percent had a college degree or more. And for Hispanic women the figure is only 12 percent.[10]

This may explain why we see such discrepancies in occupational data when we examine it by race. Whereas 39 percent of all white women and 45 percent of all Asian women worked in management, professional, and related occupations in 2005, only 30 percent of black women and 22 percent of Hispanic women did so. Women are making up more of the professional and managerial classes, but there are still important differences across race.

Although the gender wage gap has been closing, this is not because women's average wages are rising. In fact, in recent years women's earnings have not kept pace with inflation. The gap with male earnings continues to close only because men's wages are falling faster than women's. Furthermore, even though some groups of women have been able to achieve much higher wages than the average, they still tend to lose significant income throughout their childrearing years. A study by the Institute for Women's Policy Research shows that women between ages 26 and 59 earned only $273,592 on average over fifteen years, whereas the average man of that age earned $722,693 (in 1999 dollars) in the same time period. This suggests that even though the hourly gender pay ratio may be 77 percent at any one time, the lifetime gender gap is much more substantial, 38 percent in this case. While recent numbers show that the hourly wage gap for younger workers is closing, with the average gender pay ratio up to 84 cents, it is not clear if this represents a generational change or simply a pattern in life-cycle earnings.

Women are still primarily responsible for raising children and taking care of the house. Although there has been an increase in the number of single-father-headed households and the amount of child care done by fathers in general, there continues to be a large gap between the average hours that mothers and fathers devote to raising children. Contrary to the popular view that many young fathers are leaving the labor force to care for their children, the labor force participation rate for fathers with children under three years old is 95 percent: higher than any other group. Even when both parents work outside the home and fathers share in child-care tasks, mothers are more likely to take jobs with flexible hours that allow them to drop off and pick up children from school or take the day off when the children are sick. According to the Bureau of Labor Statistics, working women with small children spend more than twice the hours per day doing primary child-care activity than their spouses. Husbands do a slightly greater share of household tasks but still average only about half of the work done by their wives.[11] Over time, as more women entered the paid labor force, men have increased their share of housework somewhat, but the gap between men and women has closed primarily because women have reduced their total hours. Although more companies now offer family leave, data show that women are economically penalized for taking advantage of that leave, particularly women in professional jobs. This may be one reason why professional couples have increased their reliance on domestic help services primarily provided by other women.

Lower wages and greater child-care responsibility relate to the third trend that has remained steady, which is that women are more likely than men to be living in poverty. It is important to point out that most scholars believe that the federal poverty line is too low and does not accurately reflect the cost of living today. Nevertheless, one-third of all women live at or below 200 percent of the federal poverty line. Though the overall poverty rate of female-headed families has fallen over the past few decades, the rate began to increase in 2000, and it has been rising steadily since then. Today 36 percent of female-headed families with children under 18 years are living in poverty.

What keeps women in poverty? One significant factor is the low wages women earn in the labor market. Average wages in female-dominated occupations are very low, and as Barbara Ehrenreich pointed out so clearly in her book, *Nickel and Dimed*, the math just doesn't add up. But women who try to move into higher-wage occupations, particularly ones that don't require a college degree, face real barriers. For example, despite the many programs that attempt to bring women into nontraditional occupations, there are still very few women in higher-wage construction or manufacturing occupations. Women who do move into such occupations often experience harassment and isolation on the job, and many eventually decide to leave these occupations altogether.

But occupational segregation isn't just a reality in manufacturing or the building trades. According to Stephen Rose and Heidi Hartmann, even within occupational groups there are still male and female tiers, with women concentrated in the lower-paid tiers. The occupations that are most common for women workers today are remarkably similar to what they were in the 1940s: nurses, nurses' aids, typists, and secretaries.[12] Irene Padavic and Barbara Reskin also point out that though women were making strides in changing occupational segregation in the 1970s and 1980s, there was stagnation in the 1990s. (A trend toward occupational integration by race between the 1960s and the 1980s reversed itself in the 1990s.)

Not only do some occupations continue to remain highly segregated by gender, but wages in those occupations still show large discrepancies among comparable jobs. For example, janitors, who are primarily men, earned an average wage of $10.15 an hour in 2005, while maids and housekeepers, an occupation that requires similar amounts of training and skill, earned $8.74 an hour. Machinery maintenance workers and nursing aides receive similar amounts of training, but the former earned $16.96 an hour in 2005, and the latter earned $10.67.[13]

Explaining the Trends

What explains why some things have changed so dramatically while others have stayed the same? First and foremost, class matters, and its importance is rising. Women in professional and managerial positions have benefited enormously from changes over the past forty years. But, as Johanna Brenner points out, much of their success has been due to individualized solutions, particularly the fight for equal access to labor markets.[14] Women have pushed for admission into colleges and professional schools, and have used lawsuits and other legal strategies to fight for better access to labor markets. Their successes have contributed to the closing wage gap between men and women, as well as some of the areas of substantial occupational desegregation. The women who have benefited from these individual solutions have been disproportionately white and those with prior access to resources. For most women, entering the paid labor force also does not change their class position, as class mobility remains relatively low in the United States. Indeed, recent research suggests that class mobility has been decreasing in recent years.

The numbers also show that race matters. This is not a new point, but still a crucial one, since recent trends among women suggest a widening racial gap, evidenced by increasing occupational segregation between white and black women in the 1990s and the differential rates of employment between young white and black women in recent years.[15]

Having children also matters. Not all women with children do poorly in the labor market, but 75 percent of poor families have children under eighteen years of age.[16] And having children remains one of the best predictors of how well women will be able to negotiate the labor market. This relationship is mitigated by the presence of a husband or second parent, but women continue to hold the primary responsibility for child rearing.

But these facts are not enough to explain the trends discussed above. It is not just that working-class women and women of color have less power and fewer resources, on average, than elite women or white women. And it is not just that having children is expensive and makes it difficult to find well-paid work. Other factors and relationships significantly influence changes in social conditions.

Organizing matters. Women, including working-class women, have attempted to exert their agency both individually and collectively in this period. However, the way in which power and resources are distributed, as well as the way social reproduction is organized, have shaped how that agency has been exerted.

Similarly, the framework within which people make demands can affect the outcomes of their struggles. Nelson Lichtenstein argues that the American labor movement failed to develop a comprehensive collective approach to organizing the working class coming out of the Second World War.[17] For example, rather than fighting for a universal health care system, they won employer-based health care. Rather than fighting to improve the working conditions and employment opportunities for all workers, they fought primarily on behalf of their members. As a result, large groups of workers were not only outside the union movement, unions failed to address issues central to them like health care and retirement security. Women and people of color were particularly marginalized by the postwar development of the U.S. labor movement, and forced to look for other solutions to workplace problems. The civil rights movement of the 1960s was one expression of this search for alternatives, pressing for the passage of landmark legislation that prohibited employment discrimination on the basis of race or gender (and other categories), and required employers to pay equal wages to men and women performing the same work. However, because these rights were the product of a legislative victory, they were primarily enforced through individual lawsuits. This contributed to the approach adopted by today's women's organizations.

Since many of these approaches have enjoyed success, organizations continue to emphasize individualized strategies for working-class women. To confront occupational segregation, they advocate job training that would enable women to enter skilled trades. To decrease the wage gap, they push for more programs to get women into college and legislation that would mandate equal pay.

Although having access to individual solutions is important, it is also true that working-class women and women of color are much less likely to pursue them. There are, of course, cases like *Betty Dukes v. Wal-Mart,* as well as other initiatives on behalf of working-class women. But these cases can take many years to resolve, and most working-class women have neither the time nor resources necessary to pursue them. With legal and other individual strategies out of reach, and vehicles for collective action (like unions) on the decline, working-class women are largely left out, with no large organization of their own.

Of course, not all organizing has focused on individual solutions. Some working-class women have benefited from collective approaches that improve wages and job quality—namely unionization. There have been unions in the United States that have organized women for a long time, but efforts have increased dramatically in the past several decades. For example, women in teaching and nursing have experienced wage gains and better benefits through unionization. Working class women's organizations such as 9to5, which was founded in 1973 and now has members in all fifty states, organized to help pass the Civil Rights Act of 1991, the Family and Medical Leave Act, state health and safety laws, as well as local living-wage ordinances.

But where collective action exists it runs into a second challenge of organizing: locating sources of power. Steve Jenkins, analyzing the dynamics of the workers' center movement, makes a useful distinction between two sources of power available to workers. The first is social power, the ability to disrupt production or business, while the second is advocacy power, the ability to get lawyers, lobbyists, voters, or others to win things on your behalf.[18]

What kind of power do women workers have? One set of women who have done relatively well in the job market in the last several decades are those with access to scarce skills: in particular, women who received a college degree or more and go into managerial and professional occupations. These women have been able to rely on their individual or sometimes collective bargaining power to gain access to better jobs and wages.

A second set of women have combined collective action, primarily through unionization, with their individual skills and education to improve their wages and working conditions. Table 1 illustrates this point, listing the largest twenty occupations for women. These occupations account for 43 percent of all women workers. Note that both registered nurses and grade school teachers recorded significantly higher weekly earnings ($930 and $813, respectively) than all women workers ($585), as well as much higher rates of unionization. However, access to education and scarce skills, or even union membership, is no guarantee of success in the labor market. For example, teacher assistants and preschool and kindergarten teachers both have higher than average union density but lower than average weekly earnings. One explanation may be the difficulties associated with working in a caring profession.

As Nancy Folbre argues in her book *The Invisible Heart,* this is a by-product of the gender division of labor, where all forms of caring labor are undervalued in the marketplace. Even though caring labor has been increasingly privatized as more women enter the paid labor force, it is still heavily subsidized by the free work that women continue to do (which Folbre estimates would amount to somewhere between 30 and 60 percent of all goods and services bought in the United States). Folbre also argues that even when women in caring professions unionize they end up with lower pay than they would in comparable jobs outside the care sector. This follows from the fact that unionized workers may be more reluctant to exercise that leverage—whether through strikes or other job actions—because of the caregiving element of their jobs.

Particularly important, however, is a third group of women workers: those without individual power and those without unions. These are the women with less higher education and little ability to get jobs beyond the traditional female occupations. These jobs, such as cashier, retail salesperson, and waitress, come with little social power. The employees are seen as easily replaceable, and their occupations have very low rates of union density. As Table 1 shows, many of the largest occupations for women have lower than average union density rates. Thus most women workers benefit from neither the individual based solutions nor collective efforts like unionization.

What's more, individual-based solutions are not likely to be effective for this group of women, since they do not address the heart of the problem, the lack of "good jobs." It is possible that the Wal-Mart cashier job of today could carry pay and benefits comparable to the Ford assembly job of the 1950s, but it would take collective organizing, not job training or more education, to change those jobs into "good jobs." Indeed, that is how the onetime "bad jobs" in the auto industry were converted to higher-wage, benefited ones.

Whereas we believe women in this third category are more likely to benefit from collective strategies versus individual ones, it is important to point out that even collective approaches are still limited. First, in the short term, they can only address job quality, and not class position. Even with greater union density in all

Table 1: Top 20 Occupations for Women Workers, 2005 (Employment in thousands)

	Total employed women	Total employed (men & women)	Percent women	Women's median weekly earnings*	Union density (all workers)
Total	65,762	141,730	46.4	$585	12.5
Secretaries & admin. assistants	3,405	3,499	97.3	559	7.4
Cashiers	2,334	3,075	75.9	322	6.2
Registered nurses	2,230	2,416	92.3	930	16.6
Elementary & middle school teachers	2,150	2,616	82.2	813	52.5
Retail salespersons	1,686	3,248	51.9	401	1.2
Nursing, psychiatric, & home health aides	1,685	1,900	88.7	385	12.2
First-line supervisors/mngrs. of retail sales workers	1,462	3,523	41.5	525	4.0
Waiters & waitresses	1,384	1,927	71.8	332	1.7
Bookkeeping, accounting, & auditing clerks	1,329	1,456	91.3	551	4.7
Receptionists & information clerks	1,271	1,376	92.4	463	3.8
Child care workers	1,260	1,329	94.8	330	5.0
Customer service representatives	1,259	1,833	68.7	505	7.7
Maids & housekeeping cleaners	1,237	1,382	89.5	328	6.2
First-line supervisors/mngrs. of office & admin. support workers	1,115	1,598	69.8	656	7.3
Accountants & auditors	1,042	1,683	61.9	784	5.0
Teacher assistants	861	947	90.9	398	32.8
Office clerks, general	815	965	84.5	509	7.5
Cooks	777	1,838	42.3	314	4.6
Preschool & kindergarten teachers	702	719	97.7	520	18.9

*Weekly earnings are for full-time wage and salary workers.

Sources: U.S. Census Bureau, Current Population Survey, 2005; Barry T. Hirsch & David A. Macpherson, Union Membership & Coverage Database from the CPS (Unionstats.com).

female-dominated occupations, if we are still living in a class economy, working women would still be exploited by their employer and alienated from their labor.

Second, collective approaches that are only aimed at improving wages and job quality are still limited in the impact they can have on the lives of working women, because they do not address the social reproduction of labor. Women need collective solutions to non-market activity as well as market activity. Improving access to the market and to better-quality jobs can benefit individual women, but this often simply redistributes the caring labor among women. As Johanna Brenner and Barbara Laslett argue, it is not only power and resources that affect organizing opportunities but the entire organization of social reproduction.[19] The ways in which social reproduction—especially the gender division of labor— is structured can open or close spaces for women's self-organization. For example, a privatized system of care means that housework and child-care responsibilities fall on individuals and families. The gender division of labor has resulted in most of this work falling on women. However, there has been variation in the impact of this, particularly by class and race, and depending on the state of social movements. In times like the Progressive Era and the 1960s and 1970s, there was a strong feminist movement that challenged the gender division of labor and created a space for mostly middle-class and white women to self-organize and mobilize around their demands. In the current period, the bulk of social reproduction is privatized. Parents are responsible for solving their own child-care (and other care-work) needs. This further individualizes women's lives, and inhibits space for self-organization and collective solutions of any kind.

We would of course be remiss to ignore the other material conditions that matter in shaping women's experiences in the labor market. It is not only the structure of social reproduction that matters but also of production. Some of the most dramatic changes in women's labor force participation happened when employers and/or government actively recruited women to work outside the home for wages, such as the Lowell textile mills that recruited farm girls in the early 1800s or the defense industry that hired women during the Second World War. Women can significantly change their labor market experiences through their own self-organization, but they are not doing so under "conditions of their own choosing."

What does all of this mean for women's self-organization? As we've already noted, when framed as a fight against workplace discrimination the struggles of working-class women tend to elicit individual solutions rather than collective ones and also neglect the very real constraints imposed by social reproduction. This framework, founded on claims of equal access to markets, also avoids posing much larger political questions, most notably whether markets can lead to living-wage jobs for all and a more humane approach to production and social reproduction. Indeed, most organizations today that are concerned with issues related to women and work are ultimately hemmed in by the framework of equalizing market access: recommending more job training for women so that they can fill higher-wage jobs; child-care subsidies so that more women can enter the labor market; and comparable worth policies that force employers to recognize and fairly compensate women's human capital.[20] In the end, these solutions can only improve the chances that women can gain access to well-paid working-class jobs, or at best, leave the class altogether. What this approach leaves hidden is an acknowledgment that class, at the core, is a system where workers and employers have inherently opposing interests. The primary challenge facing working-class women and their allies today is how to fight for better conditions for workers under capitalism, while recognizing—and struggling to overcome—the limits of capitalism as a system. The experience of women in the United States in the last forty years has made abundantly clear that there will always be competition for the living-wage jobs that exist under capitalism, and the ways in which those jobs are parceled out will be influenced by systems of patriarchy and racial oppression. Individual solutions based on market access won't be enough: women also need class-based solutions. In fact, individual solutions have only exacerbated the problem for many women.

As feminists, we want to see individual women succeed: to gain access to higher education, to have the opportunity for economic independence, and to find meaningful work. But it isn't enough for a few women, or even a lot of women, to succeed. Because under capitalism, their success in leaving the class only means others are left behind. Under capitalism, you can't have a manager without the managed, and you can't have a winner without a loser. And who is losing? It remains primarily women and people of color who lose the most under capitalism, overrepresented among the working class and the poor. In addition, many of those women who are "winners" by virtue of their new degrees and higher-paying jobs aren't really winning, either. They may have more money and more power, but because of our privatized system of social reproduction, capitalism still constrains their options for caring for others and being cared for. In this way, the women who "win" under capitalism, as well as those who lose, have an incentive to build a cross-class women's movement to fight for a different model of production and social reproduction that allows us to construct our lives around human needs.

11

The Pedagogy of Oppression

Peter McLaren and Ramin Farahmandpur

The rhetoric associated with the term "democracy" which currently saturates the political landscape of civil society has lurched so far to the right that debates not easily situated within the clashing extremities of good and evil have been effectively sidelined, if not permanently excluded. The apocalyptic grandeur permeating the public spectacle of fighting terrorism has forced Americans to succumb to the fervor of the sound-and-fury packaging of the message rather than to question its substance, thus providing ideological cover for what Henry Giroux calls the "terror of neoliberalism."[1]

Like a vast all-permeating sea, capitalism increasingly is swallowing all aspects of social and cultural life. The assault by big business on the public trust proceeds apace with little mainstream opposition, as corporations relentlessly pursue the highest margins of profits on their investments with little or no consideration for the welfare of the millions of the working poor; the war in Iraq is looking more like a replay of the expansionist agenda of 1890s America, with Bush Junior taking his cues from William McKinley's Philippines playbook; education, now synchronized to the pulse of Wall Street, is forcing millions of students in public schools to compete against one another through high-stakes standardized tests; the Bush camarilla has set feathers to the heels of the military industrial complex's wildest fantasies, pouring trillions of dollars into fighting Iraqi insurgents and securing production-sharing agreements that will enable the United States to control Iraq's oil. Such acts of largess, accompanied by skillful propaganda and strategically located military bases, will secure the U.S. military presence in the Middle East for decades to come.

Back in the Homeland, where the banner of free-market democracy flies the highest in a chilling vacuum of political probity, millions of Americans experience chronic homelessness and unemployment. Much like the war on terrorism, capitalism is ratcheting up the brutality of its deployment, creating a proletariat workforce, but on a grander scale than has been seen in recent decades. Religion, racism, and the ruling class continue to provide the motifs that shape our social universe. The state senate of Georgia recently passed a bill providing money to high schools that offer elective classes in Bible studies; anti-Muslim sentiments are on the rise along with activity by the Ku Klux Klan, neo-Nazis, and other vigilante groups that share ideological propinquities; and the public has learned about the tenacious ten-year efforts by eighteen super-wealthy families (with their accumulated wealth estimated at a staggering $185.5 billion) to repeal the federal estate tax.[2] The current climate is ripe for an assault on not only immigrant groups of color but also on the educational system to which these groups often turn as a means of providing a better future for their children.

It is true that we no longer live in a country where Blake's "dark satanic mills" fleck the landscape of America's heartland. We have exported those mills elsewhere, but still profit from the misery of those forced to work in them. The transnational capitalist class still adheres to the "vile maxim" of the masters of mankind, condemned by Scottish political economist Adam Smith, that of "all for ourselves and nothing for other people."

We now face some of the most urgent problems of the twentieth century, one of which Manning Marable identifies as "the problem of global apartheid."[3] This Marable describes as "the racialized division and stratification of resources, wealth, and power that separates Europe, North America, and Japan from the billions of mostly black, brown, indigenous, undocumented immigrant and poor people across the planet." The processes of global apartheid within the United States are represented by what Marable refers to as the "New Racial Domain." This new domain of exploitation and suffering is different from the old racial domain of slavery, Jim Crow segregation, ghettoization, or strict residential segregation that were grounded in the political economy of U.S. capitalism, where antiracism was grounded in the realities of domestic markets and the policies of the U.S. nation-state. Whereas the struggles involving the old racial domain were debated "within the context of America's expanding, domestic economy, and influenced by Keynesian, welfare state public policies," the New Racial Domain, by contrast, "is driven and largely determined by the forces of transnational capitalism, and the public policies of state neoliberalism."⁴ Marable describes these forces as "an unholy trinity" or "deadly triad," which he names as unemployment, mass incarceration, and mass disenfranchisement. What is important about Marable's insights is that he avoids excessive subjectivism and traces this process to the point of capitalist production. He links the processes of the New Racial Domain to the advent of neoliberal capitalism and to the emergence of the transnational capitalist class. He sees the social consequences of these policies inside the precincts of the United States as the creation of "an unequal, two-tiered, uncivil society, characterized by a governing hierarchy of middle-to-upper-class 'citizens' who own nearly all private property and financial assets, and a vast subaltern of quasi- or sub-citizens encumbered beneath the cruel weight of permanent unemployment, discriminatory courts and sentencing procedures, dehumanized prisons, voting disenfranchisement, residential segregation, and the elimination of most public services for the poor." Exacerbating this already perilous condition is the racism that operates under the cover of race-neutral, color-blind language as well as the dismantling of unions and a xenophobia and ethnic and religious intolerance against Muslims and Arab Americans that fires the new American hyper-patriotism in a way that could "potentially reinforce traditional white racism against all people of color." Marable sees hope for the future, as we do, in a broad united front that includes the valiant struggles of those who fight on a daily basis against police brutality and mandatory minimum sentencing laws, the work of prisoners' rights activists, the efforts of those who advocate for a living wage and workers' rights, the work undertaken by those who struggle for day care, health care, public transportation, and decent housing, and the accomplishments of those who participate in the anti-globalization movement.

The anti-WTO protests in Seattle in 1999, the widespread demonstrations against the G8 summit in Genoa, Italy, in 2001, and the many anti-globalization protests since that time (including the recent G8 summit in Heiligendamm, Germany) have not only enlarged the compass of pubic understanding about the transnational sweep of contemporary capitalism but have also sparked the growth of coalitions composed of social movements, progressive organizations, labor unions, community activists, and ordinary citizens who are collectively engaged in various forms of struggles and resistance against global capitalism and U.S. imperialism. The recent anti-immigration Sensenbrenner Bill, named after its author and leading sponsor, Rep. James Sensenbrenner, which criminalizes undocumented immigrants and makes living and working in the United States illegally a felony, has outraged and angered many immigrant communities across the United States. In Los Angeles, for example, more than 500,000 demonstrators poured into the streets in protest against the anti-immigration legislature on March 25, 2006. The following day, more than 36,000 students in the Los Angeles Unified School District walked out of their classrooms. Similar student demonstrations and walkouts were reported in Dallas, Detroit, and Phoenix.

The fight for immigration rights could become one of the largest and most influential social movements in decades, a protracted struggle that draws from the ranks of the most oppressed and exploited layers of the U.S. working class. Although actions set in motion by immigrant rights organizations throughout the country—known variously as *paro económico* or *boicot económico* (economic stoppage or boycott) or *paro cívico* (moratorium)—continue to be effective in fighting proposed state laws that would not only victimize undocumented workers but also their employers, and the businesses that deal with them, such actions treat the symptoms of neoliberalism rather than the disease. They do not, for instance, address Latin America's lack of inclusive economic growth vis-à-vis the more developed capitalist countries; more significantly, they do not challenge the nature and persistence of predatory capitalism and imperialism.[5] The protest marches against draconian immigration policies are sure to rekindle debates over the effectiveness of bilingual education (President Bush has denounced the recent singing of "Nuestro Himno"—a Spanish variation of "The Star Spangled Banner"—by claiming that the national anthem should be sung in English) and the goals of multicultural education (with its recent emphasis on critical citizenship), but they are unlikely to motivate large numbers of U.S. citizens and noncitizens to question the legitimacy of capitalist social relations, at least not in the foreseeable future.

Along with the recent mass protests in the United States against the domestic policies of the Bush administration and his cronies (which Bush has warned might cost Americans the loss of "our national soul"), there has been a growing and increasingly visible international movement against neoliberal social and economic policies (that continue to force unskilled and skilled wages downward). In France, for example, over a million workers clashed with police over the new labor laws that allow private corporations more flexibility to release or fire workers under the age of twenty-six. In Argentina, the workers' autonomous movement has emerged as a response to the country's recent financial downfall. More than 20,000 unemployed workers organized and took over and reopened factories that were closed down and abandoned by companies that had moved their operations abroad to China, where labor costs are much lower and profits are much higher than in Argentina. In Bolivia, the victory of Evo Morales, the first indigenous president in the country's history, is a sure sign of hope for the millions of indigenous people who make up 75 percent of Bolivian population. In recent years, the enforcement of neoliberal social and economic policies in Bolivia, spearheaded by such international bodies and organizations as the IMF and World Bank, have only contributed to the acceleration of social and economic polarization. In the case of Bolivia, for instance, free trade policies have downsized the standard of living of more than 66 percent of Bolivians, who have been forced to survive on two dollars a day. Recently, in a symbolic gesture of solidarity with the Bolivian people, President Morales announced he would cut his salary by half in order to hire more teachers. Of course, Venezuela under the leadership of Hugo Chávez leads the field (after Cuba) in its attempt at resisting U.S. economic and military imperialism and creating a socialism for the twenty-first century.

The No Child Left Behind Reform Movement

Teachers and educational activists have increasingly played an important role in the fight against neoliberal capitalism. This has become most clearly evident in their opposition to the No Child Left Behind (NCLB) law, which is grounded in the half-century conservative fight to impose strict national standards in U.S. public schools. The origins of the current standards-based reform movement in public education can be traced back to the early twentieth century when curriculum theorists like Ellwood Cubberley and others attempted to align school curricula to the needs and demands of the U.S. economy by developing a scientific approach to designing and planning them.[6] From the 1950s to the 1970s, with the Cold War in full swing, the "back to basics" movement gained momentum in teacher education programs and graduate schools of education. Supporters of the movement were determined to ensure that school curricula reflected not only the ideologies and political views of the dominant social classes in the United States, but that they also prepared students for employment in the growing military industrial complex to defend the country against the "communist threat."

A report published in 1983, *A Nation at Risk*, was another significant milestone in the history of the education reform movement.[7] The report vilified schools for the relatively weak economic performance of the United States compared to its Asian and European rivals.

The driving forces behind the recent educational policies of the NCLB Act, passed in 2001, are neoliberal social and economic policies that favor flexibility, efficiency, outsourcing, and downsizing methods of production. Under the neoliberal economic model, schools must perform similar to corporate entities.

Just as the Dow Jones stock indices measure the performance of companies and represent the pulse of Wall Street, so too the Adequate Yearly Progress Report (A.Y.P.) measures and ranks the performance of public schools. One of the most pernicious results of the No Child Left Behind law is that the state can now indefinitely close or restructure "underperforming schools," those that fail to meet the requirements established by the A.Y.P. Greg Palast's description of the effects of the provisions within the NCLB reform movement is informative:

> Under No Child Left Behind, if enough kids flunk the tests, their school is marked a failure and its students win the right, under the law, to transfer to any successful school in their district. You can't provide more opportunity than that. But Bush does not provide it, he *promises* it, without putting up a single penny to make it happen. In New York, in 2004, a third of a million students earned the right to transfer to better schools—in which there were only 8,000 places open. New York is typical. Nationwide, only one out of two hundred students eligible to transfer manage to do it. Well, there's always the army.[8]

Take the case of Arizona, which spends $7,000 per pupil in their current schools, and runs a program that provides vouchers for $1,000. Where can you find a school to teach your child for $1,000 a year? In reality, a voucher is what Greg Palast calls a "coupon" that "lets you get something for no cost." Palast asks:

> So who benefits from this "free" private school program? According to No Child Left Behind expert Scott Young, 76% of the money handed out for Arizona's voucher program has gone to children already in private schools. In other words, the $1,000 check from the state turned into a $1,000 subsidy for wealthy parents, a $1,000 discount on private schools for the privileged. How astonishing: a program touted as a benefit for working-class kids that turns into a subsidy for rich ones.[9]

As a stipulation of NCLB, supplemental Educational Services assists schools in hiring tutors from for-profit companies for students who fail tests. Schools are required by the federal government to pay out 20 percent of their tiny "Title I" subsidy to hire tutors from private companies. This often means cutting back their own teaching staff to pay for contracts with private tutoring companies. Many of these tutors, however, are not credentialed because federal law does not require them to be. Perhaps schools will hire the youngest of the Bush clan— Neil—to help educate their students. Neil Bush's education company, Ignite!, promotes automated teaching via television screen. An advisor to Ignite! is exiled

Russian tycoon Boris Berezovsky, whose presence in Latvia has been banned by the Latvian government.[10]

At the same time, an emphasis on testing (resulting in a teaching-to-the-test mania), strict accountability schemes, prepackaged and scripted teaching for students of color, and a frenetic push toward more standardized testing (what Jonathan Kozol refers to as "desperation strategies that have come out of the acceptance of inequality") has been abundantly present since the mid-1990s. But what has this trend produced?[11] As Kozol points out, since the early 1990s, the achievement gap between black and white children has substantially widened, and at about the same time we began to witness the growing resegregation of the schools (when the courts began to disregard the mandates of the *Brown* decision).[12] This has led to what Kozol calls "apartheid schooling." Kozol reports that in 48 percent of high schools in the country's largest districts (those that have the highest concentrations of black and Latino students), less than half of the entering ninth graders graduate in four years. Between 1993 and 2002, there has been a 75 percent increase in the number of high schools graduating less than half of their ninth-grade high school class in four years. In 94 percent of districts in New York State where the majority of the students are white, nearly 80 percent of students graduate from high school in four years. In the 6 percent of districts where black and Latino students make up the majority, the percentage is considerably less—approximately 40 percent. There are 120 high schools in New York (enrolling nearly 200,000 minority students) where, Kozol notes, less than 60 percent of entering ninth graders make it to the twelfth grade. Such a statistical record has prompted Kozol to exclaim: "There is something deeply hypocritical about a society that holds an eight-year-old inner-city child 'accountable' for her performance on a high-stakes standardized exam but does not hold the high officials of our government accountable for robbing her of what they gave their own kids six or seven years earlier."[13]

Moreover, many of these multiple-choice, norm-referenced tests are unreliable and are unable to provide valid score interpretations. Tests are only worthwhile when they further instructional design, that is, when they can help teachers teach more effectively. The other key question is: What, exactly, do we want our teachers to teach effectively? In other words, effective teaching for what? And in whose interests? Who benefits from such effective teaching, the capitalist class or future wage earners totally dependent on selling their labor power in order to survive? Teachers and students are often excluded from participating in their own learning when the one-size-fits-all approach to standards focuses on uniformly covering material that is selected on the basis of its testability or ability to be quantified as measurable outcomes rather than focuses on discovering ideas. Noninstructional factors (such as the number of parents living at home, parents' educational background, type of community, and poverty rate) account for most of the variance among test scores when schools or districts are compared.[14] It is likely that standardized tests almost always hurt the education of working-class students and unlikely that they can help, especially given the fact that norm-referenced tests are designed to even out the averages. The questions for the tests (reflecting the biases of the test makers) are related to the world outside of school, a world that requires a set of skills and knowledge more likely possessed by students from affluent families. Affluent families, schools, and districts are better able to afford test preparation materials and services. When poorer schools scrape into their budgets to acquire such materials and services it is often at the expense of basic educational resources such as books. And teachers who are required to "teach to the test" are using low-level, drill-and-skill teaching methods. Alfie Kohn calls the disproportionate pressure on teachers of minority and low-income students to raise tests scores, coupled with the fact that minority students are most likely to be denied diplomas as a result of failing a high-stakes exit exam, a form of "educational ethnic cleansing."[15]

What's Behind the No Child Left Behind Act

The NCLB Act championed by President George W. Bush is an egregiously flawed act that doesn't—as it claims to do—support school improvement. In the context of the Bush administration's storied hostility to public education and its neoliberal ideology of privatization, it does just the opposite. It uses flawed standardized tests and reactionary approaches to the notions of assessment and accountability to punish schools that it labels as "failures" with sanctions that make the situation worse rather than improving it. Instead of rewarding schools for their success, NCLB is saturated in an ideology of "weed out the worst" in a war against the poor.

The mandates of NCLB call for the elimination of the academic "achievement gap" that exists between different groups of students, particularly at-risk students, but it is woefully unable to fulfill its promises. The teeth of its measures has democracy in a death clamp. NCLB imposes standardized annual testing—from third to eighth grade—in language arts, and math. Science was added in 2006. Based on annual test scores, NCLB prescribes an accountability schema ("adequate yearly progress") that focuses on sanctions for failing schools. Schools that fail to improve their test scores must use federal funds to pay for extracurricular tutoring and for transferring students to a so-called high-achieving school.

Sanctions encompass a wide variety of activities, but there is little doubt that they open the doors to corporate and faith-based sponsorship of instructional services—a move that at the federal level is unprecedented. NCLB imposes numerous other regulations on teaching practices in the area of literacy. It also includes a phonics-based initiative that is heavily influenced by SRA/McGraw-Hill's business plan known as Open Court. Some proponents of this enfeebling initiative include members of the Christian Right movement that refer to phonics as "Judeo-Christian." These same champions of phonics would refer to constructivist approaches to reading or Freirean approaches to literacy as pernicious forms of secular humanism.

And finally, NCLB mandates that local authorities not only provide access to military recruiters on their campuses but that they also provide them with student names and contact information. Schools that receive federal financial support risk having their funds withheld if they do not provide access to military recruiters. Prior to the legislation, one-third of the nation's high schools refused the military access to student information. San Francisco and Portland, for example, had board policies against military recruitment because of its discriminatory policies against gays and lesbians. The only true option provided to students who do not wish to be contacted by the military is to have their parents initiate restricted access to their children. But many students and parents don't have adequate information on how to do this—before it is too late. We know that the military is now using more relaxed defense department rules to sign up more high school dropouts and students who score lower on mental-qualification tests.

Legislative provisions of the NCLB Act clearly make the process of privatizing education a lot easier through a testing and accountability scheme that will increase the likelihood of failure of students in economically disadvantaged schools. NCLB is directed toward transferring funds and students to profit-making private school corporations through vouchers. This is essentially a neoliberal model of education. It promotes the full marketization and "businessification" of public education, a move that will destroy much of its quality. A cardinal constituent of reform in NCLB is relying on the so-called self-regulating market to "fix" educational services. The neoliberal ideology that permeates the NCLB does not share the interest of the majority of its citizens, does not relate to the lived experiences of the poor, and does not provide adequate opportunities for youth to develop into critical agents and active participants in the development of a society freed from the alienation wrought by capitalism.

The bell curve rationality of the tests that antiseptically cuts off scores irrespective of a student's linguistic background, class background, or national origin, and that sorts students into categories on the basis of single test scores, does little to motivate students to do anything other than to leave school. This punitive test-driven "reform" puts inordinate pressure on teachers to teach to the test—to narrow their focus on what subjects should be taught and what themes and topics should be addressed. Doing well on multiple-choice questions becomes the cardinal focus of the curriculum and thus pedagogical approaches to teaching subjects critically, through a dialectical approach to social life, are diminished if not lost altogether. Conspicuously absent in this exercise in futility are critical pedagogical approaches that include examining the contradictions between what is happening to students in their everyday lives and how the wider social order is constructed economically, how its legal institutions operate, and how the public and private spheres organize their priorities, and for whom. Little time in the school day is left to examine the politics of social life and how the world is driven by the capitalist law of value. In other words, there is virtually no time for public pedagogy—for learning to think and act in a manner that speaks to creating a socially and economically just society.

High-stakes testing should flatly be prohibited for graduation or grade promotion, and schools should be encouraged to focus on the use of multiple forms of assessment. Participatory democracy—local parents, educators, students, and other residents working together to make policy, curriculum, and pedagogical decisions about the school—should be at the heart of public school accountability systems. Schools need quality teachers, adequate support staff, an engaging antiracist curriculum, critical approaches to teach against sexism and homophobia, an anti-imperialist approach to understanding national and world events and the relationship between them, useful assessments, adequate planning time and staff development, significant parent involvement, small class sizes, a de-colonizing pedagogical approach that validates indigenous ways of knowing, and leadership that reflects the courage to brush against the grain of the prevailing neoliberal agenda in education and the society at large.

In the present rush toward accountability schemes, corporate management pedagogies, and state-mandated curricula, an ominous silence exists regarding the ways in which new attempts to streamline teaching represent an attack on both the democratic possibilities of schooling and the very conditions that make critical teaching possible.

Framed in the language of hypernationalism and neoliberal economics, the current conservative attack on schools represents, in large part, a truncation of the democratic vision. Underlying the new reform proposals set forth by the recent coalition of conservatives and liberals is an attack on schools for producing a wide-ranging series of national crises, from the growing trade deficit to the break-down of family morality. Not only does such an attack misconstrue the responsibility schools have for wider economic and social problems, but it is characteristic of a dangerous ideological shift regarding the role that schools should play in relation to the wider society.

At the heart of the ideological shift is an attempt to define academic success almost exclusively in terms of capital accumulation and the logic of the marketplace. The authors of the "blue ribbon" committee reports have cast their recommendations in a language that reflects the resurgence of chauvinistic patriotism and have reformulated their goals along elitist lines. In doing so, they have attempted to eliminate a social concern for nurturing a critical and committed citizenry. They have passively surrendered educational reform to a fetishism of procedure rather than demonstrating a concern with emancipatory social goals. Furthermore, the increasing adoption of management-type pedagogies has resulted in policy proposals that promote the de-skilling of teachers and the creation of a technocratic rationality in which planning and conception are removed from implementation, and the dominant model of the teacher becomes that of the technician or white-collar clerk. (Consider the narrowly scripted Open Court reading program published by the Science Research Associates in which teachers are told what to do at every moment of instruction. Here, dialogue and student interaction is undervalued as a vehicle for learning how to read.) At the same time, the model of the school has been transformed, in Giroux's terms, into that of the "company store." In general, the new efficiency-smart and conservative-minded discourse encourages schools to define themselves essentially as service institutions charged with the task of providing students with the requisite labor-power capacities to enable them to find a place within the social division of labor.

This New Right ideology of school reform—exemplified by the NCLB Act—provides only a sterile and truncated range of discourses and conceptions that undermines what it means to be a critical citizen. Under the logic of the reforms, students are taught to link citizenship to the profit imperative and the norms of market relations and brokerage politics wherein the vested interests of the individual, the corporation, or one's country are always valued over the collective interests of humanity. Rarely is the concept of profit maximization considered immoral, even when it is at the expense of the poor or minority groups, or, further afield, at the expense of the social and educational development of Central American and third-world populations. Absent from this discourse is any recognition of the importance of viewing schools as sites for social transformation and emancipation, as places where students are educated not only to be critical thinkers but to view the world as a place where their actions might make a difference. Absent are any discussions of socialism as an alternative to capitalist society, of direct, participatory democracy as an improvement over representative democracy, of ecosocialism or revolutionary ecology as ways of challenging the endlessly proliferating commodity economy with its ecological destruction.

With the neoliberal agenda in full swing, the NCLB Act has shifted the discourse of progressive educational policy from "equality" to "adequacy."[16] The language of "higher standards" and "higher expectations" has replaced the low-intensity social justice agenda of the center–left educators. Kozol debunks the conceptual frameworks used to explain the causes of underachievement among students of color. As part of the daily rituals and practices designed to raise student morale, schools now employ what Kozol refers to as "auto-hypnotic slogans." In schools that are identified as "underperforming," students of color are encouraged to memorize phrases such as "I can," "I am smart," and "I am confident" to boost their self-confidence and to improve their academic performance.

Today's Urban School Factories

Today urban schools are adroitly organized around the same principles as factory production lines. According to Kozol, "raising test scores," "social promotion," "outcome-based objectives," "time management," "success for all," "authentic writing," "accountable talk," "active listening," and "zero noise" constitute part of the dominant discourse in public schools.[17] Most urban public schools have adopted business and market "work-related themes" and managerial concepts that have become part of the vocabulary used in classroom lessons and instruction. In the "market-driven classrooms," students "negotiate," "sign contracts," and take "ownership" of their own learning. In many classrooms, students can volunteer as the "pencil manager," "soap manager," "door manager," "line manager," "time managers," and "coatroom manager." In some fourth-grade classrooms, teachers record student assignments and homework using "earning charts." In these schools, teachers are referred to as "classroom managers," principals are identified as "building managers," and students are viewed as "learning managers." It is commonplace to view schoolchildren as "assets," "investment," "productive units," or "team players." Schools identify skills and knowledge students learn and acquire as "commodities" and "products" to be consumed in the "educational marketplace." Under the current climate of the NCLB school reform movement, teachers are regarded as "efficiency technicians" and encouraged to use "strict Skinnerian control" methods and techniques to manage and teach students in their classrooms. Kozol writes that in the market-driven model of public education, teachers are viewed as "floor managers" in public schools, "whose job it is to pump some 'added value' into undervalued children."[18]

To the disdain of progressive educators, the "test craze" is now a growing trend in most large metropolitan public school districts. In some districts, standardized testing begins in kindergarten. Some public schools have been forced to cut back or entirely remove art and music classes from their school curriculum. Other schools have reduced or altogether eliminated recess and/or nap time. Most public schools now have a testing coordinator. During homeroom, for example, school administrators encourage teachers to teach students test-taking skills and strategies. The Los Angeles Unified School District has developed its own quarterly assessment tests in math, science, social studies, and English. The district tests students every two months. We are told that the purpose of these district assessment tests is to prepare students for the statewide standardized tests in late spring. At teacher and staff development meetings, most of the time is spent on sharing and discussing effective strategies and methods to prepare students for quarterly assessment tests and to review state and districts standards. Teachers are also encouraged to attend workshops and conferences to learn more on how to align their teaching practices to the state standards.

As the standardized curriculum and standardized testing widen the achievement gap between poor and wealthy school districts, working-class students and students of color continue to be tracked into vocational programs and classes that teach life skills or offer basic training that prepares them for jobs in the retail and service industry.[19] Perhaps even more disturbing is the placement of high school female students in sewing and cosmetology classes. As we know by now, these classes do little for students who must compete with advanced placement and college-tracked students. It is painfully ironic that just as we are witnessing the factory model of schooling returning with a vengeance, the factories of yesteryear in which working-class students traditionally sought employment are moving out of the country, escaping unions and depriving workers of medical benefits.

The NCLB and the Militarization of Public Schools

Provisions within the NCLB legislation have removed obstacles to the recruitment efforts of the military to target high school students, in particular vulnerable students of color in urban public schools. The military has engaged in dirty recruitment campaigns and tactics to lure high school students to enlist in the army, including visiting classrooms and making weekly home phone calls to potential high school students to pressure them to join the army. Other strategies include driving Humvees to schools blasting hip-hop music and distributing free T-shirts and "Yo Soy El Army" stickers. What is unsettling is that the army spends $13,000 in advertisements for each potential recruit, which is about the same amount of money to educate one child for one year in the New York public school system. In response, many students, teachers, and principals have organized local and national coalitions such as the Coalition Against Militarism in our Schools (CAMS) to resist military recruitment efforts in their community schools. Recently, the School Leadership Council at Roosevelt High School, located in the working-class Latino community of East Los Angeles—recognized as the number one "marine-recruited school in the nation"—passed a resolution to restrict military recruitment efforts at their high school.[20]

And if all this isn't bad enough, the military defense budget continues to swell at the expense of funding public education. In the 2002–2003 annual budget, state tax revenues fell sharply by $22 billion compared to the previous year. The Bush administration's decision to abolish the estate tax will cause an additional $10 billion loss in revenues. The impact of the Bush administration's social and economic policies has been devastating. As David Goodman notes:

> Schools around the country are reeling from the cuts. In California, where 3,800 teachers and 9,000 other school employees received pink slips last year, districts have cut textbook purchases, summer school, bus routes, maintenance, athletics, student newspapers, and electives. Half of the school districts in Kansas have cut staff; several districts have gone to a four-day week; and 50 schools in Kansas now charge students to participate in some extracurricular activities. In Michigan, funding for gifted and talented students is down 95 percent; Buffalo, New York, has been forced to close eight schools and eliminate 600 teaching jobs over the past years.[21]

Faced with the shortage of revenues to support their existing educational programs, many school districts have been forced to develop partnerships with corporations eager to step into the lucrative education market. Consider McDonald's recent adoption of a new strategy to promote its products in the highly profitable market dominated by children. This comes after the highly publicized libel suit, now famously referred to as the McLibel Case, and the recent film *Super Size Me*, which raised ethical and moral questions regarding McDonald's food processing and preparing practices that many believe have significantly contributed to obesity and other health risks among children. Nancy Hellmich reports that in an effort to restore its much-tarnished public image as the family-friendly fast-food chain, and to further protect its market shares, McDonald's has decided to capitalize on physical education programs in public schools.[22] Over 7 million students in 31,000 public schools have agreed to participate in McDonald's "Passport to Play" program. The program consists of a number of multicultural physical education activities including boomerang golf from Australia, Mr. Daruma Fell Down from Japan, and Holland's Korfball. Students who complete each of these activities receive a stamp in a passport issued by McDonald's. According to Bill Lama, McDonald's chief marketing officer, the objective of the Passport to Play program is to educate students on the "importance of eating right" and "staying active." Such a strategically calculated move allows McDonald's not only to recover from much of the negative publicity it has received in the past few years but helps the food chain to secure a greater presence and visibility in public schools.

Beyond the NCLB: Toward a Critical Pedagogy of Hope

As the drums of war drown out dissent and as accountability and testing regimes are imposed upon public schools, critical educators advocate for a curriculum that enables students to conceptualize, analyze, theorize, and critically reflect upon their experiences in the world. Despite their seeming singularity, experiences are not fashioned in isolation. Because experiences, though idiosyncratic, are part of a larger ensemble of social relations, it is important for students to interrogate their own experiences in the context of understanding how oppression and exploitation function within the larger totality of capitalist society. The long-term goal of education is the transformation of the existing social order. And that means teachers and students should have a number of theoretical approaches to work from—with a Marxist analysis of class as the centerpiece.

This approach is not new, having been developed over the years by exponents of the work of the late Brazilian educator Paulo Freire. Fortunately, the work of Freire has managed to avoid the halting attention to which many other radical educators seem depressingly prone. For decades his work has been at the helm of critical pedagogy and popular education and his legacy seems assured. That is good news for the educational Left.

Although insufficiently heralded in the United States, Freire's masterwork, *Pedagogy of the Oppressed*, can claim a one-of-a-kind status in the annals of the educational Left. More than any other single book, Freire's signature opus continues to shape the ways in which many leftist teachers and educators frame political and ideological questions related to teaching and learning in their classrooms.[23] Freirean pedagogy has inspired and motivated a new generation of educators and activists to defend democratic principles, values, and practices in their classrooms and schools against the neoliberal onslaught in an age of terror, fear, and permanent war.

Viewing human beings as a "presence in the world" (this holds true even in a consumer-driven, mass-produced culture run by taste merchants and reality-television producers), Freire maintains that taking risks is an essential characteristic of our "existing being."[24] He reminds us that education, both as a political and ideological activity, involves taking risks. Our presence in the world is not a neutral presence. As political and ideological agents, we are compelled to take a stance within it. As Freire notes: "Nobody can be in the world, with the world, and with others in a neutral manner."[25] Thus "being" is a *being in the world*. Freire sees history impregnated with possibility and hope. However, to make that possibility tangible in the lives of the oppressed, he believes that we must actively engage and intervene in the world.

What does "being in the world" entail? Freire explains that our presence in the world is not to adapt to it but to work toward transforming it. Freire emphasizes that adapting to the world is only a process—a temporary phase—toward intervening and transforming the world. Thus adaptation is a "moment in the process of *intervention*."[26] Furthermore, Freire argues that we live in an ethical world. Our ideological and political orientation compels us to make moral and ethical decisions. Freire reminds us that our actions have a universal dimension, and that "being in the world" entails recognizing our responsibilities and commitments toward other human beings.

Freire views human beings as both subjects and objects of history. In other words, though the forces of history shape our past and present, we can change the course of history, and in the process make history. As Freire puts it, "The future does not make us, we make ourselves in the struggle to make it."[27] We can break away from the chains of history passed down to us from previous generations and make our own history. In short, Freire acknowledges that human beings are conditioned by history, but he refuses to accept that they are determined by it, because for Freire history is possibility.

Freire maintains that a critical reading of the world involves *denouncing* the existing oppression and injustices in the world. At the same time, it involves *announcing* the possibility of a more humane and just world. For Freire, reading the world is both a pedagogical-political and a political-pedagogical undertaking.

Denouncing the world is an act that involves criticizing, protesting, and struggling against domination and domestication. The act of announcing a new world entails hope and possibility, and this stipulates envisioning a new democratic society outside of capitalism's law of value.

Elsewhere, Freire makes an important distinction between the role of education in helping students develop critical thinking skills and as training and preparation for entering the workforce.[28] He cautions us against reducing education to a set of techniques and skills. Freire incessantly asserts that education can effectively be employed to "make and remake" ourselves. Education, as Freire conceives it, involves knowing that you know, and knowing that you don't know. It entails developing a "critical curiosity" and a radical reorientation toward the world.

For Freire, critical pedagogy involves learning to question the world by cultivating an "epistemological curiosity." He encourages teachers and educators to imagine, dream, and struggle toward building the foundations of a new democratic society. They must also be willing to be a "presence" in the world by engaging in a dialectical process of what he calls "reading the word and the world."

Donaldo Macedo and Ana Maria Araújo Freire underscore what is meant by "reading the word and the world" when they assail those literacy specialists who teach reading as a method disarticulated from the world of exploitation and oppression, antiseptically detached from the totality of capitalist social relations. Specialists who equate the process of becoming literate to acquiring a discrete set of cognitive skills "domesticate the consciousness via a constant disarticulation between the reductionistic and narrow reading of one's field of specialization and reading of the universe within which one's specialization is situated."[29] Such "pseudocritical educators" are thus "semiliterate"—they can read the word but are woefully unable to read the world, that is, they are able to read the texts of their specialty but remain "ignorant of all other bodies of knowledge that constitute the world of knowledge."[30] Jose Ortega y Gasset calls such a specialist a "learned ignoramus" who—as Macedo and Freire explain—is "mainly concerned with his or her own tiny portion of the world, disconnected from other bodies of knowledge . . . [and] never able to relate the flux of information to gain a critical reading of the world."[31] Paulo Freire emphasized that a critical reading of the world implies "a dynamic comprehension between the least coherent sensibility of the world and a more coherent understanding of the world."[32]

Learned ignoramuses are all around us. For instance, how can education specialists in science and math and computer technology ignore how teaching advances in these areas have aided the military industrial complex that enables the United States to exercise its domination of less developed countries of the world, that allows industry to subject the poor to the ravages of capital, that facilitates the devastation of our ecosystems, and that makes possible breakthroughs in medicine that benefit only those who can afford to pay for treatment?

In our own classrooms we are careful not to approach the struggle for socialism from the Olympian standpoint of eternity—as a primrose path that leads the faithful to that luminous workers' council on the hill. We eschew utopian blueprints in favor of serious discussions that deal with questions of power, the state, and various forms for organizing for socialist democracy. For instance, we explore the current debate between the Zapatistas (who do not wish to take state power) and the supporters of Hugo Chávez (Chavistas who believe that the state can be transformed from the bottom up by taking state power). In some cases we have traveled with our students to Venezuela and Mexico and have participated in such debates firsthand.

The critical revolutionary pedagogy that we support advances these and other issues from the perspective of a problem-posing rather than a solution-giving pedagogy. It eschews magic bullet solutions and instead favors the practice of historical materialist critique. It mandates approaching the process of teaching and learning within the larger context of certain fundamental questions. In the wake of the dictatorship of the financial markets, where, in the words of Robert Went, the "invisible hand" of the market is mercilessly and ruthlessly strangling millions of working-class men, women, and children, how do we liberate creative human powers and capacities from their inhumane form, namely, capital?[33] What does it mean to be human? How can we live humanely? What ethical and moral actions must we take to live humanely? How can teachers recognize the important role they play in the battle between labor and capital?

These questions along with others can only be answered in the course of revolutionizing educational practices, which will largely depend on the willingness of teachers to join anti-imperialist struggles. Teachers need to support de-colonizing pedagogies and make efforts to work with new social movements, including indigenous groups, in their fight against capital's deadly assault on the poor and the planet that sustains all of us. Teachers must recognize that, as workers, their interests and those of their fellow educators worldwide are tied to the defeat of neoliberal capitalism and the creation of a postcapitalist, socialist society.

12

Class: A Personal Story

Michael D. Yates

I was born in 1946 in a small mining village in western Pennsylvania, about forty miles north of Pittsburgh, along a big bend in the Allegheny River. The house in which I lived during my first year of life had neither hot water nor indoor plumbing. It was a company house, and my grandmother had purchased it for $1,000 from the mining company after the town had ceased to be a company town, thanks to the United Mine Workers. A small coal stove in the living room heated the entire house.

My grandmother came to this town in the mid-1930s to be close to relatives after her husband died. She and her two children—my mother and my uncle—lived in the small tarpaper-shingled house, and she tried to eke out a living in a town with few job opportunities for women. Most of the miners were Italian; Italian was more or less the town's lingua franca. Miners everywhere show unusual cohesion and solidarity and have often been among the shock troops of labor movements. The common ethnicity of these miners deepened their fraternity. However, they believed that mining was men's work and women were to raise children and take care of the household. My grandmother's parents had taken in boarders, and Grandma had learned women's work, including helping to prepare the enormous batches of polenta made every day to feed the men.

Now she had a hard time finding work. She cleaned the town doctor's house, took in laundry, and mended clothes. She and her children got jobs unloading dynamite at the mine site. Miners were responsible for opening new seams of coal, and they used dynamite to do this. Every day, the three of them, all suffering from asthma, trudged down the steep hill to the riverbank where the entrance to the mine was located. They unloaded the heavy boxes of explosives, never getting help from the miners, some of whom were relatives. After work, they climbed the hill home to rest silently until they could again breathe freely. Later, my mother got a Saturday job cleaning the managers' offices. One of the supervisors tried to molest her, but none of the miners raised a protest.

There was a degree of spontaneous class consciousness in the village. During the Great Depression everyone was in the same boat: poor and in need of work. People were generous with one another; when beggars came to the door, the miners fed them. When the union arrived, the men were nearly unanimous in their support. During strikes, no one scabbed. The Catholic Church exerted a conservative influence, but priests in poor towns are often sympathetic to workers and their families. The town's physical isolation helped to insulate workers from the hegemonic forces at work in the larger society. Italians already had a long history of radical agitation in the United States, strengthened by the strong prejudice they faced.

Both my mother and grandmother developed some sense of belonging to the working class. However, this was not a consciousness that would lead to collective actions. Their main concern was their immediate family. After her children were grown, Grandma took a number of jobs. She was a cook on a tugboat that pushed barges loaded with steel from Pittsburgh to New Orleans. She worked as a governess for the very rich in Manhattan and Pittsburgh. She cooked in a restaurant. She understood the inferior position of wage laborers. But only individual acts of rebellion were available to her, as when she shamed the rich woman who was her employer by telling her that she didn't work for her because she liked her but because she needed the money. The strict and oppressive gender division of labor she had seen and experienced since childhood made the kind of solidarity that builds a labor movement impossible. Of course, my grandmother was not alone in this. Tens of millions of women then could have helped create much stronger labor movements than the ones actually built, and unfortunately the same thing is often true today.

The Second World War brought the mining village out of the Depression. It also helped to assimilate many Italian Americans into the more conservative American mainstream. After the war, nationalism and anticommunism became much stronger, and individual acquisitiveness began to replace the more communal life of the prewar era. The union of mine workers became a place where a few miners could move up the economic ladder. As the national union declined and lost its militancy under the corrupt leadership of Tony Boyle, the local's leaders became Boyle stalwarts. Within a few years, the mine itself was closed, and miners and their children began to move from the town or found work at other mines, in construction, or in factories up and down the river. People renovated their houses; the one in which I was born was one of the few remaining with its original tarpaper shingles. The townsfolk gradually joined the postwar mainstream, gaining some in material goods but losing most of the collective character of the earlier village.

What values did I assimilate from the mining town? This is a complicated question. The working-class solidarity always shown by underground miners seeped into my consciousness as did the ethnic clannishness of the Italian immigrants. This meant a certain distrust of anyone with money and authority and anyone outside the community. But these incipient seeds of class consciousness were counteracted by other, more troubling feelings. Mining towns in the United States were typically owned by the mining companies, and the companies exerted a near totalitarian control over the residents. They owned the houses, the only store (the infamous "company store"), all utilities, the schools, the library, everything. They had their own private police—the Coal and Iron Police in Pennsylvania—sanctioned by state law. The climate in such a town is one of perpetual insecurity and fear, emotions compounded by the danger of the work in the mines. While such authoritarian rule generates anger and hate, it also gives rise to feelings of inadequacy and worthlessness. Misery is one's lot in life. There must be something wrong with us. Those in power must have special abilities and powers we don't have. We deserve our fate. Organized religion contributes to this sense of helplessness and shifts attention away from material conditions and toward God and the afterlife.

Poverty and social isolation added fuel to the fire of fear. People lacked self-confidence and had deep-seated feelings of inferiority. When kids from the village went to the high school in the factory town three miles upriver, they faced a mocking condescension. They had the wrong clothes. They were greasy "dagos." They were "dumb coal miners." Some, like one of my cousins, reacted with anger; he hung a teacher out a third-floor window for calling him a dumb coal miner. But others took it to heart and were scarred forever.

It is difficult to overstate the power of fear and poverty in shaping how working men and women think and act. Fear of losing a job. Fear of not finding a job. Fear of being late with bill payments. Fear of the boss's wrath. Fear your house might burn down. Fear your kids will get hurt. I inherited these emotions. I have a Ph.D. and have always had a job that brings forth instant respect from others. Yet I have a deep-seated lack of confidence and anxiety in the face of authority. I can confront the powerful in a group, even if I am a leader of it, but as an individual, I hate any kind of confrontation with authority and always wonder if I have the right to confront. I prefer to remain in the background, to be invisible.

As working-class men and women are sucked into the capitalist milieu, they try to make sure that their children do not end up like them. They sacrifice so that the kids can exit the working class and become entrepreneurs and professionals. This can have painful results. If the children are successful, they may come to be ashamed of their parents, and their parents may come to resent them. These feelings may never be explicitly stated, but they will show themselves in sometimes not so subtle ways. A successful child who marries a person from outside the working class will hesitate to visit home as often as in the past. Children might blame parents for not giving them the advantages their spouses, new friends, and coworkers take for granted. Parents will be proud of their successful children, but at the same time might resent their children's new lifestyles, which stand in sharp contrast to their own. A child's big house, professional spouse, fancy car, and the grandchildren's private schools seem almost to mock the way they themselves live. I remember arguing with my father. He said to me, "You read too much." I shot back, "If you'd read a book once in awhile instead of getting all your information from television, maybe you'd be better off."

Ambivalence marks the emotions of the working class. In a society where worth is measured by money, the lack of money signifies a lack of worth. However, daily life, including religion, tells workers that there is more to a person's character than money. It also tells them that money is often tainted with corruption and violence. There is a man from the mining village who became very wealthy. People love to talk about how he was one of the poorest persons in the town, but now he owns many businesses and several mansion-like homes. He is a friendly fellow and generous to his family and friends. On the one hand, those who "knew him when" now bask reflectively in his glory. It is quite a thing to get invited to his house, and those who are will regale you with descriptions of the grounds and furnishings. On the other hand, not far below the surface, there is a sense that this man has come by his money illegitimately. If you suggest that, given the nature of his businesses, he was perhaps involved with organized crime, most people will not vehemently deny this. Wonder, jealousy, admiration, and hatred are all mixed together in a confusing brew. The rich may be, in one interpretation, God's chosen, but then again, it is more difficult for a rich man to get into heaven than for a camel to pass through the eye of a needle.

Attitudes toward work are also ambivalent. Most working-class employment sucks, and everyone knows it. And it is impossible not to be aware of the tensions existing in every workplace or to see that most bosses want only your labor and as much of it as they can get. So workers may cut corners, pretend to be working, and find unproductive ways to kill time and make the workday go faster. Yet work is a natural human endeavor, and even the most menial job requires some ingenuity. So workers want to do a good job at the same time they might know that doing a good job will not necessarily be to their advantage. Doing a good job certainly did not make the job a good one, fit for a human being. My father took a dim view of slackers, but he was not above "lifting" small items from the shop that might be useful at home. I felt much the same way when I was a full-time college teacher. As our work became more alienating, many of us began to cut corners—refusing to give essay examinations, shortening classes, especially the long evening lectures, and getting the "take-a-day flu" as often as we dared. I didn't like to see teachers slacking even though I could understand it and even though I did some of it myself.

The attitude of working-class youth toward school mirrors their parents' ambivalence toward success and work. Schools are oppressive places, and kids naturally rebel against the agents of this oppression: teachers and administrators. When I was in school, most boys were destined to be future factory workers. Only a few were deemed mentally fit to succeed in college. In the minds of most pupils, these few were the enemy as much as were the teachers. "Ordinary" students knew instinctively that they were not going to "succeed," so they built defense mechanisms to make this understanding less painful. It was not "manly" to do well in school. Physical toughness was the mark of a real man. A scholar was like a girl, who could be smart but wasn't likely to succeed in any event. At the same time, the "brains" had to be respected; the success of the few was the other side of the coin of their "failure." A student who did well could be admired and hated at the same time. From the point of view of the rulers of the economic system, schools have been great successes. Only a few working-class youth are needed to fill the relatively few skilled labor slots in the workplace. The values absorbed by the rest of the working-class boys and girls will fit them very well for the work they will do and make it difficult to blame anyone but themselves for their failure to escape their class.

My family moved from the mining village when I was two, to a small house on a farm about three miles east of the factory town where my father worked. We had hot water but still had to use an outhouse. Dad often walked to work; it would be a couple of years before we got a car.

Three years later, my parents took advantage of the government-backed home loans that were so important to the development of the white suburbs and the demise of urban working-class culture. There was another child now, my sister, and the four of us moved into a three-bedroom house with modern conveniences on a large lot. This is where my four siblings and I grew up. There weren't many houses nearby when we moved, but over the next two decades, a few hundred more were built as workers began to live the "American Dream" in the postwar "American Century."

The town was small, not quite 10,000 residents at its peak, but it housed the biggest plate-glass factory in the world. There was also a large pottery, right next to the glass factory. The city of Pittsburgh was a center of glass manufacturing, and the owner of the town's factory was the Pittsburgh Plate Glass Company. Everyone just called it "PPG." The factory was many blocks long and took up in width what would have been the town's first two avenues. Inside there was a workforce divided along several dimensions. Most of the workers were relatively unskilled, but there were a significant number of craft workers, some of whom still made glass without assembly-line mechanization and some of whom were trades-men, such as carpenters, millwrights, and electricians. The workers were mostly white men, but there were large numbers of women, typically unmarried, in cer-tain departments, like the one in which optical glass was examined. There were also black workers, who, as was typical in northern factories, were locked into unskilled jobs with little chance of advancement. There were no Asian workers and only a couple of Hispanics.

Until the workers unionized the plant in the late 1930s, the company ran the town; it was as much a company town as the mining village. But it was larger and more complex. There was a more nuanced class structure: not just workers, fore-men, and absentee owners but also shopkeepers and professionals.

Reflecting divisions in the workplace, the townspeople were also divided. Although nearly everyone in the mining town was Catholic, people in the factory town practiced many Protestant faiths as well. There were a few Jews, mainly shopkeepers and professionals. Catholics faced a certain amount of discrimina-tion in that they were unlikely to become top managers in the glass plant; these slots were reserved for those in the mainstream Protestant denominations. Anti-Semitism was widespread, although Jews were for the most part tolerated. They couldn't join certain clubs and they were called vicious names, but at the same time they were grudgingly admired for their economic success.

The ethnic and racial makeup of the town probably most differentiated it from the mining village. There was no "melting pot." Whites were rigidly separated from blacks, but whites themselves were not a uniform group. Besides religious differences, there were important ethnic splits. Those with Northern European ancestries were more likely to hold supervisory positions in the plant, and there was considerable bigotry expressed by them against Italian Americans and those from Eastern Europe. These prejudices were aligned with religious animosities as well, since the Anglo-Saxons were typically Protestant, and the "Hunkies," "Polacks," and "Dagos" were Catholic. I remember my father disdainfully telling me how the kids in these groups had their heads shaved for the summer. It was not uncommon for parents to discourage their children, especially their daughters, from dating anyone from the "wrong" ethnic groups.

Too much should not be made of ethnic (and religious) differences, however. Even by my early childhood, these had begun to break down, and cross-ethnic marriages were common. Inter-ethnic class solidarity was evident in the glass workers' union, both in strikes and in the union's internal politics. For many years, the president of the local was an Arab American, who rose to become a national officer.

The one divide within the town that was never breached was race. There was a small black community in the town, segregated at the southern or "lower" end. People there had their roots in the rural South and had, for the most part, come north in the great migration following the First World War. Many of the men found work in the glass factory and pottery, though always in the least skilled and most onerous jobs. Although white persons did associate with black townsfolk— some poor whites also lived in the "lower" end, whites and blacks played sports together, and there was no segregation in the schools—close relationships were rare. Black workers could not aspire to union office, nor could black citizens hope to win local political office. Racial epithets were always ready to come out of the mouths of white persons. It was a rare conversation in bar or club that did not include these. A fair number of whites seemed obsessed with black people, never missing a chance to denigrate them or blame them for whatever the whites perceived as bad. It was definitely taboo for whites and blacks of the opposite sex to socialize too closely, much less date or marry.

What effects did life in the factory town have on class consciousness? In many respects, the effects were the same as in the mining village. Workers generally disdained their bosses but had the same ambivalence toward "a fair day's work" as the miners did. But the factory had a more complex hierarchy of jobs than the mine, so workers could aspire to better jobs, including the job of foreman or first-level supervisor. Since the company had some control over who got the jobs covered by union contract and complete control over who became a supervisor, a worker might think that it would be better not to oppose the company too overtly or militantly. The company could also use co-optation to weaken class solidarity, draining off the most thoughtful workers into management.

The factory town also had a range of small businesses, and a worker could aim for the petit bourgeoisie. My uncle once opened a small restaurant with a fellow worker in an effort to escape the factory and be his own boss. My father had hopes of becoming a radio repairman and later took a correspondence school course to learn drafting. This kind of thinking and acting, though easy to understand, also sapped class consciousness.

As with the miners, the Second World War profoundly affected the ways in which workers thought and acted. On the one hand, the factory men came home from the war unwilling to tolerate the corporate despotism their fathers had suffered before unionization. They struck and filed grievances and won more control over what went on at work than they ever could have imagined before the war. I well remember the two summers I worked in the plant. My grandfather, a time-study engineer, got me a summer job while I was in college. I did mostly clerical work, cataloging accidents and analyzing accident reports to see where and when they were most likely to occur. Many children of workers got such jobs, and the company found this a good way to recruit local college kids into management (as with the miners, parents had mixed feelings about this but in general were proud to help their children to get out of the working class). My job was housed in the fire department—the factory was large enough to have its own. The firemen were typically on call and often had few regular daytime duties. So they spent a lot of time drinking coffee and talking. The atmosphere was casual, and the supervisors never, while I was there, told the men to do anything. The union officers, themselves full-time union staffers (drawing pay from the company), stopped everyday for coffee. The firemen moved around the plant freely and were good sources of gossip that might be useful to the union. The union president was a gruff man with one arm; he had lost the other to a grinding machine. The vice president was a dapper man, a superlative bowler and pool player, and a chronic gambler (gambling was an important part of what it meant to be a male worker). Conversation ranged freely from football pools to ongoing disputes with management. I was impressed with the degree of freedom the workers and the union officers had, the product of long years of class struggle after the war most of them had fought in. Without using the word in a sexist way, I would say that the war had made them "men," and they demanded to be treated as such.

However, at the same time, the war and its aftermath locked most of these workers into mainstream America. Wars are always about getting people in one country to hate those in another. If this can be done once, it can be done again; all that is needed is for the state to declare a new enemy. After the war, the new enemy was the Soviet Union and, by implication, all radical thinking and acting. It was no accident that the labor movement was held up as an entity infiltrated by communists and that, further, workers would have to repudiate the Reds in their unions if they were to maintain membership in U.S. society. War gets people used to obeying orders issued by the state, and this habit of mind worked to good advantage from the employers' perspective after the war when they strove to regain the power they had lost during the heyday of the Congress of Industrial Organization (CIO). Workers who insisted on trying to deepen what the CIO had achieved before and during the war—greater control by workers of their workplaces, a weakening of racism, solidarity with workers in other countries, the beginnings of a social welfare state—were simply declared enemies of the state, on a par with the Germans and Japanese just defeated in the war. The workers in my hometown, never especially radical to begin with and deeply influenced by the war and by the Catholic Church, bought into the new patriotism of anticommunism wholeheartedly and in the process never seized the opportunity to use the new union strength to deepen their class consciousness.

To help workers embrace the Cold War, the government initiated a variety of programs aimed at giving them a greater material stake in U.S. society. The most important of these was the subsidization of home mortgages. Millions of working-class families bought homes on the cheap, usually away from the cities and towns in the new and more isolated and diffuse suburbs. Home ownership came to define the "good life" for workers, and the constant care and worry that had to be devoted to it left workers with little time for anything else, except perhaps to sit around the television every night to live through the characters on the various drama and comedy shows. An enormous amount of propaganda was devoted (and still is) to the wonders of owning a house and the satisfaction to be gained by living in one with a family whose members were devoted to one another. This and the array of consumer goods needed to maintain a home were all that workers needed to be happy. My parents bought a house in 1950, on a large lot a few miles away from the town. For both of them this represented both a bold move and a declaration that they were part of the "American Century." Their lives devolved away from work and class solidarity toward a more limited and insular family life.

Subsidized home ownership was restricted to whites, who often signed covenants in which they obligated themselves not to sell their houses to minorities. The denial of home ownership to blacks further separated the races and made interracial solidarity all the more unlikely. When I was twelve years old, I took a very large paper route, with more than one hundred customers scattered over a five-mile set of interconnected roads. Every customer lived in a single-family house; no one rented. I had no black customers.

The impact on my consciousness of living in the factory town came mainly through the schools. Like everyone else, I was in school for thousands of hours during my most formative years, so it was impossible not to be influenced by what I was and was not taught. In retrospect, I think it is fair to say that, in terms of what really went on in the town and in the larger society, the schools were in one sense a mirror image and in another a fantasy world. Working-class boys and girls have always been cannon fodder for society's least desirable jobs, and the schools did their best to make this appear inevitable. The few with high IQs, as evidenced by their scores on tests that were designed not to measure anything of relevance about us except our skill at taking such tests, were placed in special classes and given an opportunity to escape our class or at least move into its upper reaches. The rest were consigned to classes that would prepare them to take the orders and perform the mundane tasks necessary to produce the mass consumption goods that would make them happy. In my high school, during the first year (ninth grade), students were divided into seven "sections," from the college-bound in sections one and two to the hopelessly ineducable in section seven. It was understood that we were in our section because that is where our intelligence objectively placed us, and, for the most part, we believed this. And I have no doubt that the teachers believed this as well. Not only did this separation of "smart" from "dumb" make it unlikely that students would develop any sense of solidarity, but it also, as it became part of our self-consciousness, made us believe that we were ourselves responsible for our fate. I was in section one because I was superior; you were in section seven because you were not. I would go to college because I deserved it, and you would go to the factory for the same reason. I would show the world that class was no obvious barrier to success. You would show everyone that you were just too lazy to deserve what I got. The fact that the kids in the lower sections were more likely to be very poor and black reinforced class and race stereotypes. Teachers did nothing to discourage any of this.

The schools I attended never told us the truth about the world in which we lived, and it is in this sense that I say that they were fantasy worlds. There were two parts to the lies at the heart of my education: what the teachers told us and what they did not tell us. They told us that the United States was a kind of paradise on earth and that other countries were either inferior or evil. They told us that Christopher Columbus was a great explorer and discoverer. They told us that the people decided through their votes how the nation would be governed. But of far greater importance was what they did not tell us. Nothing about racism, nothing about American Indians, nothing about the misery foisted upon the poor nations and peoples of the world by the rich ones, and nothing about progressive social movements. Nothing about the factories that dominated our town. Nothing about unions, despite the fact that nearly every man in town belonged to one. Nothing about the arts except the Shakespeare of *Julius Caesar* and a few other "safe" writers. Nothing but clichés and trivialities about the rest of the world. Nothing about capitalism. I cannot today remember a single inspirational thing said by any of my teachers. Some were nice; a couple of the science and math teachers were smart and gave us a decent background in these subjects; most were harmless. But none were scholars, and none gave me insight into the political economy that makes the world go 'round.

My high school was a public school. Before that, I attended a Catholic school. There ignorance reigned supreme, and the main goal was to suppress thinking and desire and to encourage blind faith. Obedience, fear of authority, guilt—these were the staples of this education. In eighth grade, learning took the form of writing down a term on the left side of our notebook and memorizing a definition of that term on the right side. Here is the definition of Thomas Paine: "As great an infidel as Voltaire." Today I have to laugh when I hear someone pontificating about the superiority of Catholic to public schools.

Naturally, some students rebelled against such an insipid education. However, most rebellion just reinforced the social outcomes the schools were established to guarantee. Rather than demand that we be taught something relevant and useful to our making a good life for ourselves, boys and girls rebelled by cutting classes and refusing to do any work at all. This led to poor grades and evaluations by the teachers and a certain ticket to a dead-end working-class life.

After high school, I left the factory town for good, first to attend college and graduate school and then to take a job as a college teacher. I got out of the working class, at least the industrial worker part of it. But my class background and consciousness, such as it was, followed me.

When I became a professor, I encountered new ambivalences. Professors have not historically thought of themselves as workers; if anything they have thought themselves superior to workers and much more closely aligned with society's elites. Though professors might disdain the bourgeoisie, they would doubtless prefer to dine with a successful businessman than a ditch digger.

So here I was in an elite job, fulfilling my parents' hope that I wouldn't be a factory worker. But I was among "colleagues"—an odd word for me—who had little knowledge of or sympathy for working people. If I was to succeed on this new job, I would have to take on most of the habits of mind and behavior of the other professors, thinking and acting in ways alien to the lives of my parents and nearly all of the residents of my hometown. I would have to dress differently. I would have to curb my instinct to use words like "fuck" and "asshole." I would have to adopt a more impersonal style of speech. In a word, I would have to behave myself.

Of course, college and graduate school had taken off some of the rough edges of a working-class youth. But they had not prepared me for what I encountered as a professor. There were enough boys like me in college, so I could act pretty much as I did at home. It was exhilarating to be in a school where I didn't have to apologize for being smart and eager to learn. And even better, I was considered by my teachers as a diamond in the rough worth polishing. In graduate school I kept to myself and hung out with friends from my hometown, which was not far away. I never learned to act like a professor.

When I became a professor, I didn't like my new environment, and I didn't fare very well at first. I enjoyed teaching, especially since so many of the students were from working-class families. The college was located in Johnstown, Pennsylvania, a famous old steel town, best known for the great flood of 1889, caused by the neglect of the dam at a private retreat of Pittsburgh's business elite. Johnstown was my hometown writ a little larger; when I arrived there in 1969 there were more than 12,000 steel workers at the enormous Bethlehem Steel plant and the smaller one owned by U.S. Steel. The students were a lot like me, and I felt that I could teach them some of the things I wished I had been taught. The teachers and the administrators were another matter. They seemed alien to me, pretentious and disconnected from the real world. I had to stay because I would have been drafted and very likely sent to Vietnam if I quit. But I couldn't imagine ever liking the place or prospering there. My colleagues and I just didn't speak the same language. I remember one of them saying, in response to something I said that betrayed my class background, "Well, you can take Mike out of Ford City [my hometown], but you can't take Ford City out of Mike."

Although I didn't much like the college, I was proud that I was a professor. My parents wanted me to get an education and a professional job and they sacrificed so that I could. And I didn't want to live in my hometown or work in the factory. By nineteen, I knew that I wanted to continue studying, and by the time I began to teach, I had gone far beyond my parents and nearly all of the townspeople in terms of what I knew about. My values were by this time a lot different than theirs. I had scrapped religion and patriotism. This created some tension and some guilt, too. I tried to live in both worlds. The college hired some good teachers in the early 1970s, and I became friendly with them. They seemed more knowledgeable and sophisticated than I, so I took crash courses of self-education in music, literature, and art so that I could hold my own in conversations. Then I would go to my parents' home on weekends and go to the racetrack with friends and my father's factory buddies. This was my way of saying I was still a regular guy.

One of the best things about being a college teacher is that you have time to read and reflect. And teaching is the best way to learn things. You cannot explain things to others unless you know them well yourself. The war in Vietnam had forced me to think about my beliefs. The drug-sodden and shattered friends returning to my hometown from the war belied the propaganda of the government. My own life and that of my students put the lie to the mainstream economics I had learned and was teaching. I couldn't ignore these things. Once you embark upon an intellectual life, you want to know why things are happening and you want to make sense of your own life.

By accident, my thinking was given a jolt that changed my life. I was so disgusted after one of my introductory economics classes that I went to the library to read a sports magazine. As I was glancing at the rack of periodicals, I noticed one containing an article about the economy. I picked up the journal, a small, booklet-sized periodical called *Monthly Review*. It was described on the cover as "an independent socialist magazine." I wondered how it managed to get into our library, whose librarian would not allow students to sign out certain books. The article was interesting, so I read the whole issue. Then I went into the stacks and started reading back issues. The writing was clear and insightful and nothing like anything I had ever read in economics. Later I returned looking for similar periodicals, and I happened upon *Ramparts* and *The Nation*. I was so impressed that I took out subscriptions. Writers I had never heard of—Paul Sweezy, Harry Magdoff, Carey McWilliams, and Noam Chomsky—provided me with new insights into the workings of our economic system, or as these folks called it, "our political economy."

Armed with this new material, I walked into class around the middle of the term, started to lecture on the week's topic, and then suddenly threw my notes on the floor and slammed the textbook down on the desk. I declared that we were going to talk about something more interesting and relevant today. With that I launched into a discussion of the war in Vietnam, the inequality of wealth and income, and the economic disparities between blacks and whites. A lively give-and-take followed, my first experience with teaching as it should be done. During the remainder of the term, we covered most of the traditional topics, but we also spent time debating the issues of the day.

In these classes, I began to stake out my territory as a radical, someone with unorthodox ideas who was not afraid to express them. I knew that not all students would like my new approach. Some of them, like the ex-marine who said that he wanted to strangle me after one particularly outrageous class, would hate me. But most would rather be challenged than bored, and I decided that I would rather be provocative than boring.

Becoming a radical helped me find a way back to the working class. To see the profound and systemic inequality in my society meant that I had to try to change things. Intellectual understanding is a form of hypocrisy if it isn't matched by action. Marx said, "The philosophers of the world have only interpreted the world in various ways; the point is to change it." If I was no longer a member of the working class, I could ally myself with it, actively. I could help workers to organize unions. I could help them with individual grievances. I could teach workers. I could abandon traditional academic professional development and write for workers. I could even try to reconceptualize professors as workers, something which became easier as I witnessed teaching becoming more like other jobs as administrators began to run the colleges like businesses and began to treat the professors more like replaceable employees.

I understand that it is dangerous to generalize from one's own experiences. But I have lived long enough, studied long enough, and taught enough working-class men and women to know that my life is in no way unique. Hundreds of millions of people around the world have undergone similar things and been shaped in more or less the same way. So are there things we can learn from my life? It is one thing to study class and to see that it is a major explanatory variable in just about every aspect of our lives. It is another thing, however, to radically transform society so that class no longer matters. To do this a revolution is required, plain and simple. But in the making of this revolution, are there obvious guiding principles? My own experiences tell me there are. Here are some "theses" that might guide us. I preface them by stating that these ideas can only be brought to fruition by a mass movement centered in the working class (or in a peasant-worker coalition in some poor countries). Labor movements, take heed:

1. Those who would lead a mass movement must confront the fear that envelops the lives of workers. In practical terms, this means that we must engage in struggles to make life more secure. Efforts to keep intact and extend Social Security, disability benefits, workers' compensation, and unemployment compensation are radical efforts. The same is true of the fight for universal, socialized health care, for the freedom and security of

all immigrants, for a living wage for all workers, for an end to the doctrine of employment at will, for the right of workers to organize without employer interference, and many others. Even the environmental movement can and should be promoted in terms of human security. Working people always bear the brunt of environmental degradation and so-called natural disasters. Whatever benefits nature benefits workers. Insecurity and its attendant fear breed passivity toward authority and make it easier for the powerful to promote dissension and hatred of those who might otherwise be allies.

2. Although many have said it, let me repeat that there is no point to talk about class without making it clear that it is backward to talk about class without speaking about gender and race. We must unabashedly demand equality across all differences. We cannot tolerate restrictions on the right of women to obtain abortions. We cannot tolerate gender inequalities either at work or in the home. We cannot tolerate more than one million black men and women in prison. We must tolerate nothing less than full equality for immigrants, regardless of their legal status. If equality were the foundation of our ideology and if we succeeded in making it an accepted thing to believe in and fight for, it would surely be more difficult for employers to pit one group against another and for the state to get workers here to kill workers in other countries.

3. Workers receive a thoroughly uninspiring and mentally and physically destructive education. Struggles to expand and improve public education are, therefore, also radical struggles. The training of teachers is scandalously inadequate, and the freedom of teachers to teach critical thinking is uniformly circumscribed. Where are the teachers' unions? Indeed, where is the labor movement? If only unions themselves took the time to educate their own members. If only the labor movement financed a network of labor radio stations, television programs, and newspapers. Working people are so misinformed and uninformed that it is no wonder governments everywhere can feed us daily doses of the most ridiculous propaganda.

4. Radical intellectuals need to stop talking to each other and actively engage the masses who alone can carry out a radical social transformation. Speak clearly. Write clearly. Seek a mass audience. And take democracy and an end to hierarchy seriously.

13

Class for a Downwardly Mobile Generation

Angela Jancius

My generation has trouble telling its story. Having begun our lives in the post-hip-pie, "deindustrializing," and disillusioned climate of the early seventies, perhaps we lack a sense of solid footing, from which to speak.

Michael Yates's biographical essay makes an interesting comparison to my own class story. On my father's side, I also stem from Pennsylvanian coal miners. As a child, I used to visit my great-grandparents in White Haven, south of Wilkes-Barre. My great-grandmother prepared food on a still-functioning coal stove homemade applesauce, rhubarb pies, and hand-kneaded warm loaves of white bread. She and her second husband (the first died in the mines) lived well into their nineties. They were kindhearted, storytelling people who, for me, represent-ed a world very different from the rough Baltimore neighborhood I grew up in.

My grandmother married a draftsman and carpenter from a recently immigrat-ed Lithuanian family. He took a Westinghouse job and the couple moved to Baltimore. Aiming for a respectful middle-class life, they sent their three children to Catholic schools. Boyhood photographs show my father in a shirt and tie, wearing "corrective shoes." My grandfather died young, however, and my grand-mother took a job at a plastics factory. Rebelling against upward mobility, my father fell in love with a girl from "the bottom"—the poorest corner of a white working-class mill town (Hampden), not far away from his own neighborhood.

My mother, aged fifteen, was working the night shift at a bookbinding shop and unsuccessfully trying to stay in school. During the summer she also processed raw cotton in one of the last remaining cotton mills. The cotton would stick in her hair. But the money helped pay the bills for my grandmother, who'd taken the youngest three of six children and finally gotten away from the husband who kept breaking her nose. My grandfather was a semiprofessional boxer and a medic in the Second World War. He drank too much, despite "the plate in his head." Before the war, he'd dreamed of being an artist. Much of my extended family lived in row houses that they owned or rented, within walking distance of our own home. In college, I learned that this was unusual. Most college friends had grown up in suburbia, relocated several times, and had relatives spread throughout the country. They often lacked a sense of being rooted to a particular place, but were well coached to cope with the social pressures of flexible mobility that were expected of our generation.

These students were the first offspring of the 1960s countercultural movement. When I asked my parents why they hadn't gone to demonstrations and rock concerts during the sixties, both gave the same answer—that they'd been "too busy working." Formal politics was rarely a topic in our household. Whereas the term "class" was not mentioned directly, my mother referred to us as "working people," and my father raved on for hours about how "the people in charge of things knew nothing about reality." To avoid Vietnam, he wait-listed himself with the Coast Guard at the age of sixteen. Still, he lost friends in the war and observed several deaths during basic training. After six years in the Coast Guard, he took a construction job, let his hair grow, and swore never again to work anywhere, where one "had to jump when some educated, know-nothing prick" told you to. Nevertheless, the subculture of the military had a strong effect on his worldview. After being forced into early retirement due to work injuries and severe alcoholism, today my father spends his days playing military games on the computer.

I was the second child, born in 1972. My younger brother and foster sister followed. My mother worked part-time until I entered middle school, and full-time after that. She held different jobs. While working at the bakery, for example, she took us to the babysitter's house at four in the morning. This made it possible for her to be off in time to pick us up from school, and she usually brought a bag of day-old doughnuts. Because my mother couldn't drive, we walked or took buses to get from place to place. To carry shopping and laundry, she had a two-wheeled metal grocery cart. The car was my father's transportation and the rest of us rarely used it. Aside from a few trips to visit family in Pennsylvania, my siblings and I never traveled beyond the city limits while growing up.

Hampden was the kind of community where relatives and friends were everything, and outsiders weren't always welcome. During Baltimore's half-century of redlining, being a closed community secured nepotistic access to factory jobs and reinforced lines of segregation from the historically African American communities that bordered the neighborhood to the south. But it also protected residents from the social ridicule of students and faculty at the nearby main campus of Johns Hopkins. For several generations, including my own, only 25 to 30 percent of Hampden teenagers completed high school. With an elite university bordering our neighborhood to the east (and today spurring its rapid gentrification), and with two magnet city high schools that the local children rarely gained admittance into, within walking distance to the north, we grew up in an insular world, literally sandwiched by people who could take their higher education for granted. Sharing more in common with neighboring African American communities than was often recognized, Hampden children, like other disadvantaged inner-city kids, were "zoned" to attend a violent high school at the far outskirts of the city, where no one seemed to learn anything. Like their peers, my siblings all dropped out of school following the ninth grade.

A generation ago, they would have taken factory jobs. But during the 1980s, the economic effects of the mill and factory closings were hard-hitting. Half of the local stores on 36th Street ("the Avenue") had closed. Some girls I'd gone to grade school with were now turning tricks for heroin in an apartment above a closed furniture shop. This was a worst-case scenario. Most local teenagers found fast-food jobs. At fourteen, I began working at Hardee's. Intuitively, we understood that this kind of employment "led nowhere." I had other jobs, too, sometimes overlapping: a paper route, babysitting work, and cashiering at a recreation center and a movie theater. I put the money into a bank account, with the dream of one day going to college. Later, I felt naive learning that the five thousand dollars I'd saved would not come close to covering tuition, room, and board for even the first semester.

For three generations, institutions of higher learning in the United States had responded to labor force demands by expanding to incorporate the masses. The G.I. Bill opened postsecondary education to thousands of (largely male and white) first-generation college students after the Second World War, and the Higher Education Act of 1965 extended these opportunities further. Manufacturing jobs disappeared rapidly on the East Coast, and by the 1980s experts were aggressively nudging all blue-collar kids toward college. In the new "knowledge economy" a post-secondary education was seen as the only way to avoid significant downward socioeconomic mobility. However, under Reaganism the cost of education had shifted from the state to the individual: The base of government financial aid had moved from grants (that did not have to be paid back) to interest-bearing student loans while simultaneously, according to the College Board, tuition rates began rising more than three times as quickly as the median family income. To make matters worse, state disinvestment in public schooling, particularly in ethnically diverse urban areas, left first-generation college students ill equipped to acquire available merit-based scholarships.

Local teenagers from Hampden and the neighboring working-class communities were frustrated and self-destructive. Enacting their worldview, my older brother and his friends had a game of driving out to the suburbs in order to dent people's mailboxes by running at them with their heads. They owned knives, and sometimes guns. Officially, Hampden was still at war with Remington, the racially mixed working-class neighborhood immediately to the south. This conflict had faded, however, and teenagers from the two communities often hung out together. There were definitely still racial tensions, but the desegregation of public schools and the flight of the middle-class to private schools and the suburbs had created a multicultural generation of disenfranchised inner-city youth. During high school, more of my friends were black or Asian than white, and I was one of three white girls in my funk-inspired, all-girls' public high school marching band. As we played and did our steps, classmates jokingly teased: "Look at that white girl dance!" Johns Hopkins University students were a common enemy for Hampden and Remington teens. On summer evenings the boys sometimes returned home bragging of how they'd harassed students who'd strayed onto their turf. Meanwhile, the girls put on miniskirts and yelled provocations to the university athletes during their outdoor practice. Going to the Johns Hopkins summer fair seemed as close as we'd ever get to attending college. Thinking back, it is clear today that we were engaged in a class war, and that education had become the battleground.

I was never the typically good student. Assessed as being too disruptive, too talkative, or too quiet, in grade school I was placed in a class for "slow learners." However, in sixth grade a new vice principle gave us IQ tests, and when I achieved a high score he encouraged me to apply for a "gifted" middle school program. This made it possible to enter into the "B-track" program at a "magnet" public high school. Although the B-track, or business and technical track, contrasted with the college-preparatory A-track, it was still considered a blessing, a way to avoid attending the zoned high school. For the have-nots, Baltimore's public secondary education was deplorable in the 1980s, and it remains deplorable today.

The family did not know how to react when I told them of my plan to attend an expensive, out-of-state liberal arts college. I had good grades but average SAT scores and had received a partial, need-based scholarship. This was considerably less than the full "merit" scholarships awarded to many incoming Bard College freshmen—students whose parents were mostly well-paid, high-status professionals, and who (if not for the offer of a free education) might otherwise have chosen to attend Harvard or Yale. The family was so worried about my risk-taking decision that my grandmother, mother, and aunt decided to visit a reputed fortune-teller downtown. A tired-looking woman in her mid-forties laid my cards on the table, studied them, and said: "I worry about a lot of people, but the cards look good for you." With this ritualized reassurance I received the blessings of my maternal kin. At the bus station my friend Eugenia warned me to "keep it real" and to promise her I'd never become "one of them." I promised.

During my freshman year, I chose anthropology as my major after reading Thomas Belmonte's *The Broken Fountain*, an ethnography of poverty and family life in Naples, Italy. I wanted to become a social scientist in order to empower the disenfranchised—to do something to lessen the hardships of working people. I felt attracted to a discipline that could produce such a vivid portrayal of the urban poor. Still, I often wondered how the instructors who had assigned such engaging literature—books like Stephen Jay Gould's *Mismeasure of Man* and Eric Wolf's *Europe and the People Without History*—could themselves participate in an aggressively tooth-and-claw institutional culture. How could they send privileged students into inner-city neighborhoods for service-learning credits while fostering an environment of social Darwinism on campus? And how could they purport to be humanists, or even Marxists, while supporting an educational system that re-created the very patterns of social inequality that they so enjoyed debating with us in class?

It was in college that I first learned how to think about inequality through the lens of social theory. Polemically, however, the environment of this elite institution was not conducive to an honest engagement with the literature. In a freshman seminar class we read Karl Marx's *Eighteenth Brumaire* and met at the professor's home to discuss the essay. In his large villa, we sat in the living room on stripe-upholstered couches, our coffee cups resting on an authentic set of Bauhaus end-tables. The professor wore a suit and horn-rimed glasses. He asked us what we had gotten from reading Marx and, like typical freshmen, we looked at one another bashfully, too intimidated to speak. The professor prodded further. What were our gut responses? I could never have told him mine. For I was thinking of the irony that I had needed to travel so far from home, and had taken out so many student loans, in order to read Karl Marx.

At a summer barbecue I attempted to engage a faculty member in a discussion of financial aid, arguing (hypothetically, of course) that funding for students who had been admitted to the college should thereafter be distributed according to need, rather than "merit-based" scholarships. He disagreed, saying: "We have to draw the line somewhere." Class—which I would define in part by occupation, income, and education, but in essence by status and power—is a key variable influencing people's decisions about whether to humanize or to dehumanize others they meet. When faculty in the social sciences "draw the line," they are contributing to the reproduction of the very patterns of social inequality that are often the subject of their research.

In a 2004 report for the Century Foundation, Richard Kahlenberg assessed that 74 percent of students at the nation's 146 most selective colleges and universities had parents who were in the wealthiest quartile, whereas only 3 percent had parents in the lowest-income quartile. Some of the most selective post-secondary institutions, including Harvard and Princeton, have initiated new policies—such as tuition waivers for low-income students—in an effort to reverse this trend. But making education more affordable does not address the absence of adequate role models. In a rare analysis of the class backgrounds of faculty, in their 2001 study public planning scholars Kenneth Oldfield and Richard Conant found that more than half of all University of Illinois at Urbana-Champaign faculty had parents in high-prestige professions—such as professors, doctors, and lawyers. Less than 2 percent had parents who were employed in professions ranked in the bottom 20 percent of their socioeconomic scale—such as farmworkers, launderers, and cooks.

I made it into this statistic. The graduate anthropology program I attended, at Michigan State University, placed a strong emphasis on applied research. Hoping to discover post–Cold War alternatives to the peripheries wrought by neoliberalism in the United States, my dissertation work was a study of the politics of mass unemployment in the East German city of Leipzig. During fieldwork, I spent time at the unemployment and welfare offices, community centers for the jobless, the Office of Economic Development, trade union halls, and a municipal work-creation firm that had been the largest employer in Saxony for a decade. At millennium's end, though, Leipzig's West German–led business and political elite just wanted to be more like America. Following a "social market economy" variant of neoliberalism, a quarter of the city's working-age population was shuffled into a low-wage, government-regulated employment sector for people who'd been deemed unfit to work in the "competitive labor market." The city's experimental reforms became a model for the Harz Commission's controversial restructuring of the German welfare state. In the final months of my research, the German and EU governments offered half a billion euros in subsidies to lure BMW to Leipzig. Last summer I visited their new production center—the shop floor was 98 percent automated and many of the 2,500 human beings who worked there had short-term job contracts through a temp agency.

Daily life for working people in the United States had gotten worse during my time in school, and after completing my Ph.D. I searched for a way to mix scholarship and teaching with activism. I took a faculty position at the Center for Working-Class Studies at Youngstown State University, in Ohio. The position called for someone to teach part-time and to work as a community liaison and fund-raiser. Within a few months it became clear that my colleagues wanted a faceless, low-ranking grant writer who would serve coffee and raise money from large donors for an endowed chair. The idea of real grassroots community building scared the hell out of them. The married couple who ran the center lived in a mansion and employed a Latino gardener. They collected artwork depicting images of laborers, and joked about their experiences in "dive bars." Seeing this side of academia scared the hell out of me. I'd received research grants and published in peer-reviewed journals. But, as a younger woman in a non-tenure track post, I had suddenly become the person that the permanent faculty need not bother greeting in the halls. Luckily, radical activists Staughton and Alice Lynd also lived in Youngstown, and my husband and I were able to work with them in their struggle for prisoners' rights. It's a tight market for anthropology, and the following year I was only able to secure another visiting assistant professorship. I still believe in the possibility of promoting positive social change from a university post, but I am uncertain whether the corporatizing university system will ever empower me to do so.

When I received my Ph.D. in 2004 my family did not attend the ceremony. For one, Michigan was simply too far away. Also, some family members had used their vacation time caring for relatives who were sick. And finally, why should they be happy about my graduate degree, after all? To the contrary, the topic of whether I "still lived in the real world" was always up for debate. During visits home, this debate takes place in the evening, at the dinner table of my parents' cramped, smoke-filled dining room. Meatloaf's *Bat Out of Hell* plays on the stereo. My mother's deviled eggs and coleslaw sit next to a drink tray with bottles of Jack Daniels, vodka, and Everclear. The siblings and their families pack into the house. The children take over the living room. In a slurred voice, my alcoholic father debates rock trivia, war games, and whether or not women have any common sense. After he passes out, others get to speak.

"What do you know about the real world?" my older brother asks.

"In Ohio, we're not living with the university people," I say. *"It's Appalachia and we rent a small bungalow in a community full of trailer homes, where many of the kids don't have winter coats. And I'm doing advocacy work with prisoners. And I don't have any job security. Isn't that the real world?"*

My brother retorts: *"Last summer I was walking down the alley and a guy rode by on a bike and punched me in the shoulder. Just punched me, for no reason. So I ran after him, knocked him off the bike, threw the bike on top of him, and stomped on it. That's the real world."*

"We love you, Angie," my sister pitches in. *"But you don't live anywhere near the real world."*

My sister should know. After all, she's raising three kids on minimum wage, with a partner who's addicted to methamphetamine. She's been homeless on and off for the past three years, but has been doing better lately.

Academia and the real world exist on alternative planes of the universe. Sometimes I imagine that I've chiseled a small corner, where these planes may overlap. But my siblings are right. I don't live anywhere near the real world. I just still empathize with the people there. To accurately portray social inequality, or make any headway toward reversing current trends, one must begin with empathy. I will never grow used to the coldness and conformity of middle-class life. When I discuss social inequality with professionals, at dinner parties, I always come away feeling quite sad. "How can you talk about poverty and designer cutlery in the same sentence?" I want to shout. "What kind of bullshit is that?"

14

Six Points on Class

Michael Zweig

1. We need to change the understanding of class in the United States, going from the division of "rich and poor" to the division of "worker and capitalist." When we popularize this more accurate and useful terminology, we will convey a better grasp of class dynamics and make it easier to address the continuing operation of racism and sexism in American society. We will also contribute to the construction of political movements capable of reversing the decades-old trend toward ever more consolidated corporate power at the expense of working people, regardless of race and gender.

We should identify the class divisions as between the *working class*, 62 percent of the U.S. labor force—a substantial majority of the American people—and the *corporate elite* (or *capitalist class*), who make up only 2 percent. In between these classes is the *middle class* (36 percent of the U.S. labor force).[1]

The "Two Americas" John Edwards identified in 2004 and the "Two New Yorks" Fernando Ferrer identified in his 2005 mayoral bid refer to crucial realities that should be front and center in our political conversations and social policy. But these divisions are not best understood as simply the difference between "rich and poor."

"Class" must be understood in terms of power rather than income, wealth, or lifestyle, although these do vary by class. Using power as the starting point allows us to see class as a dynamic relationship rather than as a static set of characteristics. Investigating class as a question of power also makes it possible to find the organic links among class, race, and gender. Looking at class in terms of income, wealth, lifestyle, or education separates it from race and gender, which are best understood as power relationships rather than inherent characteristics individuals possess.

The working class are those people with relatively little power at work—white-collar banktellers, call-center workers, and cashiers; blue-collar machinists, construction workers, and assembly-line workers; pink-collar secretaries, nurses, and home-health care workers—skilled and unskilled, men and women of all races, nationalities, and sexual preferences. The working class are those with little personal control over the pace or content of their work and without supervisory control over the work lives of others. There are nearly 90 million working-class people in the U.S. labor force today. The United States has a substantial working-class majority.

The capitalist class are the corporate elite, senior executives, and directors of large corporations, whose job it is to give strategic direction to the company, who interact with government agencies and other corporate executives while leaving the day-to-day operation of their company to intermediate levels of management and the workforce. In this they are different from small business owners, who tend to work beside their relatively few employees and manage them directly. These small business owners, while literally capitalists in that they employ wage labor, are better understood to be in the middle class, as will be discussed below.

The ruling class is considerably smaller than the full capitalist class and includes non-capitalists as well. If we think of the ruling class as those who give strategic direction to the country as a whole, extending beyond their own business or institution, we can identify those corporate directors who sit on multiple boards, thus having an opportunity to coordinate capitalist activity across enterprises, and add to them the political elites of the three branches of national government and cultural and educational leaders who contribute to the furtherance of corporate interests. The entire U.S. ruling class could fit into the seats at Yankee Stadium (capacity: 54,000).

The middle class are professionals, small business owners, and managerial and supervisory employees. They are best understood not as the middle of an income distribution but as living in the middle of the two polar classes in capitalist society. Their experiences have some aspects shared with the working class and some associated with the corporate elite.

Small business owners, for example, share with capitalists an interest in private property in business assets, defeated unions, and weak labor regulations. But they share with workers the work itself, great vulnerability to the capitalist market and government power, and difficulty securing adequate health insurance and retirement security.

Professionals are also caught in the middle of the crossfire in the principal class conflict between labor and capital. If we look at the experience over the last thirty years of professionals whose lives are closely intertwined with the working class—community college teachers, lawyers in public defender offices or with small general practices, doctors practicing in working-class neighborhoods, and public school teachers—their economic and social standing have deteriorated, along with the class they serve. But if we look at those whose lives are more fully involved in serving the capitalist class—corporate lawyers, financial service professionals, Big Four CPAs, and doctors who practice beyond the reach of HMOs' and insurance companies' oversight—these professionals have risen in fortune with the class they serve, albeit to a lesser extent, absolutely and proportionately.

Professionals in most parts of the academic community (especially in colleges closely linked to working-class constituencies) are experiencing the pain of corporate pressure as working-class people do. In the process many academic jobs have been degraded. They are no longer relatively secure tenure-track middle-class positions, but adjunct and visitor positions staffed by a growing second tier of people working at will with virtually no professional standing, a new academic working class.[2]

"Working class" is best understood differently from the Department of Labor (DOL) category "production and non-supervisory" employee. This DOL category includes every employee who is not a supervisor, like most professors and other middle-class professionals working for a salary. However, lumping all employees who have no supervisory power over others into the working class masks the real differences in social position that professional people enjoy, beleaguered as they may be. Appreciating the contradictory class location of professional and other middle-class employees helps to understand the political vicissitudes characteristic of this section of the population and suggests ways of approaching them as allies to working-class politics.

2. The usual talk of a mass middle class with some rich and poor at the fringes is deeply misleading and contributes to two central problems in American politics.

A. We get trapped in confusions about race and lose sight of class. In the popular imagination and in political campaign speeches "the poor" usually stands for "black and Hispanic" or "minority." But in the United States two-thirds of all poor people are white and three-quarters of all black people are not poor.[3] Racism continues to operate and accounts for the fact that poverty is experienced *disproportionately* among blacks and Hispanics (and among women because of sexism). But we should not allow their comparatively heavy burden to blind us to the full realities of poverty in America.

Poverty is something that happens to the working class. Most poor people in the United States are in families where the adults experience periodic spells of unemployment or work only part-time or at low wages. A family with two wage earners, one year-round full-time and one year-round half-time, each earning minimum wage, does not make enough to bring a family of three out of poverty. To address and reverse poverty we need to improve the conditions working-class people experience. The "underclass"—people entirely marginalized from the legal economy—is only a small fraction of the poor and does not characterize most poor people. The "underclass" has special needs which must be understood and addressed, but a majority of the poor are not in this "underclass"—they are working-class people experiencing hard times.

B. The political target gets confused between the false choices of "blame the poor, fix their character, and give them job skills" and "take down the rich a notch or two."

It is a mistake to identify "the rich" as the source of America's political misdirection and the target of our political organizing. When Al Gore challenged George W. Bush in the 2000 campaign by dismissing Bush's plan for tax cuts as a benefit for the richest 1 percent only, polls showed, astonishingly, that 19 percent of Americans believed themselves to be in that top 1 percent, and another 21 percent believed they would be there in the next ten years. When we attack "the rich" *too many people think we are attacking them and their future.*

The real source of the political and economic misdirection in this country is the increasingly unbridled power of the capitalist class and their arrogant pursuit of profit for the few at the expense of the vast majority of Americans and peoples of the world. This should be the target of our politics. Being rich is not the key point—winning $380 million in the Powerball lottery makes a person rich but not part of the corporate elite. The people Dick Cheney met with in early 2001 to set energy policy were rich, but much more to the point they were captains of industry, senior executives of U.S. energy corporations.

Conservatives have convinced too many Americans that their problems stem from government coddling the poor. We need to redirect this anger, not toward "the rich" but toward the corporate elite. Such an approach could not be twisted into "threats to rob working people of their future."

Targeting "the rich" may, however, have some legitimate role in the environmental movement, not in the usual sense but in the sense that the people of industrial countries, especially the rich, need to limit their consumption. Unrestricted consumption is more a question of income than it is of class power, although one can be sure that the capitalist class, eager for expanding markets, will resist any challenges to unlimited consumption.

3. The reality of race and class in the Katrina-devastated Gulf Coast is dramatically different from the "lessons of race and class" the media touted immediately after the catastrophe.

Headlines and news analysis across the country following Katrina announced the "rediscovery of race and class in America." But even as the U.S. media and an attentive public reawakened to the reality of hard lives long quietly and privately endured by millions of people, old confusions continued to obscure the facts of race and class in America. In typical media coverage *race* meant "black" and *class* meant "poverty," both joining in the common identity of the African Americans trapped at the New Orleans Superdome and Convention Center.

Looking at the situation through the lens of class brings important new information into focus. Of the total labor force in the New Orleans Metropolitan Area (including seven parishes in southeast Louisiana) 70 percent are in working-class occupations.[4] Taking the entire metropolitan area before Katrina, 37 percent of the labor force is minority, almost all of that black, a fraction that varies widely across the three largest parishes (which together account for 85 percent of the total metropolitan area): Jefferson Parish (the largest), 26 percent minority; Orleans Parish, 66 percent minority; and St. Tammany Parish, 11 percent minority.[5]

One white worker in four is employed in a job that pays at or near official poverty wages. This is equally true in both predominantly black Orleans Parish and predominantly white Jefferson Parish. They are in low-paid working-class jobs (health-support occupations, food preparation, building maintenance, personal care, and sales), occupations that pay from $12,000 to around $18,000 a year—at best not enough to bring a family of four out of poverty. Eighty-five thousand whites are among the working poor in the New Orleans–area labor force. By contrast, there are about 65,000 minority members (almost all black) in this situation (30 percent of minority employment in the area).

Looking at the other end of the employment picture, managerial and professional employment, blacks are by no means absent even though they are proportionately underrepresented. Minorities held over 47,000 (26 percent) of all such jobs in the New Orleans metropolitan area in 2004 (but were 37 percent of the labor force), and in the city of New Orleans (Orleans Parish) minorities held 45 percent of managerial and professional jobs (compared with their 66 percent share of the overall labor force).

In the construction trades, blacks and whites hold jobs in just about equal proportion to their numbers in the area, minorities holding 11,000 out of a total
29,000 such relatively well-paying jobs. President Bush's suspension of the
Davis-Bacon Act—which requires federally financed construction projects to pay
union-scale wages—for Gulf-area reconstruction hit equally hard at black and
white communities of construction workers. Similarly, federal Section 8 housing
programs are designed for the families of the working poor. The refusal by the
Bush administration to use this program in the aftermath of Katrina has affected
white as well as black working-class families.

Katrina's impact on blacks and whites in metropolitan New Orleans continued long after the storm itself passed. One year later, Orleans Parish had suffered a 27 percent drop in employment. Over the same period, overwhelmingly white St. Bernard Parish had lost 38 percent of its jobs, Jefferson Parish
24.5 percent.[6]

If we look at Katrina and see and speak of black victims only we make a ter-
rible mistake. Without neglecting or underplaying the disproportionate suffering of the African American community, it is essential—for moral as well as
political reasons—to recognize the devastation that hit tens of thousands of
white families, almost all in the working class, along with their African
American neighbors. Neglecting white suffering only contributes to racial
resentment and undermines the development of political unity that both black
and white, working- and middle-class residents will need to rescue the reconstruction for the common good.

**4. Identifying class forces accurately is an essential starting point for more
effective politics to turn back the right-wing tide that has swept across the
United States with growing power for nearly forty years.**
We need to reevaluate the constituent base of progressive politics and reformulate
our work with class as an important component. A *New York Times* news story eval-
uating the 2005 New York City mayoral race reported: "[Bloomberg's] wide support
among minority voters is a sign that the strategy of the Democrat, Fernando Ferrer,
to build a dependable base of black and Hispanic voters fell victim to emerging political realities: that blacks and Hispanics no longer vote reflexively as a bloc, and that
a middle-class coalition can trump traditional ethnic-based appeals."[7]

Class differences now divide ethnic and racial populations in ever more
important ways. Although blacks and Hispanics are disproportionately found
more often in the working class and less often in the middle and capitalist classes,
compared with their shares of the labor force (and in lower-paying jobs in all

classes compared with whites), there are nevertheless millions of black and Hispanic professionals, managers, and small business owners, and growing numbers in the corporate elite as well. Each class is divided by race and ethnicity; each race and ethnic group is divided by class.

Recombining forces within this mosaic of class and race in a progressive coalition requires a direct appeal to class interests and identity while continuing to address the problems of racism and sexism that remain important sources of suffering across class lines. Only a class-based politics that is attuned to issues of race and gender can produce the social force necessary to turn back and limit the corporate power that has gotten so destructively out of control in recent decades.

The closest recent experience in this direction was Jesse Jackson's presidential races in 1984 and 1988, in which he got significant numbers of white male working-class votes by tirelessly championing working people's aspirations, unions, strikes, and other worker campaigns while never neglecting the continuing significance of race and gender.

Asserting the interests of working people can be the basis of political alliances that benefit large sections of the middle class as well. As noted above, over the past thirty years, as working-class lives have become more difficult, millions of professionals, lower-level supervisors, and small business owners—those in the middle class whose lives are most closely linked to working people—have also suffered setbacks. At the same time, those in the middle class most closely associated with serving the corporate elite have done very well. Class-based politics can link working- and middle-class people in their common interest to limit the power of the corporate elite. A politics for the vast majority of Americans is hard to dismiss as "special interest business as usual."

Class should play an important part in the evaluation of Supreme Court and other federal court nominees, a point the corporate community already well understands. When John Roberts was nominated in July 2005, the *Wall Street Journal* reported his corporate *bona fides* as a successful and effective corporate lawyer, notably defending Toyota against a worker's compensation claim.[8]

The *New York Times* reported that the Bush administration had worked behind the scenes for a year preparing the religious right to accept the Roberts nomination. This was accompanied by an organized corporate lobbying effort on federal court appointments, to ensure that nominees backed by the religious right would also be sensitive to business interests. Similar reports followed the nomination of Samuel Alito, who, in one story, in the midst of many about his views on abortion, was said to have "sided with employers over employees."[9]

The protection of reproductive rights for women is an integral part of a progressive political agenda, but it should not be pursued without close attention to the working-class dimensions of the agenda as well. For instance, access to abortions will be much more severely restricted for working-class women than for middle- and capitalist-class women should abortion become illegal. Highlighting the antilabor stand of anti-abortion judges and their political backers will help expose the contours of power at play in the country and broaden the coalition opposed to right-wing court nominees and committed to progressive policies for women and working people alike.

The conventional wisdom has it that most Americans identify themselves as members of the middle class so political appeals to the middle class are appropriate for building winning messages. It is true that large majorities say they are in the middle class when the choices given are "upper, middle, lower" or "rich, middle, poor." But when "working class" is given as a choice, 45 to 55 percent of Americans put themselves in the working class.[10]

We do not yet know just what people mean when they identify themselves as working class. We do not know who else they think is in that class with them, and who is not. Nor do we know the strength of that identity in comparison with other identities, whether racial or in terms of particular interests such as being a hunter, a volunteer firefighter, a Little League coach, or a "pink lady" hospital volunteer. But it may well be that Americans are ready to hear and identify with class talk when it illuminates the realities of their lives and points to political practice that will improve theirs and their children's lives.

Eight or ten years ago it seemed that class categories expressed in terms of power, a working class, a capitalist class, were so far out of polite conversation that they were useless for constructive political debate. But today even mainstream commentators are increasingly referring to the working class, class warfare, and in general framing their writing in class terms. The *New York Times* series on class in America, published as a book in 2005, is a prominent example.[11] Jeff Faux's book *The Global Class War* is another.[12] Serious class talk is again possible and should be pursued with rigor, subtlety, and confidence.

Back in 1981, after the first destructive round of concession bargaining in the auto industry, UAW president Douglas Fraser characterized the process as "one-sided class warfare," in which labor was unprepared. The corporate elite—with a thorough understanding of *its* class interests—has continued these attacks on labor ever since. It is past time for progressive people to call this class warfare out for what it is and create a political vision and policies squarely in the interests of working people and all whose interests are turned aside by corporate power.

5. Class operates on a global scale.

The global economy is not separate from the domestic. The common view that globalization refers to what is "out there" while the domestic economy is "here"— with the "out there" threatening the "here" with job loss, cheap labor, and capital flight—fails to see how capital accumulation operates in all of its dynamics, both nationally and globally.[13]

The global accumulation process under the neoliberal regime of the past thirty years has generated robust capitalist classes in many developing countries (Brazil, China, and India are principal examples) and has also begun to integrate these into a coherent international capitalist class operating on a global scale.[14] At the same time, the global reach of the accumulation process is bringing into existence a global working class which already has implications for cross-border labor organizing and within-country responses to immigration.[15]

The introduction of class analysis based on power rather than income reorients our view of WTO and IMF dynamics. Rather than seeing the conflict as one between the poor Global South and the rich Global North, we can see that class divisions divide both North and South and recombine the people of each into international, as well as national, groupings. While national interests certainly continue to operate, as long as the national aspirations of the South are articulated by capitalists there, who lead the political representation of those interests, working people will be disadvantaged in both the South and the North. Broad acceptance of the idea that the South is progressive while the North is oppressive empties the global playing field of the working class in the North as a progressive force and turns a blind eye to murderous Southern elites.

Integrating domestic and international aspects of the single economic system in which we live also makes it easier to build movements among working people for just foreign policy and against the Iraq war and occupation.[16] A class analysis allows us to see beyond the financial costs and lost public services resulting from the enormous military budget. It helps make clear that the war and U.S. foreign policy seek to empower globally the same corporate capitalist class that challenges working people on virtually every economic and social issue at home.

6. Class is an idea for a movement of ideas.

If there is any hope of a progressive revival of the Democratic Party, or the rise of a third party that seeks to represent working people, it must become a party of broad vision, not just a party of interest-based policy proposals. The same is true of social movements that hope to influence public policy and political outcomes.

Policy is essential, but it must be placed in the context of the broadest understanding of how the world works, how our life prospects are shaped, and how we create and use our great capacity for wealth and community involvement. Introducing class into the national conversation can invigorate the political process and bring new energy and understanding to a broad range of questions, including the continued importance of race and gender as points of tension and needed progress.

Class talk allows us to recall the language of economic and social justice and to revive calls for economic democracy that have been the foundation of progressive social movements for over a hundred years. The corporate agenda has stripped all reference to morality from economic affairs. For the Right, unrestricted markets are all that is relevant in economic matters. This is a core question that progressives must address directly. Class understanding will help us to illuminate and ground the ethical dimensions of our politics and help us imagine and create organizations, coalitions, and social forces capable of turning back the destructive power of capital and replacing it with values and policies that relieve human suffering and promote the social good.

Contributors

Mark Brenner (mark@labornotes.org) is co-director of *Labor Notes Magazine,* http://www.labornotes.org.

Ramin Farahmandpur (farahmandpur@comcast.net) teaches in the department of Educational Policy, Foundations and Administrative Studies in the Graduate School of Education at Portland State University and, with Peter McLaren, is coauthor of *Teaching Against Global Capitalism and the New Imperialism: A Critical Pedagogy* (Rowman & Littlefield, 2005).

Joe Feagin (jrfeagin@yahoo.com) teaches sociology at Texas A&M University and is the author of *Systemic Racism: A Theory of Oppression* (Routledge, 2006). His teaching and research focus on the areas of racial, class, and gender oppression.

John Bellamy Foster is editor of *Monthly Review* and professor of sociology at the University of Oregon. His most recent book is *Naked Imperialism: The U.S. Struggle for Global Dominance* (2006). Some of his other books include *Marx's Ecology, Ecology Against Capitalism, Hungry for Profit* (with F. Magdoff and F. Buttel), and *The Vulnerable Planet,* all published by Monthly Review Press.

Martha E. Gimenez is Professor of Sociology at the University of Colorado at Boulder. She is the author of many articles and book chapters about Marxist theory, feminist theory, population issues, inequality, and U.S. policies of racial and ethnic classification. She is co-editor of special issues of *Latin American Perspectives* ("Population and Capitalism, and U.S. Politics of Ethnic Construction"), *Gender & Society* ("Marxist Feminist Theory"), and *Science & Society* ("Marxist Feminist Thought Today").

Angela Jancius (jancius@ohio.edu) teaches anthropology at Ohio University and recently guest-edited a special issue of *Ethnos* on the "Anthropology of Unemployment." Following an interest in inequality and the future of wage labor, she is studying unemployment and community economy in eastern Germany, and has also recently begun a prisoner advocacy project in Ohio (www.prisonersolidarity.org).

Kristen Lavelle (klavelle@tamu.edu) is a doctoral student at Texas A&M University and does research on white antiracist identity development as well as whites' memories of the Jim Crow South.

Stephanie Luce (sluce@econs.umass.edu) teaches at the Labor Center of the University of Massachusetts–Amherst. She is the author of *Fighting for a Living Wage* (Cornell University Press, 2004).

Peter McLaren (mclaren@gseis.ucla.edu) teaches in the Graduate School of Education and Information Studies of the University of California, Los Angeles. His most recent book is *Rage and Hope: Interviews with Peter McLaren on War, Imperialism, and Critical Pedagogy* (Peter Lang Publishing, 2006).

Vincent Navarro (vnavarro@jhsph.edu) is Professor of Public Policy, Sociology, and Policy Studies at Johns Hopkins University and Professor of Political and Social Science at Pompeu Fabra University. He is Editor-in-Chief of the *International Journal of Health Services* and author of the *Politics of Health Policy* (Blackwell, 1994), *Dangerous to Your Health: Capitalism in Health Care* (Monthly Review, 1993), *The Political Economy of Social Inequalities* (Baywood, 2000), *Political and Economic Determinants of Population Health and Well-Being* (with Charles Muntaner) (Baywood, 2004), and *Neoliberalism, Globalization, and Inequalities: Consequences for Health and Quality of Life* (Baywood, 2007).

Michael Perelman (michael@rocko.csuchico.edu) teaches economics at California State University at Chico and is the author of fifteen books, including *Manufacturing Discontent: The Trap of Individualism in Corporate Society* (Pluto Press, 2005) and *Railroading Economics: The Creation of the Free Market Mythology* (Monthly Review Press, 2006).

Sabiyha Prince (blanthro@yahoo.com) teaches anthropology at American University in Washington, D.C., and is the author of *Constructing Belonging: Race, Class and Harlem's Black Professional Workers* (Routledge, 2004).

David Roediger (droedige@uiuc.edu) teaches history at the University of Illinois at Urbana-Champaign. His most recent book is *Working Toward Whiteness: How America's Immigrants Became White: The Strange Journey from Ellis Island to the Suburbs* (Perseus Publishing, 2006).

William K. Tabb (william.tabb@gmail.com) taught economics at Queens College for many years, and economics, political science, and sociology at the Graduate Center of the City University of New York. His books include *Economic Governance in the Age of Globalization* (Columbia University Press, 2004), *Unequal Partners: A Primer on Globalization* (New Press, 2002), and *The Amoral Elephant: Globalization and the Struggle for Social Justice in the Twenty-First Century* (Monthly Review Press, 2001).

Richard D. Vogel (irvogel@aim.com) is an independent socialist writer and the author of *Stolen Birthright: The U.S. Conquest of the Mexican People*, http://www. houstonculture.org/hispanic/conquest.html.

Michael D. Yates (mikedjyates@msn.com) is associate editor of Monthly Review. For many years he taught economics at the University of Pittsburgh at Johnstown. He is the author of *Cheap Motels and a Hotplate: An Economist's Travelogue* (2007), *Naming the System: Inequality and Work in the Global System* (2004), *Why Unions Matter* (1998), and *Longer Hours and Fewer Jobs: Employment and Unemployment in the United States* (1994), all published by Monthly Review Press. His website is http://www.cheapmotelsandahotplate.org.

Michael Zweig (michael.zweig@stonybrook.edu) teaches economics and is director of the Center for Study of Working Class Life at the State University of New York at Stony Brook, http://www.workingclass.sunysb.edu. He is the author of *The Working Class Majority: America's Best Kept Secret* (Cornell University Press, 2000) and editor of *What's Class Got to Do with It? American Society in the Twenty-first Century* (Cornell University Press, 2004).

Notes

Introduction

The *Los Angeles Times* series can be found at www.latimes.com/business/la-fi-poormethoda12dec12, 1,5324668.story; the *Wall Street Journal* and *New York Times* series can be found on the papers' websites but are available only to subscribers. The *New York Times* series has been published in book form as *Class Matters*, by *New York Times* and Bill Keller (New York: Times Books, 2005). A wealth of information on income and wealth inequality and declining economic mobility can be found in Lawrence Mishel, Jared Bernstein, and Sylvia Allegretto, *The State of Working America*, 2006–2007 (Ithaca, N.Y.: Cornell University Press, 2007).

1. Aspects of Class in the United States: A Prologue

1. Bill Moyers, "This Is the Fight of Our Lives," keynote speech, Inequality Matters Forum, New York University, June 3, 2004, http://www.commondreams.org/views04/0616-09.htm/.

2. Paul M. Sweezy, "Paul Sweezy Replies to Ernest Mandel," *Monthly Review* 31, no. 3 (July–August 1979): 82.

3. Tom Hertz, *Understanding Mobility in America*, Center for American Progress, April 26, 2006, i, 8, http://www.americanprogress.org/.

4. Correspondents of the *New York Times* and Bill Keller, *Class Matters* (New York: Times Books, 2005), 186.

5. Edward N. Wolff, "Changes in Household Wealth in the 1980s and 1990s in the U.S.," April 27, 2004, draft, in Wolff, *International Perspectives on Household Wealth* (Brookfield, VT.: Edward Elgar, 2006), http://www.econ.nyu.edu/user/wolffe/.

6. Sweezy's comments were directed mainly at post-revolutionary societies, but he made it clear that the same issues related to the reproduction of class in capitalist societies. I have inserted a brief qualification in square brackets to avoid any misunderstandings related to the specific context in which he was writing. See Paul M. Sweezy, *Post-Revolutionary Society* (New York: Monthly Review Press, 1980), 79–80.

7. V. I. Lenin, *Selected Works* (Moscow: Progress Publishers, 1971), 486.

8. Sweezy, "Paul Sweezy Replies to Ernest Mandel," 79.

2. The Worldwide Class Struggle

This essay is dedicated to the memory of my good friends Paul Sweezy and Harry Magdoff, who taught us an uncompromising critical evaluation of all that exists, uncompromising in the sense that our criticism fears neither its own results nor conflict with the powers that be.

1. Michael Hardt and Antonio Negri, *Empire* (Cambridge: Harvard University Press, 2000), 39.

2. Caspar Weinberger, quoted in *Washington Post*, July 13, 1983.

3. John Williamson, "What Washington Means by the Policy Reform," in *Latin America Adjustment*, ed. J. Williamson (1990), 213.

4. The starting point of neoliberalism and of the growth of inequalities was July 1979, with Paul Volker's dramatic increase in interest rates that slowed down economic growth (plus the two oil shocks that particularly affected countries highly dependent on imported oil) (see David Harvey, *Neoliberalism,* Oxford University Press, 2005). Volker increased interest rates (thus creating a worldwide recession) as an anti-working-class move to weaken labor in the United States and abroad. The rate increase also initiated, as Giovanni Arrighi has noted (in "The African Crisis: World Systemic and Regional Aspects," *New Left Review* [May–June, 2002]), a flow of capital to the United States, making it very difficult for other countries, especially poor countries, to compete for the limited capital. The fact that petrol euro dollars (which increased enormously with the oil shocks) were deposited in the United States made the scarcity of capital particularly hard for poor countries to adapt to. This is the time when the stagnation of the poor countries started. The countries most affected by these neoliberal public policies were the Latin American countries, which followed these policies extensively, and the African countries (the poorest of the poor), which saw extremely negative economic growth. In 2000, twenty-four African countries had a smaller GNP per capita than twenty-five years earlier.

5. Mark Weisbrot, Dean Baker, and David Rosnick, "The Scorecard on Development: 25 Years of Diminished Progress," *International Journal of Health Services* 36 (2006): 211-234.

6. Branco Milanovic, *Worlds Apart* (Princeton, NJ: Princeton University Press, 2005).

7. Vincent Navarro (ed.), "Meet the New Head of the IMF: Who Is Mr. Rodrigo Rato?" *Counterpunch,* June 16, 2004, http://www.counterpunch.org/navarro06162004.html.

8. *Financial Times,* March 4, 2006.

9. Jeff Faux, *The Global Class War* (New York: Wiley, 2006).

10. *Economist,* September 25, 2003.

11. John Rawls, *The Law of Peoples: With, The Idea of Public Reason Revisited* (Cambridge: Harvard University Press, 1999).

12. Vincent Navarro (ed.), *The Political Economy of Social Inequalities: Consequences for Health and Quality of Life* (Amityville, NY: Baywood, 2002).

13. Michael Marmot, *The Status Syndrome* (New York: Henry Holt, 2005).

3. The Power of the Rich

1. G. William Domhoff, *Who Rules America Now?* (New York: Simon & Schuster, 1983), 1.

2. Kevin Phillips, *Wealth and Democracy: A Political History of the American Rich* (New York: Broadway, 2002), 214.

3. Deborah Brewster, "Senators' Stocks Beat the Market by 12%," *Financial Times,* February 25, 2006; *Washington Spectator*, "Senators Beat the Stock Market—and Get Rich—With Insider Information," January 1, 2006.

4   Center for Public Integrity, "Lobbyists Double Spending in Six Years," April 7, 2005, http://www.publicintegrity.org.

5. Associated Press, "Bush Brings Campaign Across the Potomac," August 9, 2004.

6. Robert McNatt, "Up Front," *Business Week*, November 6, 2000, 12.

7. David Kay Johnston, "Richest Are Leaving Even the Rich Far Behind," *New York Times,* June 5, 2005.

8. Thomas Ferguson, *Golden Rule: The Investment Theory of Party Competition and the Logic of Money-Driven Political Systems* (Chicago: University of Chicago Press, 1995), 28.

9. Paul Krugman, "Steps to Wealth," *New York Times,* July 16, 2002.

10. *The Economist*, "A Troubled Marriage," May 17, 2003, 27.

11. David E. Sanger, "The Big One: Washington's Political Earthquake," *New York Times*, September 24, 1995.

12. Sara Miles, "Silicon Battleground," *Mother Jones*, March 5, 2001, http://www.motherjones.com/news/special_reports/mojo_400/tech.html?welcome'true.

4. Some Economics of Class

1. President of the United States, *Economic Report of the President* (Washington, DC: GPO, 2005), table B-2, 286.

2. President of the United States, *Economic Report of the President* (Washington, DC: GPO, 2004), table B-47, 340.

3. Thomas Piketty and Emmanuel Saez, "Income Inequality in the United States, 1913–1998," in *Top Incomes Over the Twentieth Century: A Contrast Between the European and English Speaking Countries,* ed. Anthony B. Atkinson and T. Piketty (Oxford: Oxford University Press, forthcoming), http://emlab.berkeley.edu/users/saez/piketty-saez OUP04US.pdf. See also David Cay Johnston, *Perfectly Legal* (New York: Portfolio, 2003), 38–39; and Paul Krugman, "For Richer," *The New York Times Magazine*, October 20, 2002.

4. Lucian Bebchuk and Yaniv Grinstein, "The Growth of Executive Pay," *Oxford Review of Economic Policy* 21, no. 2 (2005), http://www.law.harvard.edu/faculty/bebchuk/pdfs/Bebchuk-Grinstein.Growth-of Pay.pdf.

5. Richard M. Titmuss, *Income Distribution and Social Change* (London: Allen & Unwin, 1962), 22.

6. Johnston, *Perfectly Legal*.

7. Max B. Sawicky, "Do-It-Yourself Tax Cuts: The Crisis in U.S. Tax Enforcement," Economic Policy Institute Briefing Paper No. 160, April 12, 2005, http://www.epinet.org/content.cfm/bp160.

8. Nick Mathiason, "Super-Rich Hide Trillions Offshore." *The Observer,* March 27, 2005.

9. Joseph M. Dodge and Jay A. Soled, "Inflated Tax Basis and the Quarter-Trillion-Dollar Revenue Question," *Tax Notes* 106, no. 4, January 24, 2005.

10. Johnston, *Perfectly Legal,* 129.

11. Ibid., 62.

12. Nell Minow, "The Use of Company Aircraft," http://www.thecorporatelibrary.com/special/misc/aircraft.html; Bryan Burrough and John Helyar, *Barbarians at the Gate* (New York: Harper and Row, 1990), 94; Gary Strauss, "Pricey Perk Lets Executives Fly High," *USA Today,* August 5, 2003.

13. David Yermack, "Flights of Fancy" (September 2004), http://public.kenan-flagler.unc .edu/faculty/shivdasani/uncduke%20corporate%20finance/David_Yermack_Aircraft0904.pdf.

14. Mark Maremont, "Frequent Fliers: Amid Crackdown, the Jet Perk Suddenly Looks a Lot Pricier For CEOs," *Wall Street Journal,* May 25, 2005.

15. Joseph E. Stiglitz, *The Roaring Nineties* (New York: W. W. Norton, 2004).

16. Gretchen Morgenson, "Only the Little People Pay for Lawn Care," *New York Times*, May 1, 2005.

17. Organisation for Economic Co-operation and Development, *Clocking In and Clocking Out,* October 2004), http://www.oecd.org/dataoecd/42/49/33821328.pdf.

18. Kathy Chu, "Rising Bank Fees Hit Consumers," *USA Today,* October 4, 2005; Dean Foust, "Protection" Racket?: As Overdraft and Other Fees Become Huge Profit Sources For Banks, Critics See Abuses," *BusinessWeek,* May 2, 2005.

19. Piketty and Saez, "Income Inequality in the United States"; see also Krugman, "For Richer."

20. Edward N. Wolff, "Changes in Household Wealth in the 1980s and 1990s in the U.S.," Levy Economics Institute Working Paper No, 407, May 2004.

21. Robert K. Merton, "The Matthew Effect in Science," *Science* 159, no. 3810 (January 5, 1968): 56–63.

22. Senate Banking, Housing and Urban Affairs Committee, *Federal Reserve's Second Monetary Policy Report for 2004,* 108th Congress, 2nd sess., July 20, 2004.

23. Senate Banking, Housing and Urban Affairs Committee, *Federal Reserve's First Monetary Policy Report for 2005,* 109th Congress, 1st sess., February 16, 2005.

24. Warren Buffett, "Annual Letter to the Shareholders of Berkshire Hathaway Inc.," http://www.berkshirehathaway.com/letters/2003ltr.pdf.

25. United States Department of Commerce, Bureau of Economic Analysis, National Income and Product Accounts, "Table 3.2. Federal Government Current Receipts and Expenditures" (2004), http://www.bea.gov/bea/dn/nipaweb/TableView.asp#Mid.

26. Robert S. McIntyre and T. D. Coo Nguyen, *Corporate Income Taxes in the Bush Years* (Washington, DC: Citizens for Tax Justice, Institute on Taxation and Economic Policy, 2004), http://www.ctj.org/corpfed04pr.pdf.

27. Ibid.

28. Robert S. McIntyre and T. D. Coo Nguyen, *Corporate Tax Avoidance in the States Even Worse Than Federal* (Washington, DC: Citizens for Tax Justice, Institute on Taxation and Economic Policy, 2005), http://www.ctj.org/pdf/corp0205an.pdf.

29. Richard Kogan and Robert Greenstein, "President Portrays Social Security Shortfall as Enormous, But his Tax Cuts and Drug Benefit Will Cost at Least Five Times as Much," Center on Budget and Policy Priorities, February 11, 2005, http://www.cbpp.org/1-4-05socsec.htm.

30. Daniel Altman, "Efficiency and Equity (In the Same Breath)," *New York Times,* April 20, 2003.

31. "The Non-Taxpaying Class," *Wall Street Journal,* November 20, 2002.

5. Harder Times: Undocumented Workers and the U.S. Informal Economy

1. The full report is available at: http://www.economicrt.org/summaries/hopeful_workers_marginal_jobs_synopsis.html.

2. Available at: http://www.dhs.gov/xlibrary/assets/statistics/publications/Ill_Report_1211.pdf.

3. See http://www.pewhispanic.org.

6. The Retreat from Race and Class

The books centrally discussed in this essay are Paul Gilroy, *Against Race: Imagining Political Culture Beyond the Color Line* (Cambridge, MA: Harvard University Press, 2000); and Antonia Darder and Rodolfo D. Torres, *After Race: Racism after Multiculturalism* (New York: New York University Press, 2004). Pierre Bourdieu and Loïc Wacquant's "On the Cunning of Imperialist Reason" and the debates surrounding it can be found in the journal *Theory, Culture, and Society* 16 and 17 (1999 and 2000). See also Mark Alan Healey, "Powers of Misrecognition: Bourdieu and Wacquant on Race in Brazil," *Neplantla: Views from the South* 4 (2003): 391–400; and Robert Stam and Ella Shohat, "Variations on an Anti-American Theme," *CR: The New Centennial Review* 5 (2005): 141–78. For the Patterson articles cited, see "Race Over," *The New Republic* 222 (January 10, 2000); and "Race by the Numbers," *New York Times* (May 8, 2001). Reed's "Class-ifying the Hurricane" appears in the October 3, 2005 issue of *The Nation;* and "The Real Divide" is featured in the November 2005 issue of *The Progressive.*

7. Hard Truth in the Big Easy: Race and Class in New Orleans, Pre- and Post-Katrina

1. Adolph Reed, "The Real Divide," *The Progressive* 69, no. 11 (November 2005): 31–32.

2. Michael Eric Dyson, *Come Hell or High Water: Hurricane Katrina and the Color of Disaster* (New York: Basic Civitas Books, 2006), 144.

3. Joe R. Feagin, *Systemic Racism: A Theory of Oppression* (New York: Routledge, 2006).

4. George W. Bush, "President Discusses Hurricane Relief in Address to the Nation," September 15, 2005, http://www.whitehouse.gov/news/releases/2005/09/20050915-8.html.

5. Adam Rothman, *Slave Country: American Expansion and the Origins of the Deep South* (Cambridge, MA: Harvard University Press, 2005), 83.

6. Walter Johnson, *Soul by Soul: Life inside the Antebellum Slave Market* (Cambridge, MA: Harvard University Press, 1999), 6–7.

7. Rothman, *Slave Country*, 99.

8. Johnson, *Soul by Soul*, 23, 64.

9. Roger A. Fischer, "Racial Segregation in Antebellum New Orleans," *American Historical Review* 74, no. 3 (1969): 928–29.

10. The first free blacks had become visible in the 1720s, many of them the manumitted children of white men and enslaved women. Others gained freedom through service, fighting in colonial militias, or self-purchase. Others came from northern states or Haiti during its revolution. See John W. Blassingame, *Black New Orleans, 1860–1880* (Chicago: University of Chicago Press, 1973), 9–10.

11. In Louisiana, the term "Creole" has had a number of much-disputed usages over the years but is now commonly used to refer to Louisianans who have some mixture of French, Spanish, African, and Native American ancestry. Creole also implies rather light skin and a favorable social or class status.

12. Daniel E. Walker, *No More, No More: Slavery and Cultural Resistance in Havana and New Orleans* (Minneapolis: University of Minnesota Press), 134, 139; Blassingame, *Black New Orleans*, 21.

13. Rothman, *Slave Country*, 102; Walker, *No More, No More*, 140.

14. Fischer, "Racial Segregation in Antebellum New Orleans."

15. Blassingame, *Black New Orleans*, 15, 162–63; Rothman, *Slave Country*, 102–3.

16. Blassingame, *Black New Orleans*, 83.

17. Walker, *No More, No More*, 139.

18. Blassingame, *Black New Orleans*, 17–18.

19. Ibid., 201.

20. Ibid., 77, 164.

21. "White flight" refers to predominantly white upper- and middle-class Americans who move out of inner cities into suburbs. The high tax base goes with them, as do jobs, real estate investors, and high-quality amenities. Redlining has been a major cause of white flight in the United States, a practice in which banks and insurance companies refuse services in certain racially or economically determined neighborhoods.

22. Pierce F. Lewis, *New Orleans: The Making of an Urban Landscape*, 2nd ed. (Santa Fe, NM: Center for American Places, 2003), 67, 124–25.

23. Quoted in Blassingame, *Black New Orleans*, 113.

24. Ibid., 173–74.

25. Lewis, *New Orleans*, 99, 126.

26. Porcupine, "Historical Perspective," message board post, November 22, 2004, on http://neworleans.indymedia.org/.

27. Ibid.

28. Lewis, *New Orleans*, 52, 128.

29. Arloc Sherman and Isaac Shapiro, "Essential Facts about the Victims of Hurricane Katrina," *Center on Budget and Policy Priorities,* 2005, http://www.cbpp.org/9-19-05pov.htm.

30. Lewis, *New Orleans*, 123–24.

31. Ibid., 123.

32. Harry J. Holzer and Robert I. Lerman, "Employment Issues and Challenges in Post-Katrina New Orleans" (Washington, DC: The Urban Institute, 2006), 1.

33. Edward Glaeser, "Should the Government Rebuild New Orleans, or Just Give Residents Checks?" *Economists' Voice* 2, no. 4 (2005).

34. Dyson, *Come Hell or High Water*, 8, 145.

35. Lewis, *New Orleans*, 95.

36. Mike Davis, "Who Is Killing New Orleans?" *The Nation* 282, no. 14 (April 10, 2006).

37. Dyson, *Come Hell or High Water*, 145; Sherman and Shapiro, "Essential Facts About the Victims of Hurricane Katrina."

38. John Barnshaw, "The Continuing Significance of Race and Class among Houston Hurricane Katrina Evacuees," *Natural Hazards Observer* 30, no. 2 (2005): 12.

39. Adam Nossiter, "New Orleans of Future May Stay Half Its Old Size," *New York Times*, January 21, 2007.

40. Holzer and Lerman, "Employment Issues and Challenges," 9.

41. Nossiter, "New Orleans of Future."

42. Toni McElroy and Kevin Whelan, "Rebuild New Orleans, Rebuild America" (February 5, 2007), http://www.tompaine.com/articles/2007/02/05/rebuild_new_orleans_r ebuild_america.php.

43. Davis, "Who Is Killing New Orleans?"

44. William H. Frey and Audrey Singer, "Katrina and Rita Impacts on Gulf Coast Populations: First Census Findings" (Washington, DC: The Brookings Institution, June 2006), 9.

45. CNN.com, "Poll: Effects of Katrina Differ by Race," *CNN.com* (February 27, 2006), http://www.cnn.com/2006/US/02/27/katrina.poll/index.html.

46. Davis, "Who Is Killing New Orleans?"; Barnshaw, "The Continuing Significance of Race and Class," 13.

47. Bring New Orleans Back Commission, "Urban Planning Committee: Action Plan for New Orleans Executive Summary" (2006), 10.

48. Associated Press, "Harsh Urban Renewal in New Orleans," *MSNBC.com* (October 12, 2005), http://www.msnbc.msn.com/id/9678167/.

49. Frey and Singer, "Katrina and Rita Impacts," 9.

50. E&P Staff, "Barbara Bush: Things Working Out 'Very Well' for Poor Evacuees from New Orleans," *Editor & Publisher*, September 5, 2005, http://editorandpublisher.com/eandp/news/article_display.jsp?vnu_ content_id=1001054719.

51. Barnshaw, "The Continuing Significance of Race and Class Among Houston Hurricane Katrina Evacuees," 12.

52. Michelle Chen, "Post-Katrina Throwback to Segregation Alarms Fair Housing Activists," *The New Standard*, February 10, 2006, http://newstandardnews.net/content/index.cfm/items/2797.

53. "Reports of Missing and Deceased," Louisiana Department of Health and Hospitals (April 18, 2006).

54. Eric Berger, "Poll: Locals Evacuee-Weary," *Houston Chronicle*, March 24, 2006.

55. Nicole Gelinas, "Katrina Refugees Shoot Up Houston," *City Journal* 16, no. 1 (2006), http://www.city-journal.org/html/eon2006-01-04ng.html.

56. Berger, "Poll."

57. Frey and Singer, "Katrina and Rita Impacts," 8.

58. Martin Luther King, Jr., *Where Do We Go from Here? Chaos or Community* (New York: Bantam Books, 1967), 209–10.

8. Will the Real Black Middle Class Please Stand Up?

1. It may be helpful to acknowledge that cultural theorists, essayists, social scientists, historians, and other social observers have long debated the definition of class and the composition and

function of the class structure. There is also little consensus on the concept of the middle class. After reading the work of John and Barbara Ehrenreich, Stanley Aronowitz, E. Olin Wright, Louis Wacquent, Bart Landry, William Gatewood, and others, I began using the phrase black or African American professional managerial worker(s) (PMW) as a substitute for the black or African American middle class to acknowledge that the boundaries between the middle and working classes are much more fluid than those between the elite or ruling class and other socioeconomic groupings. I also chose the term to convey my belief that people in this stratum, especially African Americans due to historic patterns of wealth disaccumulation, must labor for survival or face catastrophic conditions if the flow of income was impeded. Although PMW is a much more specific and less value-laden concept than the middle class, in this essay I opt for the more common middle-class label and alternate that with the phrases college-educated, professionals, or professional workers.

2. Bart Landry, *The New Black Middle Class* (Berkeley and Los Angeles: University of California Press, 1987).

3. Patricia Hill-Collins, "The Making of the Black Middle Class," *Social Problems* 30, no. 4 (1983).

4. Sabiyha Prince, "Changing Places: Race, Class and Belonging in the 'New' Harlem," *Urban Anthropology* 31, no. 1 (2002): 5–35; and "Race, Class and the Packaging of Harlem," *Identities: Global Studies in Culture and Power* 12 (2005): 385–404.

5. Patricia Hill-Collins, *Black Feminist Thought* (Boston: Unwin Hyman, 1990).

6. All names of individuals who participated in my doctoral study in Harlem are changed to protect their anonymity. Some of the same individuals mentioned here also appear in Sabiyha Prince, *Constructing Belonging* (New York: Routledge, 2004).

7. Carol Stack, *Call to Home* (New York: Basic Books, 1996).

8. As an anecdotal validation of this point, a family friend was gunned down in northwest Washington, D.C., by an off-duty Metropolitan Police Department officer in 2003. He was a dentist from a multigenerationally middle-class family—the only one of my black friends with a grandfather who graduated from college—but this did not protect Dr. Brian Hundley from the fate of so many unarmed African American men.

9. Joe Feagin and Melvin Sikes, *Living with Racism* (Boston: Beacon Press, 1994); and Mary Pattillo, *Black Picket Fences* (Chicago and London: University of Chicago Press, 1999).

10. Prince, *Constructing Belonging*.

11. It is important to acknowledge that progressive political views did not always carry over into all areas of their professional and personal lives. College-educated, African American radicals have also brought elitism to their societal analyses/commentary and/or interpersonal relations as Manning Marable shows in his biography, *W. E. B. Du Bois: Black Radical Democrat* (Independence, KY: Twayne Publishers, 1986). Some of his class chauvinism was expressed in Du Bois's opposition to the work of Zora Neale Hurston, a position also shared by novelist Richard Wright who was not college educated. These men were concerned about the promotion of folk images of African Americans who did not speak standard English or strive for uplift and proper comportment as defined by black middle-class leaders and organizations of the day.

12. Two studies mentioned were Ronald Mincy, ed., *Black Males Left Behind* (Washington, DC: Urban Institute Press, 2006); and Peter Edelman, Harry J. Holzer, and Paul Offner, *Reconnecting Disadvantaged Young Men* (Washington, DC: Urban Institute Press, 2006).

13. Michael Eric Dyson, *Was Bill Cosby Right, Or Has the Black Middle Class Lost Its Mind?* (New York: Basic Civitas Books, 2005).

9. Back to Class: Reflections on the Dialectic of Class and Identity

1. Paul Krugman, "Graduates Versus Oligarchs," *New York Times*, February 27, 2006.

2. G. William Domhoff, "Wealth, Income, and Power," in *Who Rules America?*, http://sociology.ucsc.edu/whorulesamerica/power/wealth.html.

3. Steven Greenhouse and David Leonhardt, "Real Wages Fail to Match a Rise in Productivity," *New York Times*, August 28, 2006.

4. U.S. Department of Labor, Bureau of Labor Statistics, "Characteristics of Minimum Wage Workers: 2005," http://www.bls.gov/cps/minwage2005.htm.

5. See, for example, Stanley Aronowitz, *The Politics of Identity: Class, Culture, Social Movements* (New York: Routledge, 1992).

6. See, for example, Diana Kendall, *Framing Class: Media Representations of Wealth and Poverty in America* (New York: Rowman & Littlefield Publishers, 2005).

7. Karl Marx and Friedrich Engels, *The Communist Manifesto* (New York: Monthly Review Press, [1848] 1998), 2–3.

8. Karl Marx, *Capital*, vol. 3 (New York: International Publishers, [1894] 1967), 885.

9. Hans Gerth and C. Wright Mills, eds., *From Max Weber: Essays in Sociology* (New York: Oxford University Press, 1973), 181.

10. Ibid., 182.

11. Ibid., 187.

12. Ibid.

13. Ibid., 176.

14. Marx, *Capital*, vol. 3, chaps. 6 and 7.

15. High school textbooks ignore labor and class issues and promote the view that the United States is the land of equal opportunity, concludes James Loewen after reviewing twelve widely used history textbooks. See James W. Loewen, "The Land of Opportunity," *Lies My Teacher Told Me: Everything Your American History Textbook Got Wrong* (New York: Simon & Schuster, 1996).

16. See, for example, Philip S. Foner, *May Day: A Short History of the International Worker's Day Holiday 1886–1986* (New York: International Publishers, 1986).

17. Marxist theory postulates the need to go beyond the appearances, the readily observable social phenomena, to investigate the social processes and contradictions that produce such phenomena; "All science would be superfluous if the outward appearance and the essence of things directly coincided." Marx, *Capital*, vol. 3, 817.

18. For a critique of the ideological effects of Weber's views on social inequality, see Deb Kelsh and Dave Hill, "The Culturalization of Class and the Occluding of Class Consciousness," *Journal for Critical Education Policy Studies* 4, no. 1 (March 2006), available at http://www.jceps.com/?pageID'article&articleID'59.

19. I am referring to the vast majority of the population who needs to work for a living, in manual, white-collar or service occupations, regardless of status differences. See Herbert J. Gans, "Race as Class," in *Contexts: Understanding People in their Social Worlds* 4, http://www.contextmagazine.org/content_sample_v4_4.php.

20. Aronowitz, *Politics of Identity*, 67.

21. See, for example, Martha E. Gimenez, "Reflections on 'The Feminization of Poverty: Myth or Reality,'" in *Enriching the Sociological Imagination: How Radical Sociology Changed the Discipline*, ed. Rhonda F. Levine (Leiden-Boston: Brill, 2004), 165–87.

22. See Kelsh and Hill, "The Culturalization of Class."

23. Gimenez, "Reflections on 'The Feminization of Poverty,' " 183.

24. See, for example, Martha E. Gimenez, "Latino/'Hispanic': Who Needs a Name? The Case Against a Standardized Terminology," *International Journal of Health Services* 19, no. 3 (1989): 557–71.

25. See Robert Blauner, "Colonized and Immigrant Minorities," in *From Different Shores: Perspectives on Race and Ethnicity in America*, ed. Ronald Takaki (New York: Oxford University Press, 1987), 149–60.

26. Manning Marable, "Cultural Awareness, Not Just Race, Is Part of Black Identity," *Daily Camera*, 1991.

27. See, for example, William Julius Wilson, *The Declining Significance of Race* (Chicago: University of Chicago Press, 1978).

28. Karl Marx, "On the Jewish Question," in *Early Writings* (New York: Penguin, 1992), 219.

29. Antonia Darder and Rodolfo D. Torres, *After Race: Racism after Multiculturalism* (New York: New York University Press, 2004), 125.

30. The notion of ideological interpellation as the source of subjectivity can be found in Louis Althusser, "Ideology and Ideological State Apparatuses," in *Lenin and Philosophy and Other Essays* (New York: Monthly Review Press, 2001).

31. Karl Marx and Friedrich Engels, *The German Ideology* (New York: International Publishers, [1845–46] 1947), 39.

32. Karl Marx, *A Contribution to the Critique of Political Economy* (New York: International Publishers, [1859] 1970), 21.

33. Aronowitz, *Politics of Identity*, 71.

34. For a comprehensive critique of diversity and identity politics see Walter Benn Michaels, *The Trouble with Diversity: How We Learned to Love Identity and Ignore Inequality* (New York: Henry Holt, 2006).

35. Aronowitz, *Politics of Identity*, 72.

36. Benn, *Trouble with Diversity*.

37. Ibid., 16.

38. Nancy Fraser, "From Redistribution to Recognition? Dilemmas of Justice in a 'Post-Socialist' Age," *New Left Review* 212 (1995): 64–93.

39. Iris Young, "Unruly Categories: A Critique of Nancy Fraser's Dual Systems Theory," *New Left Review* 222 (1997): 147–160.

40. Althusser, "Ideology and Ideological State Apparatuses."

41. Ibid., 117.

42. Manning Marable, *Beyond Black and White* (London: Verso, 1995), cited in Valerie Scatamburlo-D'Annibale and Peter McLaren, "Class-ifying Race: The Compassionate Racism of the Republican Right," in *Repturing Racism*, ed. Leeno Karumanchery (Halifax: Fernwood Press, forthcoming), 14.

43. In Lauren Langman and Valerie Scatamburlo-D'Annibale, "Identity and Hegemony: Toward a Critical Social Psychology" (Unpublished manuscript, 2001), the authors call for a different kind of identity politics which, instead of asking, "who are you?" asks "where are you?" thus seeking to make clear the ethical and political commitments underlying identities. While a welcome departure to ultimately individualistic understandings of identity, class location as the terrain for the formation of political coalitions transcending identity is more important; hence the alternative to their question with which I close this chapter.

10. Women and Class: What Has Happened in Forty Years?

We thank Johanna Brenner, Charlie Post, Catherine Sameh, and Erin Small for helping us develop the ideas in this paper.

1. Irene Padavic, "Patterns of Labor Force Participation and Sex Segregation," paper presented at 3rd Annual Invitational Journalism-Work/Family Conference, Boston University and Brandeis University, Community, Families and Work Program, May 20–21, 2004.

2. This is for full-time workers. Institute for Women's Policy Research, "The Gender Wage Ratio: Women's and Men's Earnings," Fact Sheet IWPR #C350 (Washington, DC: Institute for Women's Policy Research, August 2006), http://www.iwpr.org/pdf/Updated 2006_C350.pdf.

3. Data in this article come from the Bureau of Labor Statistics, Current Populaton Survey, Women in the Labor Force Databook 2006, unless otherwise specified. See http://www.bls.gov/cps/wlf-table4-2006.pdf.

4. Ibid.

5. Available at: http://www.bls.gov/cps/wlf-table6-2006.pdf.

6. Heather Boushey, "Are Mothers Really Leaving the Workplace?" issue brief, Council on Contemporary Families and the Center for Economic and Policy Research, March 28, 2006.

7. Available at: http://www.bls.gov/cps/wlf-table10-2006.pdf.

8. Economic Policy Institute, http://www.epi.org/datazone/06/wagebyed_w.pdf.

9. Erik Olin Wright and Rachel Dwyer, "The American Jobs Machine: Is the New Economy Creating Good Jobs?" *Boston Review* 25 (December/January 2000–01): 21–26.

10. "Educational Attainment in the United States: 2005," Current Population Survey, http://www.census.gov/population/www/socdemo/educ-attn.html (accessed February 2, 2007).

11. Bureau of Labor Statistics, Women in the Labor Force Databook 2006.

12. Irene Padavic and Barbara Reskin, *Women and Men at Work*, 2nd ed. (Thousand Oaks, CA: Pine Forge Press, 2002).

13. National Occupational Employment and Wage Estimates. Bureau of Labor Statistics, US Department of Labor. May 2005 National Occupational Employment and Wage Estimates. Available at http://www.bls.gov/oes/current/oes_nat.htm. Accessed February 2, 2007.

14. Johanna Brenner, *Women and the Politics of Class* (New York: Monthly Review, 2000).

15. Lori L. Reid and Irene Padavic, "Employment Exits and the Race Gap in Young Women's Employment," *Social Science Quarterly* 86 (December 2005): 1242–60.

16. Available at: http://www.census.gov/hhes/www/poverty/histpov/hstpov4.html.

17. Nelson Lichtenstein, *State of the Union: A Century of American Labor* (Princeton, NJ: Princeton University Press, 2003).

18. Steve Jenkins, "Organizing, Advocacy and Member Power: A Critical Reflection," *WorkingUSA* (Fall 2002): 56–73.

19. Johanna Brenner and Barbara Laslett, "Gender, Social Reproduction, and Women's Self-Organization: Considering the U.S. Welfare State," *Gender and Society* 5, no. 3 (1991): 311–33.

20. For a useful debate between different theoretical/political positions about the merits and weaknesses of comparable worth policies see Paula England, *Comparable Worth: Theories and Evidence* (New York: Aldine De Gruyter, 1992).

11. The Pedagogy of Oppression

1. Henry Giroux, *The Terror of Neoliberalism* (Boulder, CO: Paradigm Publishers, 2004).

2. Public Citizen, "Public Citizen and United for a Fair Economy Expose Stealth Campaign of Super-Wealthy to Repeal Federal Estate Tax," April 26, 2006, http://www.citizen.org/pressroom/release.cfm?ID'2182.

3. Manning Marable, "Empire, Racism and Resistance: Global Apartheid and Prospects for a Democratic Future," *The Black Commentator* (2007), http://www.blackcommentator.com/211/211_cover_manley_speech_marab le_ed_bd.html.

4. Ibid.

5. Akosua Amoo Adare, "A Short E-Mail Interview with the Dirty Thirty's Peter McLaren," *Chopbox Magazine* (Toronto, Canada: Kofi Asare).

6. Christine Sleeter, *Un-Standardizing Curriculum: Multicultural Teaching in the Standards-Based Classroom* (New York: Teachers College Press, 2005).

7. National Commission on Excellence in Education, *A Nation at Risk: The Imperative for Educational Reform* (Washington, DC: The Commission, 1983).

8. Greg Palast, *Armed Madhouse* (New York: Dutton, 2006), 313.

9. Ibid., 317–18.

10. Ibid.

11. Jonathan Kozol, *The Shame of the Nation: The Restoration of Apartheid Schooling in America* (New York: Crown Publishers, 2005), 51.

12. Kozol, *Shame of the Nation*, 51.

13. Ibid., 46.

14. Alfie Kohn, *The Case Against Standardized Testing: Raising the Scores, Ruining the Schools* (Portsmouth, NH: Heinemann, 2000).

15. Ibid.

16. Kozol, *Shame of the Nation*, 46.

17. Ibid.

18. Ibid., 285.

19. Ibid.

20. Arlebe Inouye, "Standing Up to the Military Recruiters," *Rethinking Schools Online* 20, no. 3 (Spring 2005), http://rethinkingschools.org/archive/20_03/mili203.shtml.

21. David Goodman, "Class Dismissed," *Mother Jones* 29, no. 3 (2004): 43.

22. Nancy Hellmich, "McDonald's Kicks Off School PE Program," *USA Today*, September 12, 2005.

23. Paulo Freire, *The Pedagogy of the Oppressed* (New York: Continuum Books, 1970).

24. Paulo Freire, *Pedagogy of Indignation* (Boulder, CO: Paradigm Publishers, 2004).

25. Ibid., 60.

26. Ibid., 34, emphasis in the original.

27. Ibid.

28. Ibid.

29. Donaldo Macedo and Ana Maria Araujo Freire, "Foreword," in Paulo Freire, *Teachers as Cultural Workers: Letters to Those Who Dare Teach* (Boulder, CO: Westview Press, 1998), xxii.

30. Ibid., xvii.

31. Ibid., xvii.

32. As quoted in Macedo and Freire, "Forward," xvii.

33. Robert Went, *Globalization: Neoliberal Challenge, Radical Responses* (London and Sterling, VA: Pluto Press, 2000).

14. Six Points on Class

I thank Denis DaPuzzo for research assistance.

1. See Michael Zweig, *The Working Class Majority: America's Best Kept Secret* (Ithaca, NY: Cornell University Press, 2000) for details.

2. Joe Berry, *Reclaiming the Ivory Tower* (New York: Monthly Review Press, 2005).

3. For an exchange on the statistical and conceptual treatment of Hispanic poverty, see letters by David Roediger and Michael Zweig in *Monthly Review*, December 2006. Hispanics are not a "race" in U.S. data. Most Hispanics in the United States report themselves to be "white," although many report they are "black." Racial differences are significant in Latin America as well as in the United States. See, for example, Roy Levy Williams, "Venezuela's Black Vote," *Amsterdam News*, December 20, 2006.

4. U.S. Department of Labor, "May 2004 Metropolitan Area Occupational Employment and Wage Estimates: New Orleans, LA MSA," http://www.bls.gov/oes/current/oessrcma.htm.

5. Louisiana Department of Labor, "Louisiana Labor Force Diversity Data: 2004," http://www.laworks.net/.

6. Molly Garber, Linda Unger, James White, and Linda Wohlford, "Hurricane Katrina's Effects on Industry Employment and Wages," *Monthly Labor Review* (Washington, DC: U.S. Department of Labor, August 2006), 32.

7. Sam Roberts, "Mayor Crossed Ethnic Barriers for Big Victory: Democrats Now Facing New Political Reality," *New York Times,* November 10, 2005.

8. Jess Blavin and Jeanne Cummings, "Bush Taps Roberts for Supreme Court: Conservative Nominee, 50, Is Viewed as Pro-Business; Doubts from Some Democrats," *Wall Street Journal,* July 20, 2005.

9. Stephen Labaton, "Court Nominee Has Paper Trail Businesses Like," *New York Times,* November 5, 2005.

10. Poll results reported in Zweig, *Working Class Majority,* 57–59.

11. Correspondents of the *New York Times, Class Matters* (New York: Times Books, 2005).

12. Jeff Faux, *The Global Class War* (Hoboken, NJ: Wiley, 2006).

13. See, for example, William K. Tabb, *The Amoral Elephant* (New York: Monthly Review Press, 2001) and Faux, *Global Class War.*

14. Leslie Sklair, *The Transnational Capitalist Class* (Oxford, UK: Blackwell, 2001).

15. Katie Quan, "Global Strategies for Workers: How Class Analysis Clarifies 'Us' and 'Them' and What We Need to Do," in *What's Class Got to Do with It? American Society in the Twenty-First Century,* ed. Michael Zweig (Ithaca, NY: Cornell University Press, 2004).

16. Michael Zweig, "Labor and the War: The Remarkable Story of USLAW," *New Labor Forum* (Fall 2005).

Index